101
Ready-to-Use
Excel® Formulas

101
Ready-to-Use
Excel® Formulas

by Michael Alexander and Dick Kusleika

WILEY

101 Ready-to-Use Excel® Formulas

Published by: **John Wiley & Sons, Inc.,** 111 River Street, Hoboken, NJ 07030-5774, www.wiley.com

Copyright © 2014 by John Wiley & Sons, Inc., Hoboken, New Jersey

Published simultaneously in Canada

For general information on our other products and services, please contact our Customer Care Department within the U.S. at 877-762-2974, outside the U.S. at 317-572-3993, or fax 317-572-4002. For technical support, please visit www.wiley.com/techsupport.

Wiley publishes in a variety of print and electronic formats and by print-on-demand. Some material included with standard print versions of this book may not be included in e-books or in print-on-demand. If this book refers to media such as a CD or DVD that is not included in the version you purchased, you may download this material at http://book-support.wiley.com. For more information about Wiley products, visit www.wiley.com.

Library of Congress Control Number: 2014935514

ISBN 978-1-118-90268-4 (pbk); ISBN 978-1-118-90259-2 (ebk); ISBN 978-1-118-90289-9 (ebk)

Manufactured in the United States of America

10 9 8 7 6 5 4 3 2 1

# Contents at a Glance

▶ Table of Contents

INTRODUCTION

Formulas are the true engines of Excel. Employing various Excel functions, formulas enable Excel analysts to create aggregated reporting, complex calculation engines, clever dashboard models, and much more. Indeed, Excel analysts become more productive as their proficiency with Excel functions and formulas improves.

But building proficiency with Excel functions and formulas takes time. Given that Excel contains more than 400 functions, you could spend months, even years, learning which functions are best for certain tasks and which functions can be combined with others functions.

Unfortunately, many analysts don't have the luxury of taking a few weeks' time-out to learn all they need to know about Excel functions and formulas. The scenarios and issues they face require solutions now.

This is where *101 Ready-to-Use Excel Formulas* comes in. This book approaches Excel formulas with the assumption that "learning" comes with accomplishing core tasks. Instead of offering the usual general overview of Excel formula writing, this book provides 101 of the most commonly used, real-world Excel formulas.

For each formula covered, we outline a common problem that needs to be solved and provide the actual Excel formula to solve the problem, along with detailed explanations of how the formula works. This approach lets you use this book as a handy reference for finding a formula that solves a common problem.

After reading about a given formula, you should be able to

> ➤ Immediately implement the needed Excel formula
> ➤ Understand how the formula works
> ➤ Reuse the formula in other workbooks

What You Need to Know

To get the most out of this book, you need to have established certain skills before diving in. The ideal candidate for this book has experience working with data in Excel along with familiarity with the basic concepts of data analysis such as working with tables, aggregating data, performing calculations, and creating charts.

What You Need to Have

You need the following to be able to download and use the examples highlighted in this book:

> ➤ A licensed copy of Excel 2010 or Excel 2013
>
> ➤ An Internet connection in order to download the sample files

How This Book Is Organized

We've grouped this book into nine chapters that are chock-full of tips, techniques, and formulas dedicated to a particular topic.

Chapter 1: Introducing Excel Formulas

Chapter 1 serves as an introduction to Excel formulas, giving you an understanding of how Excel formulas work and some of the ground rules for working with formulas.

Chapter 2: Common Mathematical Operations

In Chapter 2, you gain insight into some of the fundamental mathematical operations every Excel analyst should know. The formulas found here serve as the foundation for all kinds of advanced data analysis.

Chapter 3: Manipulating Text with Formulas

Chapter 3 focuses on the transformation and shaping of text strings. In this chapter, you explore some of the common text transformation exercises an Excel analyst performs, and in the process, you get a feel for many of the text-based functions Excel has to offer.

Chapter 4: Working with Dates and Times

Chapter 4 gives you a solid understanding of how Excel handles time-based data. Through the prism of the most commonly used date formulas, you discover how to more effectively utilize the dates and times within your data sets.

Chapter 5: Performing Conditional Analysis

In Chapter 5, you take a look at a wide array of conditional analysis formulas that add flexibility to your analytical processes. With the formulas found here, you'll be able to save time, organize your analytical processes, and enhance your data-crunching power.

Chapter 6: Using Lookup Formulas

Chapter 6 focuses on Excel's powerful, sometimes intimidating, Lookup formula. The formulas demonstrated in this chapter provide the foundation you need to add depth and power to your Excel data models.

Chapter 7: Common Business and Financial Formulas

Chapter 7 demonstrates a host of business and financial formulas that leverage Excel's flexible spreadsheet environment to create key business and financial metrics used in virtually every industry.

Chapter 8: Common Statistical Analysis

Chapter 8 takes you beyond simple mathematical operation and into the realm of statistical analysis. With the help of the formulas found here, you quickly get up to speed on fundamental statistical concepts, even if you've never taken a course in statistics.

Chapter 9: Using Formulas with Conditional Formatting

Chapter 9 rounds out the book's 101 formulas with a look at how you can leverage formulas to enhance conditional formatting. Here, you take in a few examples of how integrating your own custom formulas can help add a visual layer to your data analysis.

Conventions in This Book

We present menu command sequences in this book by using an arrow (⇨) between commands. For example, File⇨Open means go to the File menu, click it, and select Open on the list that appears.

Formulas usually appear on a separate line in monospace font, like so:

```
=AVERAGE(A1:A3)
```

Excel function names appear in uppercase and other formula elements are all lowercase. Text that we tell you to type appears in *bold*.

What the icons mean

Tip

We use Tip icons to indicate a pointer that you should file away for future reference. Tips usually make your life easier.

Note

The Note icon indicates something that you should pay special attention to.

Cross-Ref

This icon refers you to related or additional material found in the book.

Caution

We use Caution icons to flag an issue that can cause you trouble.

About the Sample Files

Each chapter in this book has an associated sample file with a separate tab for each formula outlined in this book. These sample files give you the ability to see the formula working, as well as the ability to copy the formula for your own use elsewhere.

You can download the sample files from the Wiley website at the following URL:

`www.wiley.com/go/101excelformula`

Introducing Excel Formulas

Microsoft Excel is, at its core, a calculation engine. Like a calculator, it accepts a question (such as 2+2) and gives you an answer. When you're working with a calculator, these questions are called mathematical operations. In Excel, you call these formulas.

Excel allows you to use formulas to perform not only mathematical operations but also a myriad of other complex actions, such as parsing textual values, searching for certain values in a range of data, performing recursive calculations, and much more.

To leverage the full power of Excel formulas, you need to understand how Excel formulas work as well as some of the ground rules for working with formulas. The goal of this chapter, therefore, is for you to get acquainted with the fundamentals of using Excel formulas.

Tip

Feel free to skip over this chapter if you already have a solid understanding of formula mechanics and want to get right into real-world examples, which start in Chapter 2.

Note

You can download the files for all the formulas at `www.wiley.com/go/` `101excelformula`.

Creating and Editing Excel Formulas

An Excel spreadsheet is simply a collection of cells that you can use to enter data. Each cell is given a name based on its position in the spreadsheet. The top-leftmost cell is called cell A1. It's the cell located in column A, row 1. When you enter a value in cell A1 (for example, the number 5), that cell's value becomes 5. If you enter the number 10 in cell B1, that cell's value becomes 10. You can use then use these values in a formula.

For instance, you can click cell C1 and begin typing **=A1+B1**, as shown in Figure 1-1. Note how you can see your formula in both the cell you're typing in and the Formula Bar above the column headings.

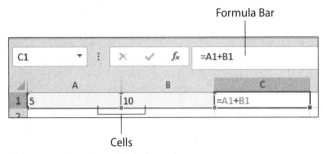

Figure 1-1: Entering a basic formula.

After you press the Enter key on your keyboard, Excel recognizes what you're asking and performs the calculation that gives you the result of 15 (5+10 = 15).

The reason Excel recognizes that you were entering a formula and not just another value is the equal sign (=). Entering the equal sign followed by other values tells Excel that you're starting a formula. In this example, we used what are known as cell references (A1 and B1). These cell references are just one of the types of values that you can use in your formulas.

Excel formulas accept the following types of values:

➤ **Constants:** You can use hard-coded numbers directly in a formula. For example, you can enter **=5+10** directly into a cell to get the answer 15.

➤ **Operators:** These include symbols that perform addition (+), symbols that perform multiplication (*), symbols that compare values (>), and symbols that join values together (&). For example, entering **=15>10** into a cell returns TRUE as the result because 15 is indeed greater than 10.

➤ **Cell references:** These include any value that points back to a single cell or range of cells. As you've already seen, entering **=A1+B1** in a cell tells Excel to use the values in those two cells in the formula.

➤ **Text strings:** Any text string can be used as an argument in a formula as long as it's wrapped in quotation marks. For example, entering **="Microsoft"&"Excel"** in any cell results in the joined text *Microsoft Excel*.

Methods for entering formulas

You have several ways to actually enter a formula into a cell:

➤ **Enter the formula directly into a cell:** Simply click a cell, begin typing your formula, and then press the Enter key on your keyboard.

➤ **Enter the formula into the Formula Bar:** Click inside the Formula Bar found above the column headers, type your formula, and then press the Enter key on your keyboard.

➤ **Enter the formula using the mouse:** If your formula involves cell references, you can use the mouse to help reduce the amount of typing you need to do. For instance, instead of typing =A1+B1, you can type the equal symbol, use your mouse to click cell A1, type the plus symbol, use the mouse to click cell B1, and then press the Enter key.

➤ **Enter the formula using the arrow keys:** If your formula involves cell references, you can use the arrow keys on your keyboard to help reduce the amount of typing you need to do. For instance, instead of typing =A1+B1, you can type the equal symbol, use the arrow keys on your keyboard to move the cursor to cell A1, type the plus (+) symbol, use the arrow keys on your keyboard to move the cursor to cell B1, and then press the Enter key.

Editing a formula

If you find that you need to edit a formula, you can do so in three ways:

➤ **Edit directly in the Formula Bar:** Select the cell that contains your formula, go up to the Formula Bar, and start editing the formula there.

➤ **Double-click the formula cell:** You can edit the formula directly in the cell it's in by double-clicking the cell. Double-clicking the cell gets you into Edit mode, where you can edit the formula as needed.

➤ **Press F2:** Select the cell that contains your formula and then press F2 on your keyboard to get into Edit mode. As stated previously, you can then edit the formula as needed.

Using Formula Operators

As mentioned earlier in this chapter, you can use symbols known as operators to define the operation your formula will accomplish. Some of these operators are mathematical operators that simply add, subtract, and multiply. Other operators allow you to perform more complex actions such as comparing values. For example, you can determine whether an employee has met his or her quota by using a comparison operator to see if actual sales are greater than or equal to a predetermined quota.

Table 1-1 lists the operators you can use in your Excel formulas.

Table 1-1: Operators for Excel Formulas

Operator	What It Does
+	The plus symbol adds two or more numeric values.
-	The hyphen symbol subtracts two or more numeric values.
/	The forward slash symbol divides two or more numeric values.
*	The asterisk symbol divides two or more numeric values.

continued

Table 1-1: Operators for Excel Formulas *(continued)*

Operator	What It Does
%	The percent symbol indicates a numeric percent. Entering a percent sign after a whole number divides the number by 100 and formats the cell as a percentage.
&	The ampersand symbol is used to join or concatenate two or more textual values.
^	The carat symbol is used as an exponentiation operator.
=	The equal symbol is used to evaluate whether one value is equal to another value
>	The greater-than symbol is used to evaluate whether one value is greater than another value.
<	The less-than symbol is used to evaluate whether one value is less than another value.
>=	The greater-than symbol used in conjunction with the equal symbol evaluates whether one value is greater than or equal to another value.
<=	The less-than symbol used in conjunction with the equal symbol evaluates whether one value is less than or equal to another value.
<>	The less-than symbol used in conjunction with the greater-than symbol evaluates whether one value is not equal to another value.

Understanding the order of operator precedence

It's important to understand that when you create a formula with several operators, Excel evaluates and performs the calculation in a specific order. For instance, Excel always performs multiplication before addition. This order is called the *order of operator precedence*. You can force Excel to override the built-in operator precedence by using parentheses to specify which operation to evaluate first.

Consider this basic example. The correct answer to (2+3)*4 is 20. However, if you leave off the parentheses, as in 2+3*4, Excel performs the calculation like this: 3*4 = 12 + 2 = 14. Excel's default order of operator precedence mandates that Excel perform multiplication before addition. Entering 2+3*4 gives you the wrong answer. Because Excel evaluates and performs all calculations in parentheses first, placing 2+3 inside parentheses ensures the correct answer.

The order of operations for Excel is as follows:

Evaluate items in parentheses.

Evaluate ranges (:).

Evaluate intersections (spaces).

Evaluate unions (,).

Perform negation (-).

Convert percentages (%).

Perform exponentiation (^).

Perform multiplication (*) and division (/), which are of equal precedence.

Perform addition (+) and subtraction (-), which are of equal precedence.

Evaluate text operators (&).

Perform comparisons (=, <>, <=, >=).

Note   **Operations that are equal in precedence are performed left to right.**

Here is another widely demonstrated example. If you enter 10^2, which represents the exponent 10 to the 2nd power as a formula, Excel returns 100 as the answer. If you enter -10^2, you would expect -100 to be the result. Instead, Excel returns 100 yet again. The reason is that Excel performs negation before exponentiation, meaning that Excel is converting 10 to -10 before the exponentiation, effectively calculating -10*-10, which indeed equals 100. Using parentheses in the formula -(10^2) ensures that Excel calculates the exponent before negating the answer, giving you -100.

Remembering the order of operations and using parentheses where appropriate will ensure that you avoid miscalculating your data.

Using nested parentheses

It's a best practice to use parentheses whenever you can in formulas, even if the use of parentheses seem to be superfluous. The liberal use of parentheses can not only help you avoid calculation errors but also help you better understand what the formula is doing.

You can even nest parentheses in formulas. Nesting means putting parentheses inside of other parentheses. When a formula contains nested parentheses, Excel evaluates the most deeply nested operations first and works its way out. The following formula uses nested parentheses:

```
=((A1*B1)+(C1*D1))*E1
```

This formula has three sets of parentheses. Excel will evaluate the two nested sets of parentheses first, then will add those two results together. The added result will then be multiplied by the value in E1.

Note   **Every open parenthesis must have a matching close parenthesis. You can imagine that when you start adding lots of parentheses to your formula, determining which open parenthesis has a matching close parenthesis can get difficult. For its part, Excel offers some help by color coding the parentheses while you're in Edit mode. Matching open and close parentheses will have the same color.**

Relative versus Absolute Cell References

Imagine that you go to C1 and enter the formula =A1+B1. Your human eyes will define that as the value in A1 added to the value in B1. However, Excel, doesn't see it that way. Because you entered the formula in cell C1, Excel reads the formula like this: Take the value in the cell two spaces to the left and add it to the value in the cell one space to the left.

If you copy the formula =A1+B1 from cell C1 and paste it into cell D1, the formula in D1 will seem different to you. You will see =B1+C1. But to Excel, the formula is exactly the same: Take the value in the cell two spaces to the left and add it to the value in the cell one space to the left.

By default, Excel considers every cell reference used in a formula as a relative reference. That is, it takes no heed of actual column row coordinates. Instead, it evaluates the cell references in terms of where they are relative to the cell the formula resides in.

This behavior is by design and works in situations in which you need the cell references to be adjusted when you copy the formula and paste it to other cells. For instance, the formula shown in cell C1 (see Figure 1-2) was copied and pasted down to the rows below. Note how Excel helps by automatically adjusting the cell references to match each row.

	A	B	C
1	5	10	=A1+B1
2	10	20	=A2+B2
3	15	30	=A3+B3
4	20	40	=A4+B4
5	25	50	=A5+B5
6	30	60	=A6+B6
7	35	70	=A7+B7
8	40	80	=A8+B8
9	45	90	=A9+B9

Figure 1-2: Relative references come in handy when you need to apply the same operation to values in different rows.

Note   **When you copy and paste a formula, Excel automatically adjusts the cell references. However, if you cut and paste a formula, Excel assumes that you want to keep the same cell references and does not adjust them.**

If you want to ensure that Excel does not adjust cell references when a formula is copied, you can lock the references down by turning them into absolute references. You turn them into absolute references by adding a dollar symbol ($) before the column and row reference. For instance, you can enter =$A$1+$B$1 to add the value in A1 to the value of B1.

By adding the dollar symbol to any cell reference and making that reference absolute, you can copy the formula anywhere else on the spreadsheet, and the formula will always point to A1 and B1.

Excel gives you the flexibility to make any part of your cell reference absolute. That is, you can specify that only the column part of your cell reference should be locked but the row part can adjust. Alternatively, you can specify that only the row part of your cell reference should be locked but the column part can adjust.

These different types of absolute references are commonly called Absolute, Row Absolute, and Column Absolute, and here's how they work:

> ➤ **Absolute:** When the formula is copied, the cell reference does not adjust at all. Example: $A$1

> ➤ **Row Absolute:** When the formula is copied, the column part adjusts but the row part stays locked. Example: A$1

> ➤ **Column Absolute:** When the formula is copied, the column part stays locked but the row part adjusts. Example: $A1

Tip

Instead of manually entering the dollar symbols, you can easily toggle between the possible reference styles by highlighting the cell reference in your formula and pressing the F4 key.

Using External Cell References

You may find that you have data in one workbook that you want to reference in a formula within another workbook. In such a situation, you can create a link between the workbooks using an external cell reference. An external cell reference is nothing more than a cell reference that resides in an outside workbook. The benefit of using an external cell reference is that when the data in the outside workbook changes, Excel automatically updates the value returned by the external cell reference.

Creating an external cell reference is relatively easy. Open both workbooks (the workbook that you're currently working in and the outside workbook). While entering a formula in the workbook you're currently working in, click the cell that you want to reference in the outside workbook.

As you can see in Figure 1-3, you'll immediately be able to tell that the cell reference is an external reference due to the full file path and sheet name prefixing the cell reference.

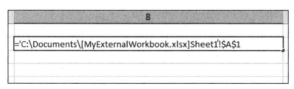

Figure 1-3: An example of an external cell reference.

All external cell references have the same component parts, as follows:

'File Path[Workbook Name]Sheet Name'!Cell Reference

Here's a breakdown of these parts:

➤ **File Path:** This part of the cell reference points to the drive and directory in which the workbook is located.

➤ **Workbook Name:** This part of the cell reference points to the name of the workbook. This part is always enclosed in brackets ([ ]) and always includes the file extension (.xlsx, .xls, .xslm, and so on).

➤ **Sheet Name:** This part of the cell reference points to the name of the sheet in which the referenced cell resides.

➤ **Cell Reference:** This part of the cell reference points to the actual cell that is being referenced.

Formula Calculation Modes

By default, Excel is set to recalculate automatically. If you change any of the cells referenced in a particular formula, Excel automatically recalculates that formula so that it returns a correct result based on the changes in its cell references. Also, if the formula that it recalculates is used as a cell reference in other formulas, every formula that is dependent on the newly recalculated formula is also recalculated.

You can imagine that as your spreadsheet grows and gets populated with interweaving formulas, Excel will be constantly recalculating. You may even find that when working with worksheets that contain many complex formulas, Excel slows dramatically as it tries to keep up with all the recalculating it needs to do.

In these cases, you can choose to set Excel's calculation mode to Manual. You can do this by clicking the Formulas tab in the Excel Ribbon and selecting Calculation Options⇨Manual.

While working in Manual calculation mode, none of your formulas will recalculate until you trigger the calculation yourself. You have several ways to trigger a recalculation:

➤ Click the Calculate Now command on the Formulas tab to recalculate all formulas in the entire workbook.

➤ Click the Calculate Sheet command on the Formulas tab to recalculate only the formulas on the currently active sheet.

➤ Click the Calculate link on the status bar to recalculate the entire workbook.

➤ Press F9 to recalculate all formulas in the entire workbook.

➤ Press Shift+F9 to recalculate only the formulas on the currently active sheet.

Leveraging Excel Functions

Functions are essentially canned formulas that Excel provides as a way to accomplish common tasks. Some Excel functions perform simple calculations, saving you from having to enter the formula yourself. Other functions perform complex actions that would be impossible to perform with simple formulas alone.

As you go through the chapters in this book, you explore many of the most useful Excel functions. For now, you start with a basic understanding of the role Excel functions play in your formulas.

Why to use Excel functions

One of the key benefits of using Excel functions is that they help simplify your formulas. For example, if you wanted to get the average of the values in cell A1, A2, and A3, you could enter this formula:

```
=(A1+A2+A3)/3
```

This particular formula isn't too bad, but what if you had to get the average of 100 values? How cumbersome would that formula be to create and manage?

Luckily, Excel has an AVERAGE function. With the AVERAGE function, you can simply enter this formula:

```
=AVERAGE(A1:A3)
```

If you had to get the average of 100 values, you could simply expand the range:

```
=AVERAGE(A1:A100)
```

Another key benefit of using functions is that they help you accomplish tasks that would be impossible with standard formulas. For instance, imagine that you wanted a couple of formulas that would automatically return the largest and smallest numbers in a range of cells. Sure, if your range was small enough, you could eyeball the largest and smallest numbers. But that's hardly automated.

There is no nonfunction-driven formula you could possibly enter that would automatically return the largest or smallest number in a range.

Excel's MAX and MIN functions, however, make short work of this task. The MAX function returns the largest number, whereas the MIN function returns the smallest.

```
=MAX(A1:A100)
=MIN(A1:A100)
```

Functions can also help save time by helping you automate tasks that would take you hours to accomplish manually. For example, say that you needed to extract the first 10 characters of a customer number. How long do you think it would take you to go through a table of 1,000 records and get a list of customer numbers that contains only the first 10 characters?

The LEFT function can help here by pulling out the left 10 characters:

```
=LEFT(A1,10)
```

You can simply enter this formula for the first row of your table and then copy it down to as many rows you need.

Understanding function arguments

Most of the functions found in Excel require some input or information in order to calculate correctly. For example, to use the AVERAGE function, you need to give it a range of numbers to average.

```
=AVERAGE(A1:A100)
```

Any input you give to a function is called an argument.

The basic construct of a function is:

Function_Name(argument1, argument2,...)

To use a function, you enter its name, open parenthesis, the needed arguments, and then the close parenthesis. The number of arguments needed varies from function to function.

Using functions with no arguments

Some functions, such as the NOW() function, don't require any arguments. To get the current date and time, you can simply enter a formula like this:

```
=NOW()
```

Note that even though no arguments are required, you still need to include the open and close parentheses.

Using functions with one or more required arguments

Some functions require one or more arguments. The LARGE function, for instance, returns the nth largest number in a range of cells. This function requires two arguments: a cell reference to a range of numeric values and a rank number. To get the third largest value in range A1 through A100, you can enter:

```
=LARGE(A1:A100,3)
```

Note that each argument is separated by a comma. This is true regardless of how many arguments you enter. Each argument must be separated by a comma.

Using functions with both required and optional arguments

Many Excel functions, such as the NETWORKDAYS function, allow for optional arguments in addition to the required arguments. The NETWORKDAYS function returns the number of workdays (days excluding weekends) between a given start date and end data.

To use the NETWORKDAYS function, you need to provide, at minimum, the start and end dates. These are the required arguments.

The following formula gives you the answer 260, meaning that there are 260 workdays between January 1, 2014, and December 31, 2014:

```
=NETWORKDAYS("1/1/2014", "12/31/2014")
```

The NETWORKDAYS function also allows for an optional argument that lets you pass a range containing a list of holiday dates. The function treats each date in the optional range as a nonworkday, effectively returning a different result (255 workdays between January 1, 2014, and December 31, 2014, taking into account holiday dates).

```
=NETWORKDAYS("1/1/2014", "12/31/2014", A1:A5)
```

Don't be too concerned with completely understanding the NETWORKDAYS function. The take-away here is that when a function has required and optional arguments, you can elect to use the function with just the required arguments, or you can take advantage of the function's additional utility by providing the optional arguments.

Finding out which arguments are needed for a given function

An easy way to discover the arguments needed for a given function is to begin typing that function into a cell. Click a cell, enter the equal sign, enter the function name, and then enter an open parenthesis. Recognizing that you are entering a function, Excel activates a tooltip (see Figure 1-4) that shows you all the arguments for the function. Any argument that is shown in brackets ([ ]) is an optional argument. All others shown without the brackets are required arguments.

⊿	A	B	C	D	E	F
1						
2						
3						
4						
5	1/1/2014	12/31/2014	=NETWORKDAYS(			
6			NETWORKDAYS(**start_date**, end_date, [holidays])			
7						

Figure 1-4: The function tooltip is a handy way to find out the required and optional arguments for a function.

Getting Help from the Insert Function Wizard

If you find that you're stuck on which function to use, or aren't sure of the syntax needed for a particular function, you can use Excel's Insert Function feature.

Place your cursor in the cell you want to enter a function in and click the Insert Function command, found on the Formulas tab. Alternatively, you can press Shift+F3 to call up the Insert Function dialog box, shown in Figure 1-5. The idea here is to find the function you need and double-click it.

Figure 1-5: The Insert Function dialog box.

If you're not sure which function you need, you can use the search field at the top of the dialog box to find the most appropriate function based on a keyword. Simply enter one or more keywords and click the Go button. The list of functions will change to display those that best match your search criteria. For example, entering the search term "loan payment" results in functions that perform loan calculations.

If you need to use a function that you've recently implemented, you can skip the search feature and simply select "Most Recently Used" from the category drop-down box. The list of functions changes to display those you've recently utilized.

You can also use the category drop-down box to select a category of functions. For instance, selecting "Statistical" from the category drop-down box displays all the statistical functions.

When you find the function that you want to use, double-click it to activate the Function Arguments dialog box (see Figure 1-6). This dialog box serves as a kind of wizard, guiding you through the arguments needed for the selected function.

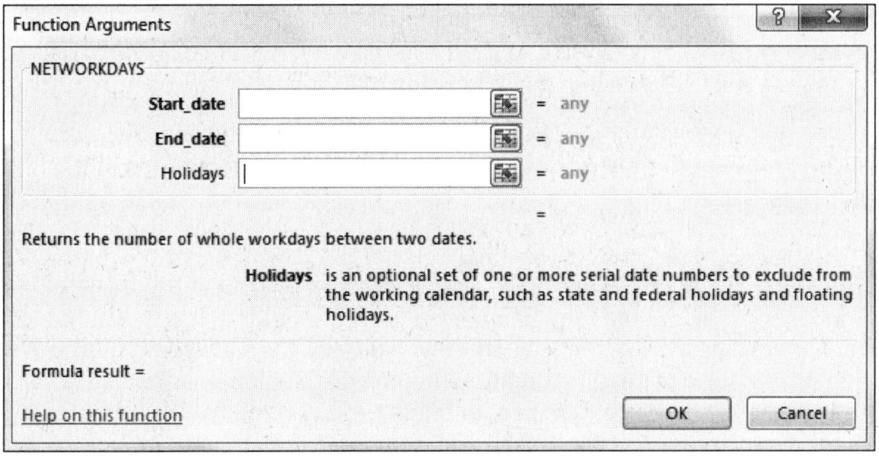

Figure 1-6: The Function Arguments dialog box guides you through creating your Excel functions.

For each required argument, enter an appropriate value or cell reference in the respective input boxes. Note that the required arguments are always listed first and shown in bold type. Do the same thing for any optional argument that you want to utilize.

Click the OK button to apply your newly configured function to your target cell.

Understanding Formula Errors

It's not always smooth sailing when you're working with formulas. Sometimes a formula returns an error value instead of the value you were expecting. Excel helps you identify what the problem may be by returning one of seven error values: #DIV/0!, #N/A, #NAME?, #NULL!, #NUM!, #REF!, and #VALUE!, explained in the following list:

➤ **#DIV/0!:** This error value means that the formula is attempting to divide a value by zero. There is mathematically no way to divide a number by zero. You will also see this error if the formula is trying to divide a value by an empty cell.

➤ **#N/A:** This error value means that the formula cannot return a legitimate result. You would typically see this error when you use an inappropriate argument in a function. You will also see this error when a lookup function does not return a match.

➤ **#NAME?:** This error value means Excel doesn't recognize a name you used in a formula as a valid object. This error could be a result of a misspelled function, a misspelled sheet name, a mistyped cell reference, or some other syntax error.

➤ **#NULL!:** This error value means the formula uses an intersection of two ranges that don't intersect.

➤ **#NUM!:** This error value means there is a problem with a number in your formula; typically an invalid argument in a math or trig function. For example, you entered a negative number where a positive number was expected.

➤ **#REF!:** This error value means that your formula contains an invalid cell reference. This is typically caused by deleting a row or column to which the formula refers. This could also mean that the formula uses a cell reference that doesn't exist (A2000000, for instance).

➤ **#VALUE:** This error value means that your formula uses the wrong data type for the operation it's trying to do. For example, this formula will return a #VALUE error (=100+"dog").

Using Named Ranges in Formulas

A named range is nothing more than a cell or range of cells that has been given a friendly, descriptive name. Naming your ranges allows you use easily recognizable names in your formulas instead of cell addresses. For instance, say that you have line-item sales in cells A1:A25 and you have a percent tax in cell B1. You could calculate a total sale amount with tax using this formula:

```
=SUM(A1:A25)*(1+B1)
```

Now imagine that you gave your ranges descriptive names, calling cells A1:25 Sale_Items, and calling cell B1 Tax_Percent. You could then calculate the total sale amount with tax by using this formula:

```
=SUM(Sales_Items)*(1+Tax_Percent)
```

Immediately, you can see how much easier it is to understand what is going on in the formula. The formula is easier not only to read but also to explain to others who aren't familiar with the workbook.

Another benefit to naming these ranges is that creating new formulas with these named ranges becomes easier because you can simply use the easily remembered descriptive name instead of trying to remember that line-item sales live in cells A1:A25.

Creating a named range

Follow these steps to create a named range:

1. Select the cell or range of cells you want to name.

2. Choose Define Name from the Formulas tab. This activates the New Name dialog box, shown in Figure 1-7.

3. In the Name input box, enter a friendly, descriptive name for your range.

4. In the Scope drop-down box, select whether you want your named range to be available for use throughout the workbook or just on a specific sheet.

5. Press the OK button to create your named range.

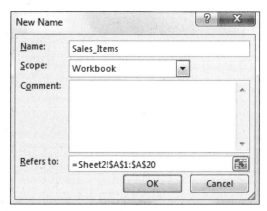

Figure 1-7: The New Name dialog box.

Keep these rules and best practices in mind when choosing a name for your range:

➤ You cannot use spaces in range names. Use an underscore to emulate a space instead (for example, Sales_Items).

➤ Range names must begin with a letter or an underscore.

➤ Range names cannot be the same as cell addresses. For instance, you cannot name your range Q1 because Excel already has a cell Q1.

➤ You can use any single letter as a range name except for R and C. These are reserved in Excel for the R1C1 reference style.

➤ You cannot use operator symbols (+, –, *, /, <, >, &) in range names. The only symbols valid in range names are the period (.), question mark (?), underscore (_), and backslash (\) symbols, as long as they are not used as the first character of the name.

➤ Avoid using names that Excel uses internally, for example, Print_Area. Although Excel allows this name, using it can cause name conflict errors in the workbook. Other names to avoid are Auto_Activate, Auto_Close, Auto_Deactivate, Auto_Open, Consolidate_Area, Criteria, Data_Form, Database, Extract, FilterDatabase, Print_Titles, Recorder, and Sheet_Title.

➤ The maximum length for a range name is 255 characters. That being said, you should avoid very long range names in general. Remember that the purpose of a range name is to provide a meaningful, easy-to-remember name that you can easily type into a formula.

Working with the Name Box

The Name Box, found to the left of the Formula Bar, offers a couple of handy features for working with named ranges. You can click the drop-down selector in the Name Box to see all the named ranges in your workbook (see Figure 1-8). Clicking any of the named ranges in the list automatically selects that range.

A1						
MyRange1		C	D	E	F	
MyRange2						
MyRange3						
3						
4						
5						
6						

Figure 1-8: Use the Name Box to view and navigate to any named range within the workbook.

The Name Box also serves as a faster way to create a named range. To create a named range with the Name Box, first select the cell or range you want to name. Next, enter a valid name directly into the Name Box. Press the Enter key to create the name.

Tip

The Name Box is resizable. If you have a name that is too long for the Name Box, simply move your mouse cursor over the right edge of the Name Box until it turns into a horizontal arrow. When your cursor becomes a horizontal arrow, click and drag to widen the Name Box.

Common Mathematical Operations

Most Excel analysts working in the corporate world are asked to perform mathematical operations that provide insight into key operational metrics. Calculations such as percent of totals, variance to budget, and running totals are the cornerstone of any basic business analysis. In this chapter, you explore 12 mathematical operations commonly used in the world of business analytics.

Note **You can download the files for all the formulas at** www.wiley.com/go/101excelformula.

Formula 1: Calculating Percent of Goal

When someone asks you to calculate a percent of goal, she is simply saying to compare actual performance to a stated goal. The math involved in this calculation is simple: Divide the goal by the actual. This gives you a percentage value that represents how much of the goal has been achieved. For instance, if your goal is to sell 100 widgets, and you sell 80, your percent of goal is 80 percent (80/100).

Note **Percent of Goal can also be referred to as percent of budget or percent of forecast; it all means the same thing.**

In Figure 2-1, you see a list of regions with a column for goals and a column for actuals. Note that the formula in cell E5 simply divides the value in the Actual column by the value in the Goal column.

```
=D5/C5
```

	A	B	C	D	E
1					
2					
3					
4		Region	Goal	Actual	Percent of Goal
5		North	$509,283	$553,887	=D5/C5
6		South	$483,519	$511,115	106%
7		East	$640,603	$606,603	95%
8		West	$320,312	$382,753	119%

Figure 2-1: Calculating the percent of goal.

How it works

There isn't much to this formula. You're simply using cell references to divide one value by another. You just enter the formula one time in the first row (cell E5 in this case) and then copy that formula down to every other row in your table.

Alternative: Using a common goal

If you need to compare actuals to a common goal, you can set up a model like the one shown in Figure 2-2. In this model, each region does not have its own goal. Instead, you're comparing the values in the Actual column to a single goal found in cell B3.

```
=C6/$B$3
```

	A	B	C	D
1				
2		Common Goal		
3		$700,000		
4				
5		Region	Actual	Percent of Goal
6		North	$553,887	=C6/$B$3
7		South	$511,115	73%
8		East	$606,603	87%
9		West	$382,753	55%

Figure 2-2: Calculating the percent of goal using a common goal.

Note that the cell reference to common goal is entered as an absolute reference ($B$3). Using the dollar symbols locks the reference to the goal in place, ensuring that the cell reference pointing to your common goal does not adjust as you copy the formula down.

Cross-Ref   See Chapter 1 for more information on absolute and relative cell references.

Formula 2: Calculating Percent Variance

A variance is an indicator of the difference between one number and another. To understand this, imagine that you sold 120 widgets one day, and on the next day, you sold 150. The difference in sales in actual terms is easy to see; you sold 30 more widgets. Subtracting 120 widgets from 150 widgets gives you a unit variance of +30.

So what is a percent variance? This is essentially the <u>percentage</u> difference between the benchmark number (120) and the new number (150). You calculate the percent variance by subtracting the benchmark number from the new number and then dividing that result by the benchmark number. In this example, the calculation looks like this: (150-120)/120 = 25%. The Percent variance tells you that you sold 25 percent more widgets than yesterday.

Figure 2-3 demonstrates how to translate this into a formula. The formula in E4 calculates the percent variance between current year sales and previous year sales.

```
=(D4-C4)/C4
```

▲	A	B	C	D	E
1					
2					
3		Region	Prior Year	Current Year	Percent Variance
4		North	$509,283	$553,887	=(D4-C4)/C4
5		South	$483,519	$511,115	6%
6		East	$640,603	$606,603	-5%
7		West	$320,312	$382,753	19%

Figure 2-3: Calculating the percent variance between current year sales and previous year sales.

How it works

The one thing to note about this formula is the use of parentheses. By default, Excel's order of operations states that division must be done before subtraction. But if you let that happen, you would get an erroneous result. Wrapping the first part of the formula in parentheses ensures that Excel performs the subtraction before the division.

You can simply enter the formula one time in the first row (cell E4 in this case) and then copy that formula down to every other row in your table.

Cross-Ref   See Chapter 1 for more information on the order of operator precedence.

Alternative: Simplified percent variance calculation

An alternative formula for calculating percent variance is to simply divide the current year sales by the previous year sales and then subtract 1. Because Excel performs division operations before subtraction, you don't have to use parentheses with this alternative formula.

```
=D4/C4-1
```

Formula 3: Calculating Percent Variance with Negative Values

In the previous section, "Formula 2: Calculating Percent Variance," you discovered how to calculate a percent variance. That formula works beautifully in most cases. However, when the benchmark value is a negative value, the formula breaks down.

For example, imagine that you're starting a business and expect to take a loss the first year. So you give yourself a budget of negative $10,000. Now imagine that after your first year, you actually made money, earning $12,000. Calculating the percent variance between your actual revenue and budgeted revenue would give you -220%. You can try it on a calculator. 12,000 minus -10,000 divided by -10,000 equals -220%.

How can you say that your percent variance is -220% when you clearly made money? Well, the problem is that when your benchmark value is a negative number, the math inverts the results, causing numbers to look wacky. This is a real problem in the corporate world where budgets can often be negative values.

The fix is to leverage the ABS function to negate the negative benchmark value:

```
=(C4-B4)/ABS(B4)
```

Figure 2-4 uses this formula in cell E4, illustrating the different results you get when using the standard percent variance formula and the improved percent variance formula.

▲	A	B	C	D	E
1					
2					
3		Budget	Actual	Standard Percent Variance	Improved Percent Variance
4		-10,000	12,000	-220%	220%

Figure 2-4: Using the ABS function gives you an accurate percent variance when dealing with negative values.

How it works

Excel's ABS function returns the absolute value for any number you pass to it. Entering =ABS(-100) into cell A1 would return 100. The ABS function essentially makes any number a non-negative number. Using ABS in this formula negates the effect of the negative benchmark (the negative 10,000 budget in the example) and returns the correct percent variance.

Note

You can safely use this formula for all your percent variance needs; it works with any combination of positive and negative numbers.

Formula 4: Calculating a Percent Distribution

Percent distribution is a measure of how a metric (such as total revenue) is distributed among the component parts that make up the total. As you can see in Figure 2-5, the calculation is relatively simple. You divide each component part by the total. This example has a cell that contains Total revenue (cell C9). You then divide each region's revenue by the total to get a percent distribution for each region.

◢	A	B	C	D
1				
2		Region	Revenue	Percent of Total
3		North	$7,626	=C3/$C$9
4		South	$3,387	18%
5		East	$1,695	9%
6		West	$6,457	34%
7				
8				
9		Total	$19,165	
10				

Figure 2-5: Calculating a percent distribution of revenue across regions.

How it works

This formula doesn't have a lot to it. You're simply using cell references to divide each component value by the total. The one thing to note is that the cell reference to the Total is entered as an absolute reference ($C$9). Using the dollar symbols locks the reference in place, ensuring that the cell reference pointing to Total does not adjust as you copy the formula down.

Cross-Ref

See Chapter 1 for more information on absolute and relative cell references.

Alternative: Percent distribution without a dedicated Total cell

You don't have to dedicate a separate cell to an actual Total value. You can simply calculate Total on the fly within the percent distribution formula. Figure 2-6 demonstrates how you can use the SUM function in place of a cell dedicated to holding a Total. The SUM function adds together any numbers you pass to it.

Again, note the use of absolute references in the SUM function. Using absolute references ensures that the SUM range stays locked as you copy the formula down:

```
=C3/SUM($C$3:$C$6)
```

◢	A	B	C	D
1				
2		Region	Revenue	Percent of Total
3		North	$7,626	=C3/SUM($C$3:$C$6)
4		South	$3,387	18%
5		East	$1,695	9%
6		West	$6,457	34%

Figure 2-6: Calculating percent distribution with the SUM function.

Formula 5: Calculating a Running Total

Some organizations like to see a running total as a mechanism to analyze the changes in a metric as a period of time progresses. Figure 2-7 illustrates a running total of units sold for January through December. The formula used in cell D3 is copied down for each month:

```
=SUM($C$3:C3)
```

◢	A	B	C	D
1				
2			Units Sold	Running Total
3		January	78	=SUM($C$3:C3)
4		February	63	141
5		March	38	179
6		April	17	196
7		May	84	280
8		June	63	343
9		July	32	375
10		August	20	395
11		September	98	493
12		October	63	556
13		November	75	631
14		December	75	706

Figure 2-7: Calculating a running total.

How it works

In this formula, you use the SUM function to add all the units from cell C3 to the current row. The trick to this formula is the absolute reference ($C$3). Placing an absolute reference in the reference for the first value of the year locks that value down. Locking the value down ensures that as the formula is copied down, the SUM function always captures and adds the units from the very first value to the value on the current row.

Cross-Ref

See Chapter 1 for more information on absolute and relative cell references.

Formula 6: Applying a Percent Increase or Decrease to Values

A common task for an Excel analyst is to apply a percentage increase or decrease to a given number. For instance, when applying a price increase to a product, you would typically raise the original price by a certain percent. When giving a customer a discount, you would decrease that customer's rate by a certain percent.

Figure 2-8 illustrates how to apply a percent increase and decrease using a simple formula. In cell E5, you apply a 10 percent price increase to Product A. In Cell E9, you give a 20 percent discount to Customer A.

	A	B	C	D	E
1					
2					
3					
4			Unit Cost	Price Increase	Final Price
5		Product A	100	10%	=C5*(1+D5)
6					
7					
7					
8			Cost per Service	Percent Discount	Discounted Cost
9		Customer A	1000	20%	=C9*(1-D9)

Figure 2-8: Applying a percent increase and decrease using a simple formula.

How it works

To increase a number by a percentage amount, multiply the original amount by 1+ the percent of increase. In the example in Figure 2-8, Product A is getting a 10 percent increase. So you first add 1 to the 10 percent, which gives you 110 percent. You then multiply the original price of 100 by 110 percent. This calculates to the new price of 110.

To decrease a number by a percentage amount, multiply the original amount by 1- the percent of increase. In the example in Figure 2-8, Customer A is getting a 20 percent discount. So you first subtract 20 percent from 1, which gives you 80 percent. You then multiply the original 1,000 cost per service by 80 percent. This calculates to the new rate of 800.

Note the use of parentheses in the formulas. By default, Excel's order of operations states that multiplication must be done before addition or subtraction. But if you let that happen, you would get an erroneous result. Wrapping the second part of the formula in parentheses ensures that Excel performs the multiplication last.

See Chapter 1 for more information on the order of operator precedence.

Cross-Ref

Formula 7: Dealing with Divide-by-Zero Errors

In mathematics, division by zero is impossible. One way to understand why it's impossible is to consider what happens when you divide a number by another.

Division is really nothing more than fancy subtraction. For example, 10 divided by 2 is the same as starting with 10 and continuously subtracting 2 as many times as needed to get to zero. In this case, you would need to continuously subtract 2 five times.

$$10-2 = 8$$
$$8-2 = 6$$
$$6-2 = 4$$
$$4-2 = 2$$
$$2-2 = 0$$

So, $10/2 = 5$.

Now if you tried to do this with 10 divided by 0, you would never get anywhere, because 10-0 is 10 all day long. You'd be sitting there subtracting 0 until your calculator dies.

$$10-0 = 10$$
$$10-0 = 10$$
$$10-0 = 10$$
$$10-0 = 10$$
$$\ldots\ldots \text{Infinity}$$

Mathematicians call the result you get when dividing any number by zero "undefined." Software like Excel simply gives you an error when you try to divide by zero. In Excel, when you divide a number by zero, you get the #DIV/0! error.

You can avoid this by telling Excel to skip the calculation if your denominator is a zero. Figure 2-9 illustrates how to do this by wrapping the division operation in Excel's IF function.

```
=IF(C4=0, 0, D4/C4)
```

▲	A	B	C	D	E
1					
2			Budget	Actual	Percent to Budget
3		Jim	200	200	100%
4		Tim	0	100	=IF(C4=0, 0, D4/C4)
5		Kim	300	350	117%

Figure 2-9: Using the IF function to avoid a division-by-zero error.

How it works

The IF function requires three arguments: the condition; what to do if the condition is true; and what to do if the condition is false.

The condition argument in this example is the budget in C4 is equal to zero (C4=0). Condition arguments must be structured to return TRUE or FALSE, and that usually means that there is a comparison operation (like an equal sign or greater-than sign).

If the condition argument returns TRUE, the second argument of the IF function is returned to the cell. The second argument is 0, meaning that you simply want a zero displayed if the budget number in cell C4 is a zero.

IF the condition argument is not zero, the third argument takes effect. In the third argument, you tell Excel to perform the division calculation (D4/C4).

So this formula basically says that if C4 equals 0, then return a 0, or else return the result of D4/C4.

Formula 8: Basic Rounding of Numbers

Often, your customers want to look at clean, round numbers. Inundating a user with decimal values and unnecessary digits for the sake of precision can actually make your reports harder to read. For this reason, you may want to consider using Excel's rounding functions.

Figure 2-10 illustrates how the number 9.45 is affected by the use of the ROUND, ROUNDUP, and ROUNDDOWN functions.

▲	A	B	C
1			
2		Formula	Result
3		=ROUND(94.45,0)	94
4		=ROUND(94.45,1)	94.5
5		=ROUND(94.45,-1)	90
6		=ROUND(94.45,-2)	100
7		=ROUNDDOWN(94.45,0)	94
8		=ROUNDUP(94.45,0)	95

Figure 2-10: Rounding numbers using formulas.

How it works

Excel's ROUND function is used to round a given number to a specified number of digits. The ROUND function takes two arguments: the original value and the number of digits to round to.

Entering a 0 as the second argument tells Excel to remove all decimal places and round the integer portion of the number based on the first decimal place. For instance, this formula rounds to 94:

```
=ROUND(94.45,0)
```

Entering a 1 as the second argument tells Excel to round to one decimal based on the value of the second decimal place. For example, this formula rounds to 94.5:

```
=ROUND(94.45,1)
```

You can also enter a negative number as the second argument, telling Excel to round based on values to the left of the decimal point. The following formula, for example, returns 90:

```
=ROUND(94.45,-1)
```

You can force rounding in a particular direction using the ROUNDUP or ROUNDDOWN functions.

This ROUNDDOWN formula rounds 94.45 down to 94:

```
=ROUNDDOWN(94.45,0)
```

This ROUNDUP formula rounds 94.45 up to 95:

```
=ROUNDUP(94.45,0)
```

Formula 9: Rounding to the Nearest Penny

In some industries, it is common practice to round a dollar amount to the nearest penny. Figure 2-11 demonstrates how rounding a dollar amount up or down to the nearest penny can affect the resulting number.

	A	B	C	D
1				
2		Dollar Amount	Round up to Nearest Penny	Round Down to the Nearest Penny
3		$ 34.243	$34.25	$34.24
4				
5			=CEILING(B3,0.01)	=FLOOR(B3,0.01)

Figure 2-11: Rounding to the nearest penny.

How it works

You can round to the nearest penny by using the CEILING or FLOOR functions.

The CEILING function rounds a number up to the nearest multiple of significance that you pass to it. This utility comes in handy when you need to override the standard rounding protocol with your own business rules. For instance, you can force Excel to round 123.222 to 124 by using the CEILING function with a significance of 1.

```
=CEILING(123.222,1)
```

So entering a .01 as the significance tells the CEILING function to round to the nearest penny.

If you wanted to round to the nearest nickel, you could use .05 as the significance. For instance, the following formula returns 123.15:

```
=CEILING(123.11,.05)
```

The FLOOR function works the same way except that it forces a rounding *down* to the nearest significance. The following example function rounds 123.19 down to the nearest nickel, giving 123.15 as the result:

```
=FLOOR(123.19,.05)
```

Formula 10: Rounding to Significant Digits

In some financial reports, figures are presented in significant digits. The idea is that when you're dealing with numbers in the millions, you don't need to inundate a report with superfluous numbers for the sake of showing precision down to the tens, hundreds, and thousands places.

For instance, instead of showing the number 883,788, you could choose to round the number to one significant digit. This would mean displaying the same number as 900,000. Rounding 883,788 to two significant digits would show the number as 880,000.

In essence, you're deeming that a particular number's place is significant enough to show. The rest of the number can be replaced with zeros. You might feel as though doing this could introduce problems, but when you're dealing with large enough numbers, any number below a certain significance is inconsequential.

Figure 2-12 demonstrates how you can implement a formula that rounds numbers to a given number of significant digits.

	A	B	C	D	E
1					
2					Significant Digits
3					1
4		Raw Number	Significant Digits		
5		605,390	=ROUND(B5,LEN(INT(ABS(B5)))*-1+$E$3)		
6		900,942	900,000		
7		591,007	600,000		
8		491,235	500,000		
9		883,788	900,000		
10		952,687	1,000,000		
11		(332,602)	-300,000		

Figure 2-12: Rounding numbers to 1 significant digit.

How it works

You use Excel's ROUND function to round a given number to a specified number of digits. The ROUND function takes two arguments: the original value and the number of digits to round to.

Entering a negative number as the second argument tells Excel to round based on significant digits to the left of the decimal point. The following formula, for example, returns 9500:

```
=ROUND(9489,-2)
```

Changing the significant digits argument to -3 returns a value of 9000.

```
=ROUND(B14,-3)
```

This works great, but what if you have numbers on differing scales? That is, what if some of your numbers are millions while others are hundreds of thousands? If you wanted to show them all with 1 significant digit, you would need to build a different ROUND function for each number to account for the differing significant digits argument that you would need for each type of number.

To help solve this issue, you can replace your hard-coded significant digits argument with a formula that calculates what that number should be.

Imagine that your number is -2330.45. You can use this formula as the significant digits argument in your ROUND function:

```
LEN(INT(ABS(-2330.45)))*-1+2
```

This formula first wraps your number in the ABS function, effectively removing any negative symbol that may exist. It then wraps that result in the INT function, stripping out any decimals that may exist. It then wraps *that* result in the LEN function to get a measure of how many characters are in the number without any decimals or negation symbols.

In this example, this part of the formula results in the number 4. If you take the number -2330.45 and strip away the decimals and negative symbol, you have four characters left.

This number is then multiplied by -1 to make it a negative number, and then added to the number of significant digits you are looking for. In this example, that calculation looks like this: 4*-1+2 = -2.

Again, this formula will be used as the second argument for your ROUND function. Enter this formula into Excel and round the number to 2300 (2 significant digits):

```
=ROUND(-2330.45, LEN(INT(ABS(-2330.45)))*-1+2)
```

You can then replace this formula with cell references that point to the source number and cell that holds the number of desired significant digits. This what you see in Figure 2-12, shown previously.

```
=ROUND(B5,LEN(INT(ABS(B5)))*-1+$E$3)
```

Formula 11: Counting Values in a Range

Excel provides several functions to count the values in a range: COUNT, COUNTA, and COUNTBLANK. Each of these functions provides a different method of counting based on whether the values in your range are numbers, numbers and text, or blank.

Figure 2-13 illustrates the different kinds of counting you can perform. In row 12, the COUNT function is counting only exams where students have passed. In column H, the COUNTA function is counting all the exams taken by a student. In column I, the COUNTBLANK function is counting only those exams that have not yet been taken.

	A	B	C	D	E	F	G	H	I
1									
2									
3			Math	English	Science	History		Exams Taken By Each Student	Exams Remaining
4		Student 1	Fail		1			2	2
5		Student 2	1	1	1			3	1
6		Student 3		1	1	1		3	1
7		Student 4	Fail		Fail			2	2
8		Student 5	1	1	1	Fail		4	0
9									
10			How many students passed each exam.						
11			Math	English	Art	History			
12			2	3	4	1			

Figure 2-13: A demonstration of counting cells.

How it works

The COUNT function counts only numeric values in a given range. It requires only a single argument in which you pass a range of cells. For example, this formula counts only those cells in range C4:C8 that contain a numeric value:

```
=COUNT(C4:C8)
```

The COUNTA function counts any cell that is not blank. You can use this function when you're counting cells that contain any combination of numbers and text. It requires only a single argument in which you pass a range of cells. For instance, this formula counts all the nonblank cells in range C4:F4:

```
=COUNTA(C4:F4)
```

The COUNTBLANK function counts only the blank cells in a given range. It requires only a single argument in which you pass a range of cells. For instance, this formula counts all the blank cells in range C4:F4:

```
=COUNTBLANK(C4:F4)
```

Formula 12: Creating a Conversion Table

You may work at a company where you need to know how many cubic yards can be covered by a gallon of material, or how many cups are needed to fill an Imperial Gallon.

You can use Excel's CONVERT function to produce a conversion table containing every possible type of conversion that you need for a set of measures. Figure 12-14 illustrates a conversion table created using nothing but Excel's CONVERT function.

With this table, you can get a quick view of the conversions from one unit of measure to another. You can see that it takes 48 teaspoons to make a cup, 2.4 cups to make an English pint, and so on.

▲	C	D	E	F	G	H	I
1							
2				Teaspoon	Tablespoon	Fluid ounce	Cup
3				tsp	tbs	oz	cup
4		Teaspoon	tsp	=CONVERT(1,$E4,F$3)	0.33	0.17	0.02
5		Tablespoon	tbs	3.00	1.00	0.50	0.06
6		Fluid ounce	oz	6.00	2.00	1.00	0.13
7		Cup	cup	48.00	16.00	8.00	1.00
8		U.S. pint	us_pt	96.00	32.00	16.00	2.00
9		U.K. pint	uk_pt	115.29	38.43	19.22	2.40
10		Quart	qt	192.00	64.00	32.00	4.00
11		Imperial quart	uk_qt	230.58	76.86	38.43	4.80
12		Gallon gal	gal	768.00	256.00	128.00	16.00

Figure 12-14: Creating a unit-of-measure conversion table.

How it works

The CONVERT function requires three arguments: a number value, the unit you're converting from, and the unit you're converting to. For instance, to convert 100 miles into kilometers, you can enter this formula to get the answer 160.93:

```
=CONVERT(100,"mi", "km")
```

You can use the following formula to convert 100 gallons into liters. This gives you the result 378.54:

```
=CONVERT(100,"gal", "l")
```

Notice the conversion codes for each unit of measure. These codes are very specific and must be entered in exactly the way Excel expects to see them. Entering a CONVERT formula using "gallon" or "GAL" instead of the expected "gal" returns an error.

Luckily, Excel provides a tooltip as you start entering your CONVERT function, letting you pick the correct unit codes from a list.

You can refer to Excel's Help files on the CONVERT function to get a list of valid unit-of-measure conversion codes.

When you have the codes you are interested in, you can enter them in a matrix-style table like the one you see in Figure 12-14. In the top-leftmost cell in your matrix, enter a formula that points to the appropriate conversion code for the matrix row and matrix column.

Be sure to include the absolute references necessary to lock the references to the conversion codes. For the codes located in the matrix row, lock the column reference. For the codes located in the matrix column, lock the row reference.

```
=CONVERT(1,$E4,F$3)
```

At this point, you can simply copy your formula across the entire matrix.

Manipulating Text with Formulas

3

Often, the work you do with Excel involves not only calculating numbers but also transforming and shaping data to fit your data models. Many of these activities include manipulating text strings. This chapter highlights some of the common text transformation exercises that an Excel analyst performs, and in the process gives you a sense of some of the text-based functions Excel has to offer.

Note

You can download the files for all the formulas at www.wiley.com/go/101excelformula.

Formula 13: Joining Text Strings

One of the more basic text manipulation actions you can perform is joining text strings together. In the example shown in Figure 3-1, you create a full-name column by joining together first and last names.

⊿	A	B	C	D
1				
2		FirstName	LastName	Full Name
3		Guy	Gilbert	=B3&" "&C3
4		Kevin	Brown	Kevin Brown
5		Roberto	Tamburello	Roberto Tamburello
6		Rob	Walters	Rob Walters
7		Thierry	Alexander	Thierry Alexander
8		David	Bradley	David Bradley
9		JoLynn	Dobney	JoLynn Dobney
10		Ruth	Ellerbrock	Ruth Ellerbrock
11		Doris	Hartwig	Doris Hartwig
12		John	Campbell	John Campbell

Figure 3-1: Joining first and last names.

How it works

This example illustrates the use of the ampersand (&) operator. The ampersand operator tells Excel to concatenate values with one another. As you can see in Figure 3-1, you can join cell values with text of your own. In this example, you join the values in cells B3 and C3, separated by a space (created by entering a space in quotes).

Note

Excel also provides a CONCATENATE function that joins values without the need for the ampersand. In this example, you could enter =CONCATENATE(B3, " ", C3). Frankly, it's better to skip this function and simply use the ampersands. This function is more processing intensive and requires using more keystrokes.

Formula 14: Setting Text to Sentence Case

Excel provides three useful functions to change the text to upper-, lower-, or proper case. As you can see in rows 6, 7, and 8 illustrated in Figure 3-2, these functions require nothing more than a pointer to the text you want converted. As you might guess, the UPPER function converts text to all uppercase, the LOWER function converts text to all lowercase, and the PROPER function converts text to title case (the first letter of every word is capitalized).

What Excel lacks is a function to convert text to sentence case (only the first letter of the first word is capitalized). But as you can see in Figure 3-2, you can use the following formula to force text into sentence case:

```
=UPPER(LEFT(C4,1)) & LOWER(RIGHT(C4,LEN(C4)-1))
```

⊿	A	B	C
1			
2			
3			
4			The QUICK brown FOX JUMPS over the lazy DOG.
5			
6		=UPPER(C6)	THE QUICK BROWN FOX JUMPS OVER THE LAZY DOG.
7		=LOWER(C7)	the quick brown fox jumps over the lazy dog.
8		=PROPER(C8)	The Quick Brown Fox Jumps Over The Lazy Dog.
9			
10		=UPPER(LEFT(C4,1))&LOWER(RIGHT(C4,LEN(C4)-1))	The quick brown fox jumps over the lazy dog.

Figure 3-2: Converting text into uppercase, lowercase, proper case, and sentence case.

How it works

If you take a look at this formula closely, you can see that it's made up of two parts that are joined by the ampersand.

The first part uses Excel's LEFT function:

```
UPPER(LEFT(C4,1))
```

The LEFT function allows you to extract a given number of characters from the left of a given text string. The LEFT function requires two arguments: the text string you are evaluating and the number of characters you need extracted from the left of the text string. In this example, you extract the left 1 character from the text in cell C4. You then make it uppercase by wrapping it in the UPPER function.

The second part is a bit trickier. Here, you use the Excel RIGHT function:

```
LOWER(RIGHT(C4,LEN(C4)-1))
```

Like the LEFT function, the RIGHT function requires two arguments: the text you are evaluating, and the number of characters you need extracted from the right of the text string. In this case, however, you can't just give the RIGHT function a hard-coded number for the second argument. You have to calculate that number by subtracting 1 from the entire length of the text string. You subtract 1 to account for the first character that is already uppercase thanks to the first part of the formula.

You use the LEN function to get the entire length of the text string. You subtract 1 from that, which gives you the number of characters needed for the RIGHT function.

You can finally pass the formula you've created so far to the LOWER function to make everything but the first character lowercase.

Joining the two parts together gives results in sentence case:

```
=UPPER(LEFT(C4,1)) & LOWER(RIGHT(C4,LEN(C4)-1))
```

Formula 15: Removing Spaces from a Text String

If you pull data in from external databases and legacy systems, you will no doubt encounter text that contains extra spaces. Sometimes these extra spaces are found at the beginning of the text, whereas at other times, they show up at the end.

Extra spaces are generally evil because they can cause problems in lookup formulas, charting, column sizing, and printing.

Figure 3-3 illustrates how you can remove superfluous spaces by using the TRIM function.

	A	B	C
1			
2			
3		Original Text	Trimmed Text
4		ABCD	ABCD
5		A B C D	A B C D
6		Alan Jones	Alan Jones
7		ABCD	=TRIM(B7)

Figure 3-3: Removing excess spaces from text.

How it works

The TRIM function is relatively straightforward. Simply give it some text and it removes all spaces from the text except for single spaces between words.

As with other functions, you can nest the TRIM function in other functions to clean up your text while applying some other manipulation. For instance, the following function trims the text in cell A1 and converts it to uppercase all in one step:

```
=UPPER(TRIM(A1))
```

Note

The TRIM function was designed to trim only the ASCII space character from text. The ASCII space character has a code value of 32. The Unicode character set, however, has an additional space character called the nonbreaking space character. This character is commonly used in web pages and has the Unicode value of 160.

The TRIM function is designed to handle only CHAR(32) space characters. It cannot, by itself, handle CHAR(160) space characters. To handle this kind of space, you need to use the SUBSTITUTE function to find CHAR(160) space characters and replace them with CHAR(32) space characters so that the TRIM function can fix them. You can accomplish this task all at one time with the following formula:

```
=TRIM(SUBSTITUTE(A4,CHAR(160),CHAR(32)))
```

For a detailed look at the SUBSTITUTE function, see Formula 18: Substituting Text Strings.

Formula 16: Extract Parts of a Text String

One of the most important techniques for manipulating text in Excel is the capability to extract specific portions of text. Using Excel's LEFT, RIGHT, and MID functions, you can perform tasks such as:

    Convert nine-digit postal codes into five-digit postal codes

    Extract phone numbers without the area code

    Extract parts of employee or job codes for use somewhere else

Figure 3-4 demonstrates how using the LEFT, RIGHT, and MID functions can help easily accomplish these tasks.

	A	B	C
1			
2	Convert these 9-digit postal codes into 5-digit postal codes.		
3	Zip	Zip	
4	70056-2343	70056	=LEFT(A4,5)
5	75023-5774	75023	=LEFT(A5,5)
6			
7	Extract the phone number without the area code.		
8	Phone	Phone	
9	(214)887-7765	887-7765	=RIGHT(A9,8)
10	(703)654-2180	654-2180	=RIGHT(A10,8)
11			
12	Extract the 4th character of each Job Code.		
13	Job Code	Job Level	
14	2214001	4	=MID(A14,4,1)
15	5542075	2	=MID(A15,4,1)
16	1113543	3	=MID(A16,4,1)

Figure 3-4: Using the LEFT, RIGHT, and MID functions.

How it works

The LEFT function allows you to extract a given number of characters from the left of a given text string. The LEFT function requires two arguments: the text string you are evaluating and the number of characters you need extracted from the left of the text string. In the example, you extract the left five characters from the value in Cell A4.

```
=LEFT(A4,5)
```

The RIGHT function allows you to extract a given number of characters from the right of a given text string. The RIGHT function requires two arguments: the text string you are evaluating and the number of characters you need extracted from the right of the text string. In the example, you extract the right eight characters from the value in Cell A9.

```
=RIGHT(A9,8)
```

The MID function allows you to extract a given number of characters from the middle of a given text string. The MID function requires three arguments: the text string you are evaluating; the character position in the text string from where to start extracting; and the number of characters you need extracted. In the example, you start at the fourth character in the text string and extract one character.

```
=MID(A14,4,1)
```

Formula 17: Finding a Particular Character in a Text String

Excel's LEFT, RIGHT, and MID functions work great for extracting text, but only if you know the exact position of the characters you are targeting. What do you do when you don't know exactly where to start the extraction? For example, if you had the following list of Product codes, how would you go about extracting all the text after the hyphen?

PRT-432

COPR-6758

SVCCALL-58574

The LEFT function wouldn't work because you need the right few characters. The RIGHT function alone won't work because you need to tell it exactly how many characters to extract from the right of the text string. Any number you give will pull either too many or too few characters from the text. The MID function alone won't work because you need to tell it exactly where in the text to start extracting. Again, any number you give will pull either too many or too few characters from the text.

The reality is that you often will need to the find specific characters in order to get the appropriate starting position for extraction.

This is where Excel's FIND function comes in handy. With the FIND function, you can get the position number of a particular character and use that character position in other operations.

In the example shown in Figure 3-5, you use the FIND function in conjunction with the MID function to extract the middle numbers from a list of product codes. As you can see from the formula, you find the position of the hyphen and use that position number to feed the MID function.

```
=MID(B3,FIND("-",B3)+1,2)
```

▲	A	B	C
1			
2		Product Code	Extract the Numbers
3		PWR-16-Small	=MID(B3,FIND("-",B3)+1,2)
4		PW-18-Medium	18
5		PW-19-Large	19
6		CWS-22-Medium	22
7		CWTP-44-Large	44
8			

Figure 3-5: Using the FIND function to extract data based on the position of the hyphen.

How it works

The FIND function has two required arguments. The first argument is the text you want to find. The second argument is the text you want to search. By default, the FIND function returns the position number of the character you are trying to find. If the text you are searching contains more than one of your search characters, the FIND function returns the position number of the first encounter.

For instance, the following formula searches for a hyphen in the text string "PWR-16-Small". The result will be a number 4, because the first hyphen it encounters is the fourth character in the text string.

```
=FIND("-","PWR-16-Small")
```

You can use the FIND function as an argument in a MID function to extract a set number of characters after the position number returned by the FIND function.

Entering this formula in a cell will give you the two numbers after the first hyphen found in the text. Note the +1 in the formula. Including +1 ensures that you move over one character to get to the text after the hyphen.

```
=MID("PWR-16-Small", FIND("-","PWR-16-Small")+1, 2)
```

Alternative: Finding the second instance of a character

By default, the FIND function returns the position number of the first instance of the character you are searching for. If you want the position number of the second instance, you can use the optional Start_Num argument. This argument lets you specify the character position in the text string to start the search.

For example, the following formula returns the position number of the second hyphen because you tell the FIND function to start searching at position 5 (after the first hyphen).

```
=FIND("-","PWR-16-Small", 5)
```

To use this formula dynamically (that is, without knowing where to start the search) you can nest a FIND function as the Start_Num argument in another FIND function. You can enter this formula into Excel to get the position number of the second hyphen.

```
=FIND("-","PWR-16-Small", FIND("-","PWR-16-Small")+1)
```

Figure 3-6 demonstrates a real-world example of this concept. Here, you extract the size attribute from the product code by finding the second instance of the hyphen and using that position number as the starting point in the MID function. The formula shown in cell C3 is as follows:

```
=MID(B3,FIND("-",B3,FIND("-",B3)+1)+1,10000)
```

This formula tells Excel to find the position number of the second hyphen, move over one character, and then extract the next 10,000 characters. Of course, there aren't 10,000 characters, but using a large number like that ensures that everything after the second hyphen is pulled.

	A	B	C
1			
2		Product Code	Extract the Size Designation
3		PWR-16-Small	=MID(B3,FIND("-",B3,FIND("-",B3)+1)+1,10000)
4		PW-18-Medium	Medium
5		PW-19-Large	Large
6		CWS-22-Medium	Medium
7		CWTP-44-Large	Large
8			

Figure 3-6: Nesting the FIND function to extract everything after the second hyphen.

Formula 18: Substituting Text Strings

In some situations, it's helpful to substitute some text with other text. One such case is when you encounter the annoying apostrophe S ('S) quirk that you get with the PROPER function. To see what we mean, enter this formula into Excel:

```
=PROPER("STAR'S COFFEE")
```

This formula is meant to convert the given text into title case (where the first letter of every word is capitalized). The actual result of the formula is the following:

Star'S Coffee

Note how the PROPER function capitalizes the S after the apostrophe. Annoying, to say the least.

However, with a little help from the Excel's SUBSTITUTE function, you can avoid this annoyance. Figure 3-7 shows the fix using the following formula:

```
=SUBSTITUTE(PROPER(SUBSTITUTE(B4,"'","qzx")),"qzx","'")
```

E4	▼ : × ✓ *fx*	=SUBSTITUTE(PROPER(SUBSTITUTE(B4,"'","qzx")),"qzx","'")					
	A	B	C	D	E	F	G	H
1								
2								
3		Company	Bad Proper Case		Better Proper Case			
4		STAR'S COFFEE	Star'S Coffee		Star's Coffee			
5		DONALD'S	Donald'S		Donald's			
6		MICHAEL'S DELI	Michael'S Deli		Michael's Deli			
7								

Figure 3-7: Fixing the apostrophe S issue with the SUBSTITUTE function.

How it works

The formula uses the SUBSTITUTE function, which requires three arguments: the target text; the old text you want replaced; and the new text to use as the replacement.

As you look at the full formula, note that it uses two SUBSTITUTE functions. This formula is actually two formulas (one nested in the other). The first formula is the part that reads

```
PROPER(SUBSTITUTE(B4,"'","qzx"))
```

In this part, you use the SUBSTITUTE function to replace the apostrophe (') with qzx. This may seem like a crazy thing to do, but there is some method here. Essentially, the PROPER function capitalizes any letter coming directly after a symbol. You trick the PROPER function by substituting the apostrophe with a benign set of letters that are unlikely to be strung together in the original text.

The second formula actually wraps the first. This formula substitutes the benign qzx with an apostrophe.

```
=SUBSTITUTE(PROPER(SUBSTITUTE(B4,"'","qzx")),"qzx","'")
```

So the entire formula replaces the apostrophe with qzx, performs the PROPER function, and then reverts the qzx back to an apostrophe.

Formula 19: Counting Specific Characters in a Cell

A useful trick is to be able to count the number of times a specific character exists in a text string. The technique for doing this in Excel is a bit clever. To figure out, for example, how many times the letter *s* appears in the word *Mississippi*, you can count them by hand, of course, but systematically, you can follow these general steps:

1. Measure the character length of the word *Mississippi* (11 characters).

2. Measure the character length after removing every letter *s* (6 characters).

3. Subtract the adjusted length from the original length.

You can then accurately conclude that the number of times the letter *s* appears in the word *Mississippi* is four.

A real-world use for this technique of counting specific characters is to calculate a word count in Excel. Figure 3-8 shows the following formula being used to count the number of words entered in cell B4:

```
=LEN(B4)-LEN(SUBSTITUTE(B4," ",""))+1
```

	A	B	C
1			
2			
3			Get Word Count
4		The Quick Brown Fox Jumps Over The Lazy Dog.	=LEN(B4)-LEN(SUBSTITUTE(B4," ",""))+1
5			

Figure 3-8: Calculating the number of words in a cell.

How it works

This formula essentially follows the steps mentioned earlier in this section. The formula uses the LEN function to first measure the length of the text in cell B4:

```
LEN(B4)
```

It then uses the SUBSTITUTE function to remove the spaces from the text:

```
SUBSTITUTE(B4," ","")
```

Wrapping that SUBSTITUTE function in a LEN function gives you the length of the text without the spaces. Note that you have to add one to that answer to account for the fact that the last word doesn't have an associated space.

```
LEN(SUBSTITUTE(B4," ",""))+1
```

Subtracting the original length with the adjusted length gives you the word count.

```
=LEN(B4)-LEN(SUBSTITUTE(B4," ",""))+1
```

Formula 20: Adding a Line Break within a Formula

When creating charts in Excel, it's sometimes useful to force line breaks for the purpose of composing better visualizations. Take the chart shown in Figure 3-9, for example. Here, the X-axis labels in the chart include the data value in addition to the sales rep. This setup works well when you don't want to inundate your chart with data labels.

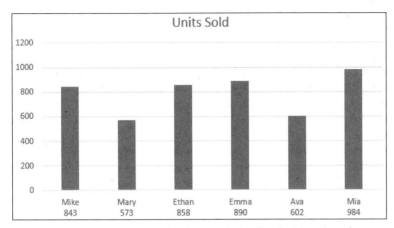

Figure 3-9: The X-axis labels in this chart include a line break and a reference to the data values.

The secret to this trick is to use the CHAR() function in a formula that makes up your chart labels (see Figure 3-10).

	A	B	C
1			
2			Units Sold
3	Mike	=A3&CHAR(10)& C3	843
4	Mary	Mary573	573
5	Ethan	Ethan858	858
6	Emma	Emma890	890
7	Ava	Ava602	602
8	Mia	Mia984	984

Figure 3-10: Using the CHAR() function to force a line break between sales rep name and data value.

How it works

Every character in Excel has an associated ANSI character code. The ANSI character code is a Windows system code set that defines the characters you see on your screen. The ANSI character set consists of 255 characters, numbered from 1 to 255. The uppercase letter *A* is character number 97. The number 9 is character 57.

Even nonprinting characters have codes. The code for a space is 32. The code for a line break is 10.

You can call up any character in a formula by using the CHAR() function. The example shown in Figure 3-10 calls up the line break character and joins it with the values in cells A3 and C3:

```
=A3 & CHAR(10) & C3
```

The cell itself doesn't show the line break unless you have wrap text applied. But even if you don't, any chart using this kind of formula will display the data returned by the formula with the line breaks.

Formula 21: Cleaning Strange Characters from Text Fields

When you import data from an external data source such as text files or web feeds, strange characters may come in with your data. Instead of trying to clean these manually, you can use Excel's CLEAN function (see Figure 3-11).

	A	B	C
1			
2		Store	Cleaned Text
3		Detroit (Store #1)▯▯▯▯▯	=TRIM(CLEAN(B3))
4		Detroit (Store #2)▯▯▯▯▯	Detroit (Store #2)
5		Detroit (Store #3)▯▯▯▯▯	Detroit (Store #3)
6		Charlotte (Store #1)▯▯▯▯▯	Charlotte (Store #1)
7		Charlotte (Store #2)▯▯▯▯▯	Charlotte (Store #2)
8		Charlotte (Store #3)▯▯▯▯▯	Charlotte (Store #3)

Figure 3-11: Cleaning data with the CLEAN function.

How it works

The CLEAN function removes nonprintable characters from any text you pass to it. You can wrap the CLEAN function within the TRIM function to remove unprintable characters and excess spaces at the same time.

```
=TRIM(CLEAN(B3))
```

Formula 22: Padding Numbers with Zeros

In many cases, the work you do in Excel ends up in other database systems within the organization you're involved with. Those database systems often have field-length requirements that mandate a certain number of characters. A common technique for ensuring that a field is made up of a set number of characters is to pad data with zeros.

Padding data with zeros is a relatively easy concept to apply. Essentially, if you have a Customer ID field that must be 10 characters long, for example, you need to add enough zeros to fulfill that requirement. So Customer ID 5381656 would need to be padded with three zeros, making that ID 5381565000.

Cell C4 shown in Figure 3-12 uses this formula to pad the Customer IDs with zeros:

```
=LEFT(B4&"0000000000", 10)
```

⬜	A	B	C
1			
2			
3		Customer ID	Pad to 10 characters
4		5381656	=LEFT(B4&"0000000000", 10)
5		832	8320000000
6		23	2300000000
7		290	2900000000
8		2036	2036000000
9		5965	5965000000
10		6	6000000000
11		7457	7457000000
12		2903	2903000000
13		6137	6137000000

Figure 3-12: Padding Customer IDs to 10 characters.

How it works

The formula shown in Figure 3-12 first joins the value in cell B4 and a text string comprising of 10 zeros, effectively creating a new text string that guarantees a Customer ID composed of 10 zeros.

You then use the LEFT function to extract the left 10 characters of that new text string. The result will be a Customer ID with a minimum of 10 characters.

Cross-Ref   For more details on the LEFT function, see Formula 16: Extract Parts of a Text String.

Formula 23: Formatting the Numbers in a Text String

It's not uncommon to have reporting that joins text with numbers. For example, you may be required to show a line in your report that summarizes a salesperson's results, like this:

John Hutchison: $5,000

The problem is that when you join numbers in a text string, the number formatting does not follow. Take a look at Figure 3-13 as an example. Note how the numbers in the joined strings (column E) do not adopt the formatting from the source cells (column C).

	A	B	C	D	E
1					
2		Rep	Revenue		Rep and Revenue
3		Gilbert	$6,820		=B3&": "&C3
4		Brown	$5,205		Brown: 5205
5		Tamburello	$246		Tamburello: 246
6		Walters	$7,136		Walters: 7136
7		Alexander	$2,921		Alexander: 2921
8		Bradley	$8,225		Bradley: 8225
9		Dobney	$5,630		Dobney: 5630
10		Ellerbrock	$7,994		Ellerbrock: 7994
11		Hartwig	$6,676		Hartwig: 6676
12		Campbell	$5,716		Campbell: 5716

Figure 3-13: Numbers joined with text do not inherently adopt number formatting.

To solve this problem, you have to wrap the cell reference for your number value in the TEXT function. Using the TEXT function, you can apply the needed formatting on the fly. The formula shown in Figure 3-14 resolves the issue:

```
=B3&": "&TEXT(C3, "$0,000")
```

	A	B	C	D	E
1					
2		Rep	Revenue		Rep and Revenue
3		Gilbert	$6,820		=B3&": "&TEXT(C3, "$0,000")
4		Brown	$5,205		Brown: $5,205
5		Tamburello	$246		Tamburello: $0,246
6		Walters	$7,136		Walters: $7,136
7		Alexander	$2,921		Alexander: $2,921
8		Bradley	$8,225		Bradley: $8,225
9		Dobney	$5,630		Dobney: $5,630
10		Ellerbrock	$7,994		Ellerbrock: $7,994
11		Hartwig	$6,676		Hartwig: $6,676
12		Campbell	$5,716		Campbell: $5,716

Figure 3-14: Using the TEXT function allows you to format numbers joined with text.

How it works

The TEXT function requires two arguments: a value, and a valid Excel format. You can apply any formatting you want to a number as long as it's a format that Excel recognizes.

For example, you can enter this formula into Excel to display $99:

```
=TEXT(99.21,"$#,###")
```

You can enter this formula into Excel to display 9921%:

```
=TEXT(99.21,"0%")
```

You can enter this formula into Excel to display 99.2:

```
=TEXT(99.21,"0.0")
```

An easy way to get the syntax for a particular number format is to look at the Number Format dialog box. To see that dialog box and get the syntax, follow these steps:

1. Right-click any cell and select Format Cell.
2. On the Number format tab, select the formatting you need.
3. Select Custom from the Category list on the left of the Number Format dialog box.
4. Copy the syntax found in the Type input box.

Alternative: Using the DOLLAR function

If the number value you're joining with text is a dollar figure, you can use the simpler DOLLAR function. This function applies the regional currency format to the given text.

The DOLLAR function has two basic arguments: the number value and the number of decimals you want to display.

```
=B3&": "&DOLLAR(C3,0)
```

Working with Dates and Times

In Excel, every possible date starting from January 1, 1900, is stored as a serial number. For example, January 1, 1900, is stored as 1; January 2, 1900, is stored as 2; and so on. This system of storing dates as serial numbers, commonly called the *1900 system,* is the default date system for all Microsoft Office applications.

To work with times, Excel simply extends the date serial system to decimal fractions of a 24-hour day, with each time value being represented by a number between 0 and 1. Together, the date serial number and time fraction make up a date and time. For instance, the serial number 1.5 represents January 1, 1900, 12 p.m. The serial number 2.75 represents January 2, 1900, 6 p.m.

The fact that, beneath the covers, dates and times are nothing more than a numbering system opens the door for all kinds of cool formula-driven analyses. This chapter walks you through some of these cool analyses. Along the way, you pick up a few techniques that will help you create your own formulas.

Note **You can download the files for all the formulas at** `www.wiley.com/ go/101excelformula.`

Formula 24: Getting the Current Date and Time

Instead of typing the current date and time, you can use one of two Excel functions. The TODAY function returns the current date.

```
=TODAY()
```

The NOW() function returns the current date along with the current time.

```
=NOW()
```

How it works

Both the TODAY and NOW functions return date serial numbers that represent the current system date and time. The TODAY function assumes 12 p.m. as the time, whereas the NOW function returns the actual time.

It's important to note that both of these functions automatically recalculate each time you change or open your workbook, so don't use these functions as a timestamp of record.

Tip

If you want to quickly enter a static date that doesn't change, press Ctrl+; (semicolon) on your keyboard. Pressing Ctrl+; inserts a static date in the active cell.

You can use the TODAY function as part of a text string by wrapping it in the TEXT function with some date formatting. The following formula returns today's date in Month Day, Year format.

```
="Today is "&TEXT(TODAY(),"mmmm d, yyyy")
```

Cross-Ref

For more details on using the TEXT function, see Formula 23: Formatting the Numbers in a Text String, in Chapter 3.

Formula 25: Calculating Age

One of the easiest ways to calculate the age of anything is to use Excel's DATEDIF function. This mysterious function doesn't appear in Excel's Help files, but it has been around since Excel 2000. This function makes calculating any kind of date comparisons a breeze.

To calculate a person's age using the DATEDIF function, you can enter a formula like this:

```
=DATEDIF("5/16/1972",TODAY(),"y")
```

You can, of course, reference a cell that contains a date:

```
=DATEDIF(B4,TODAY(),"y")
```

How it works

The DATEDIF function calculates the number of days, months, or years between two dates. It requires three arguments: a start date, an end date, and a time unit.

The time units are defined by a series of codes, which are listed in Table 4-1.

Table 4-1: DATEDIF Time Unit Codes

Code	What It Returns
"y"	The number of complete years in the period.
"m"	The number of complete months in the period.
"d"	The number of days in the period.
"md"	The difference between the days in start_date and end_date. The months and years of the dates are ignored.
"ym"	The difference between the months in start_date and end_date. The days and years of the dates are ignored.
"yd"	The difference between the days of start_date and end_date. The years of the dates are ignored.

Using these time codes, you can easily calculate the number of years, months, and days between two dates. If someone was born on May 16, 1972, you could find that person's age in year, months and days using these respective formulas:

```
=DATEDIF("5/16/1972",TODAY(),"y")
=DATEDIF("5/16/1972",TODAY(),"m")
=DATEDIF("5/16/1972",TODAY(),"d")
```

Formula 26: Calculating the Number of Days between Two Dates

One of the most common date calculations performed in the corporate world is figuring the number of days between two dates. Project management teams use it to measure performance against a milestone; HR departments use it to measure time to fill a requisition; and finance departments use it to track receivables aging.

Luckily, it's one of the easiest calculations to perform thanks to the handy DATEDIF function.

Figure 4-1 demonstrates an example report that uses the DATEDIF function to calculate the number of days outstanding for a set of invoices.

▲	A	B	C	D
1				
2				
3			Invoice Date	Days Outstanding
4			25-Apr-14	=DATEDIF(C4,TODAY(),"d")
5			04-May-14	7
6			04-May-14	7
7			28-Mar-14	44
8			22-Apr-14	19
9			31-Mar-14	41

Figure 4-1: Calculating the number of days between today and invoice date.

How it works

Looking at Figure 4-1, you see that the formula in cell D4 is

```
=DATEDIF(C4,TODAY(),"d")
```

This formula uses the DATEDIF function with the time code "d" (the number of days in the given period). The formula tells Excel to return the number of days based on the start date (C4) and the end date (TODAY).

Cross-Ref

For more detail on the DATEDIF function, see Formula 25: Calculating Age.

Formula 27: Calculating the Number of Workdays between Two Dates

Often when reporting on the elapsed number of days between a start date and end date, counting the weekends in the final number of days is not appropriate. Operations are typically shut down on the weekends, so you would want to avoid counting those days.

You can use Excel's NETWORKDAYS function to calculate the number of days between a start date and end date excluding weekends.

As you can see in Figure 4-2, the NETWORKDAYS function is used in Cell E4 to calculate the number of workdays between 1/1/2014 and 12/31/2014.

E4	▼	:	×	✓	fx	=NETWORKDAYS(B4,C4)

▲	A	B	C	D	E
1					
2					
3		Start Date	End Date		Net Work Days
4		1/1/2014	12/31/2014		261
5					

Figure 4-2: Calculating the number of workdays between two dates.

How it works

This formula is fairly straightforward. The NETWORKDAYS function has two required arguments: a start date and an end date. If your start date is in cell B4 and your end date is in cell C4, this formula returns the number of workdays (excluding Saturdays and Sundays):

```
=NETWORKDAYS(B4,C4)
```

Alternative: Using NETWORKDAYS.INTL

The one drawback to using the NETWORKDAYS function is that it defaults to excluding Saturdays and Sundays. But what if you work in a region where the weekends are actually Fridays and Saturdays? Or worst yet, what if your weekends include only Sundays?

Excel has you covered with the NETWORKDAYS.INTL. In addition to the required start and end dates, this function has an optional third argument: a weekend code. The weekend code allows you to specify which days to exclude as a weekend day.

As you enter the NETWORKDAYS.INTL function, Excel activates a tooltip as soon as you go into the third argument (see Figure 4-3). Simply select the appropriate weekend code and press Enter.

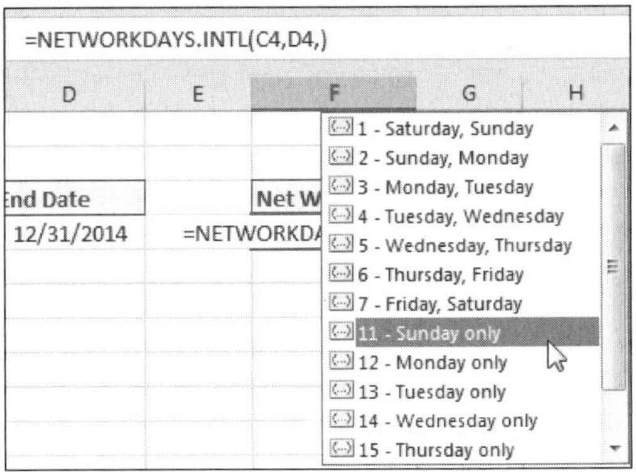

Figure 4-3: The NETWORKDAY.INTL allows you to specify which days to exclude as weekend days.

Formula 28: Generate a List of Business Days Excluding Holidays

When creating dashboards and reports in Excel, it's often useful to have a helper table that contains a list of dates that represent business days (that is, dates that are not weekends or holidays). This kind of a helper table can assist in calculations like revenue per business day, units per business day, and so on.

One of the easiest ways to generate a list of business days is to use the WORKDAY.INTL function.

Start with a spreadsheet that contains the last date of the previous year and a list of your organization's holidays. As you can see in Figure 4-4, your list of holidays should be formatted dates.

◢	A	B	C	D
1				
2				
3		12/31/2012		Holidays
4				1/1/2013
5				1/21/2013
6				3/29/2013
7				3/31/2013
8				5/31/2013
9				7/4/2013
10				9/1/2013
11				10/14/2013
12				11/28/2013
13				12/24/2013
14				12/25/2013
15				12/31/2013

Figure 4-4: The last date of the previous year and a list of holidays.

In the cell beneath the last date of the previous year, enter this formula:

```
=WORKDAY.INTL(B3,1,1,$D$4:$D$15)
```

At this point, you can copy the formula down to create as many business days as you need (see Figure 4-5).

◢	A	B	C	D
1				
2				
3		12/31/2012		Holidays
4		=WORKDAY.INTL(B3,1,1,$D$4:$D$15)		1/1/2013
5		1/3/2013		1/21/2013
6		1/4/2013		3/29/2013
7		1/7/2013		3/31/2013
8		1/8/2013		5/31/2013
9		1/9/2013		7/4/2013
10		1/10/2013		9/1/2013
11		1/11/2013		10/14/2013
12		1/14/2013		11/28/2013
13		1/15/2013		12/24/2013
14		1/16/2013		12/25/2013
15		1/17/2013		12/31/2013

Figure 4-5: Creating a list of business days.

How it works

The WORKDAY.INTL function returns a workday date based on the number of days you tell it to increment. This function has two required arguments and two optional arguments:

➤ **Start Date (required):** This argument is the date to start from.

➤ **Days (required):** This argument is the number of days from the start date you want to increment.

➤ **Weekends (optional):** By default, the WORKDAY.INTL function excludes Saturdays and Sundays, but this third argument allows you to specify which days to exclude as a weekend day. As you enter the WORKDAYS.INTL function, Excel activates an interactive tooltip from which you can select the appropriate weekend code.

➤ **Holidays (optional):** This argument allows you to give Excel a list of dates to exclude in addition to the weekend days.

In this example formula, you tell Excel to start from 12/31/2012 and increment up 1 to give you the next business day after the start date. For the optional arguments, you specify that you need to exclude Saturdays and Sundays, along with the holidays listed in cells $D$4:$D$15.

```
=WORKDAY.INTL(B3,1,1,$D$4:$D$15)
```

Be sure to lock down the range for your list of holidays with absolute references so that it remains locked as you copy your formula down.

Formula 29: Extracting Parts of a Date

The capability to pick out a specific aspect of a date is often very helpful. For example, you may need to filter all records that have order dates within a certain month, or all employees that have time allocated to Saturdays. In such situations, you would need to pull out the month and workday number from the formatted dates.

Excel provides a simple set of functions to parse dates out into their component parts. These functions are:

➤ YEAR: Extracts the year from a given date

➤ MONTH: Extracts the month from a given date

➤ DAY: Extracts the month day number from a given date

➤ WEEKDAY: Returns the weekday number for a given date

➤ WEEKNUM: Returns the week number for a given date

Figure 4-6 demonstrates the use of these functions to parse the date in cell C3 into its component parts.

▲	A	B	C
1			
2			
3			5/16/2015
4			
5		=YEAR(C3)	2015
6		=MONTH(C3)	5
7		=DAY(C3)	16
8		=WEEKDAY(C3)	7
9		=WEEKNUM(C3)	20
10			

Figure 4-6: Extracting the parts of a date.

How it works

These functions are fairly straightforward.

The YEAR function returns a four-digit number that corresponds to the year of a specified date. This formula returns 2015:

```
=YEAR("5/16/2015")
```

The MONTH function returns a number between 1 and 12 that corresponds to the month of a specified date. This formula returns 5:

```
=MONTH("5/16/2015")
```

The DAY function returns a number between 1 and 31 that corresponds to the day of the month represented in a specified date. This formula returns 16:

```
=DAY("5/16/2015")
```

The WEEKDAY function returns a number from 1 to 7 that corresponds to the day of the week (Sunday through Saturday) on which the given date falls. If the date falls on a Sunday, the number 1 is returned. If the date falls on a Monday, the number 2 is returned, and so on. The following formula returns 7 because 5/16/2015 falls on a Saturday:

```
=WEEKDAY("5/16/2015")
```

This function actually has an optional return_type argument that lets you specify which day of the week defines the start of the week. By default, the WEEKDAY function defines the start of the week as Sunday. As you enter the WEEKDAY function, Excel activates a tooltip through which you can select a different return_type code.

You can adjust the formula so that the return values 1 through 7 represent Monday through Sunday. In the following case, the formula using a 1 as the optional argument tells Excel that the week starts on Monday and ends on Sunday. Because May 16, 2015, falls on a Saturday, the formula returns the number 6.

```
=WEEKDAY("5/16/2015", 1)
```

The WEEKNUM function returns the week number within which the specified date falls. This formula returns 20 because 5/16/2015 falls within week number 20 in 2015.

```
=WEEKNUM("5/16/2015")
```

Formula 30: Calculating the Number of Years and Months between Dates

Sometimes you need to be able to determine the amount of time between dates in years and months. For example, you can determine that the amount of time elapsed between November 23, 1960, and May 13, 2014, is 53 years and five months.

The formula that you use to find out the time between two dates in years and months uses a text string with two DATEDIF functions.

Cell C4 shown in Figure 4-7 contains the following formula:

```
=DATEDIF(A4,B4,"Y") & " Years, " & DATEDIF(A4,B4,"YM") & " Months"
```

	A	B	C	D
			`=DATEDIF(A4,B4,"Y") & " Years, " & DATEDIF(A4,B4,"YM") & " Months"`		
1				
2				
3	Start Date	End Date	Number of Years and Months	
4	11/23/1960	5/13/2014	53 Years, 5 Months	
5	10/25/1944	5/13/2014	69 Years, 6 Months	
6	4/14/1920	5/13/2014	94 Years, 0 Months	
7	8/28/1940	5/13/2014	73 Years, 8 Months	
8	8/5/1987	5/13/2014	26 Years, 9 Months	
9	8/24/1982	5/13/2014	31 Years, 8 Months	
10	3/17/1959	5/13/2014	55 Years, 1 Months	
11	4/6/1961	5/13/2014	53 Years, 1 Months	
12	6/5/1944	5/13/2014	69 Years, 11 Months	
13	3/15/1930	5/13/2014	84 Years, 1 Months	
14	9/29/1921	5/13/2014	92 Years, 7 Months	
15	5/10/1953	5/13/2014	61 Years, 0 Months	

Figure 4-7: Showing the years and months between dates.

How it works

You accomplish this task by using two DATEDIF functions joined in a text string with the ampersand (&) operator.

The first DATEDIF function calculates the number of years between the start and end dates by passing the year time unit ("Y"):

```
DATEDIF(A4,B4,"Y")
```

The second DATEDIF function uses the "YM" time unit to calculate the number of months, ignoring the year portion of the date:

```
DATEDIF(A4,B4,"YM")
```

Finally, you join these two functions with some text of your own to let users know which number represents years and which represents months:

```
=DATEDIF(A4,B4,"Y") & " Years, " & DATEDIF(A4,B4,"YM") & " Months"
```

Cross-Ref   **For more details on the DATEDIF function, see Formula 25: Calculating Age.**

Formula 31: Converting Dates to Julian Date Formats

Julian dates are often used in manufacturing environments as a timestamp and quick reference for a batch number. This type of date coding allows retailers, consumers, and service agents to identify when a product was made, and thus the age of the product. Julian dates are also used in programming, the military, and astronomy.

Different industries have their own variations on Julian dates, but the most commonly used variation is made up of two parts: a two-digit number representing the year, and the number of elapsed days in the year. For example, the Julian date for 1/1/1960 would be 601. The Julian date for 12/31/2014 would be 14365.

Excel has no built-in function to convert a standard date to Julian date, but Figure 4-8 illustrates how you can use the following formula to accomplish the task.

```
=RIGHT(YEAR(A4),2)& A4-DATE(YEAR(A4),1,0)
```

	A	B
1		
2		
3	Standard Date	Julian Date
4	1/1/1960	=RIGHT(YEAR(A4),2)&A4-DATE(YEAR(A4),1,0)
5	10/25/1944	44299
6	4/14/1920	20105
7	8/28/1940	40241
8	8/5/1987	87217
9	8/24/1982	82236
10	3/17/1959	5976
11	4/6/1961	6196
12	6/5/1944	44157
13	3/15/1930	3074
14	9/29/2000	00273
15	5/10/2014	14130

Figure 4-8: Converting standard dates into Julian dates.

How it works

This formula is really two formulas joined as a text string using the ampersand (&).

The first formula uses the RIGHT function to extract the right two digits of the year number. Note that you use the YEAR function to pull out the year portion from the actual date.

```
=RIGHT(YEAR(A4),2)
```

Cross-Ref   **For more detail on the RIGHT function, see Formula 16: Extract Parts of a Text String, in Chapter 3.**

The second formula is a bit trickier. For this one, you have to find out how many days have elapsed since the beginning of the year. To do so, you first need to subtract the target date from the last day of the previous year:

```
A4-DATE(YEAR(A4),1,0)
```

Note the use of the DATE function.

The DATE function allows you to build a date on the fly using three arguments: the year, the month, and the day. The year can be any whole number from 1900 to 9999. The month and date can be any positive or negative number.

For example, this formula would return the date serial number for December 1, 2013:

```
=DATE(2013, 12, 1)
```

In the Julian date formula in this example, you use a zero as the day argument. When you use 0 as the day argument, you tell Excel that you want the day before the first day of the given month. So, for instance, entering the following formula into a blank cell will return December 31, 1959:

```
=DATE(1960,1,0)
```

Joining the two formulas together with an ampersand builds a Julian date made up of the first two characters of the year and the number of elapsed days:

```
=RIGHT(YEAR(A4),2)& A4-DATE(YEAR(A4),1,0)
```

Formula 32: Calculating the Percent of Year Completed and Remaining

When you're building Excel reports and dashboards, you'll often find it beneficial to calculate the percent of the year that has elapsed and what percent remains. You can use these percentages in other calculations or simply as a notification for your audience.

Figure 4-9 shows a sample of this concept. As you can see in the Formula Bar, the formula uses the YEARFRAC function.

B7	▾	:	×	✓	fx	=YEARFRAC(B3,C3)	

◢	A	B	C
1			
2		Start Date	End Date
3		1/1/2014	5/13/2014
4			
5			
6		Pcnt of this Year Complete	Pcnt of this Year Left
7		37%	63%

Figure 4-9: Calculating the percent of the year completed.

How it works

The YEARFRAC function simply requires a start date and an end date. When it has those two variables, it calculates the fraction of the year representing the number of days between the start date and end date:

```
=YEARFRAC(B3,C3)
```

To get the percent of the year that remains, as shown in cell C7 of Figure 4-9, simply subtract 1 from the YEARFRAC formula:

```
=1-YEARFRAC(B3,C3)
```

Formula 33: Returning the Last Date of a Given Month

A common need when working with dates is to dynamically calculate the last date in a given month. Of course, although the last day for most months is fixed, the last day for February varies depending on whether the given year is a leap year. You'll be able to spot the leap years in the results you produce from the formula.

Figure 4-10 shows how to get the last date in February for each year given in order to see which years are leap years.

⬜	A	B	C
1			
2		First Day of February	Last Day of February
3		2/1/1999	=DATE(YEAR(B3),MONTH(B3)+1,0)
4		2/1/2000	2/29/2000
5		2/1/2001	2/28/2001
6		2/1/2002	2/28/2002
7		2/1/2003	2/28/2003
8		2/1/2004	2/29/2004
9		2/1/2005	2/28/2005
10		2/1/2006	2/28/2006
11		2/1/2007	2/28/2007
12		2/1/2008	2/29/2008
13		2/1/2009	2/28/2009
14		2/1/2010	2/28/2010
15		2/1/2011	2/28/2011
16		2/1/2012	2/29/2012

Figure 4-10: Calculating the last day of each month.

As you look at Figure 4-10, keep in mind that you can use the formula to get the last day of any month, not just February.

How it works

The DATE function allows you to build a date on the fly using three arguments: the year, the month, and the day. The year can be any whole number from 1900 to 9999. The month and day can be any positive or negative number.

For example, this formula returns the date serial number for December 1, 2013:

```
=DATE(2013, 12, 1)
```

When you use 0 as the day argument, you tell Excel that you want the day before the first day of the month. For instance, entering the following formula into a blank cell returns February 29, 2000:

```
=DATE(2000,3,0)
```

In this example, instead of hard-coding the year and month, you use the YEAR function to get the desired year and the MONTH function to get the desired month. You add 1 to the month so that you go into the next month. This way, when you use 0 as the day, you get the last day of the month that you're actually interested in.

```
=DATE(YEAR(B3),MONTH(B3)+1,0)
```

Cross-Ref For more detail on the YEAR and MONTH function, see Formula 29: Extracting Parts of a Date.

Alternative: Using the EOMONTH function

The EOMONTH function is an easy alternative to using the DATE function. With the EOMONTH function, you can get the last date of any future or past month. All you need is two arguments: a start date and the number of months in the future or past.

For example, this formula returns the last day of April, 2015:

```
=EOMONTH("1/1/2015", 3)
```

Specifying a negative number of months returns a date in the past. So, for example, the following formula returns the last day of October, 2015:

```
=EOMONTH("1/1/2015", -3)
```

Specifying a zero as the number of months returns the last day of the month in which the given date falls. The following formula returns the last day of January, 2015:

```
=EOMONTH("1/1/2015", 0)
```

Formula 34: Calculating the Calendar Quarter for a Date

Believe it or not, Excel has no built-in function to calculate quarter numbers. If you need to calculate which calendar quarter a specific date falls in, you have to create your own formula.

Figure 4-11 demonstrates the following formula, which you use for calculating calendar quarters:

```
=ROUNDUP(MONTH(B3)/3,0)
```

	A	B	C
1			
2		Date	Calendar Quarter
3		1/1/2013	=ROUNDUP(MONTH(B3)/3,0)
4		1/21/2013	1
5		3/29/2013	1
6		3/31/2013	1
7		5/31/2013	2
8		7/4/2013	3
9		9/1/2013	3
10		10/14/2013	4
11		11/28/2013	4
12		12/24/2013	4
13		12/25/2013	4
14		12/31/2013	4

Figure 4-11: Calculating calendar quarters.

How it works

The secret to this formula is simple math. Here, you're dividing the month number for the given month by 3 and then rounding that number up to the nearest integer.

For instance, say that you're calculating which quarter August falls into. Because August is the eighth month of the year, you can divide 8 by 3. That would give you the answer 2.66. Round that number up and you get 3. August therefore is in the third quarter of the calendar year.

The formula in Figure 4-11 does the same thing. You use the MONTH function to extract the month number from the given date, and you use the ROUNDUP function to force the rounding up.

Cross-Ref

For more detail on the YEAR and MONTH function, see Formula 29: Extracting Parts of a Date. For more detail on the ROUNDUP function, see Formula 8: Basic Rounding of Numbers, in Chapter 2.

Formula 35: Calculating the Fiscal Quarter for a Date

Many of us work in organizations for which the fiscal year does not start in January. Instead, it starts in October, or April, or any other month. In these organizations, the fiscal quarter can't be calculated in the same way as a calendar quarter is.

Figure 4-12 demonstrates a clever formula for converting a date into a fiscal quarter using the CHOOSE function. In this example, you calculate the fiscal quarters when the fiscal year starts in April. The formula you see in the Formula Bar is as follows:

```
=CHOOSE(MONTH(B3),4,4,4,1,1,1,2,2,2,3,3,3)
```

C3			⁞	×	✓	fx	=CHOOSE(MONTH(B3),4,4,4,1,1,1,2,2,2,3,3,3)

	A	B	C	D
1				
2		Date	**Fiscal Quarter** (Fiscal Year Starts in April)	
3		1/1/2013	4	
4		1/21/2013	4	
5		3/29/2013	4	
6		3/31/2013	4	
7		5/31/2013	1	
8		7/4/2013	2	
9		9/1/2013	2	
10		10/14/2013	3	
11		11/28/2013	3	
12		12/24/2013	3	
13		12/25/2013	3	
14		12/31/2013	3	

Figure 4-12: Calculating fiscal quarters.

How it works

The CHOOSE function returns an answer from a list of choices based on a position number. If you were to enter the formula =**CHOOSE(2, "Gold", "Silver", "Bronze", "Coupon")** you would get Silver because 'Silver' is the second choice in your list of choices. Replace the 2 with a 4, and you would get 'Coupon' — the fourth choice.

The CHOOSE function's first argument is a required index number. This argument is a number from 1 to as many choices you list in the next set of arguments. Index number determines which of the next arguments is returned.

The next 254 arguments (only the first one is required) define your choices and determine what is returned when an index number is provided. If the index number is 1, the first choice is returned. If the index number is 3, the third choice is returned.

The idea here is to use the CHOOSE function to pass a date to a list of quarter numbers.

```
=CHOOSE(MONTH(B3),4,4,4,1,1,1,2,2,2,3,3,3)
```

The formula shown in cell C3 (see Figure 4-12) tells Excel to use the Month number for the given date and select a quarter that corresponds to that number. In this case, because the month is January, Excel returns the first choice (January is the first month). The first choice happens to be a 4. January is in the fourth fiscal quarter.

Say that your company's fiscal year starts in October instead of April. You can easily compensate for this fact by simply adjusting your list of choices to correlate with your fiscal year's start month. Notice how the tenth choice in the following formula is a 1. This would mean that October falls in the first fiscal quarter.

```
=CHOOSE(MONTH(B3),2,2,2,3,3,3,4,4,4,1,1,1)
```

Formula 36: Returning a Fiscal Month from a Date

In some organizations, the operationally recognized months don't start on the 1st and end on the 30th or 31st. Instead, they have specific days marking the beginning and end of a month. For instance, you may work in an organization in which each fiscal month starts on the 21st and ends on the 20th of the next month.

In such an organization, it's important to be able to translate a standard date into that organization's own fiscal months.

Figure 4-13 demonstrates a formula for converting a date into a fiscal month using the EOMONTH function in conjunction with the TEXT function. In this example, you calculate the fiscal month that starts on the 21st and ends on the 20th of the next month. The formula that appears in the Formula Bar is the following:

```
=TEXT(EOMONTH(B3-20,1),"mmm")
```

	A	B	C
1			
2		Date	**Fiscal Month** (Starts on the 21st and ends on the 20th of the Next Month)
3		1/1/2013	=TEXT(EOMONTH(B3-20,1),"mmm")
4		1/1/2013	Jan
5		1/21/2013	Feb
6		3/20/2013	Mar
7		3/31/2013	Apr
8		4/21/2013	May
9		6/20/2013	Jun
10		6/21/2013	Jul
11		7/21/2013	Aug
12			

Figure 4-13: Calculating fiscal months.

How it works

In this formula, you first take the date (shown in cell B3 in Figure 4-13) and go back 20 days by subtracting 20. Then you use that new date in the EOMONTH function to get the last day of the next month.

```
EOMONTH(B3-20,1)
```

You then wrap the resulting value in a TEXT function in order to format the resulting date serial number into a three-letter month name.

Cross-Ref

For more detail on the EOMONTH function, see Formula 33: Returning the Last Date of a Given Month. For more detail on the TEXT function, see Formula 23: Formatting the Numbers in a Text String, in Chapter 3.

Formula 37: Calculate the Date of the Nth Weekday of the Month

Many analytical processes rely on knowing the dates of specific events. For example, if payroll processing occurs the second Friday of every month, it's beneficial to know which dates in the year represent the second Friday of each month.

Using the date functions covered thus far in this chapter, you can build dynamic date tables that automatically provide you with the key dates you need.

Figure 4-14 illustrates such a table. In this table, formulas calculate the Nth weekday for each month listed. The idea is to fill in the years and months you need and then tell it what number occurrence of each weekday you are looking for. In this example, cell B2 shows that you are looking for the second occurrence of each weekday.

	A	B	C	D	E	F	G	H	I
1		Nth Occurance							
2		2							
3									
4			1	2	3	4	5	6	7
5	YEAR	MONTH	Nth Sun of the Month	Nth Mon of the Month	Nth Tues of the Month	Nth Wed of the Month	Nth Thur of the Month	Nth Fri of the Month	Nth Sat of the Month
6	2014	1	1/12/2014	1/13/2014	1/14/2014	1/8/2014	1/9/2014	1/10/2014	1/11/2014
7	2014	2	2/9/2014	2/10/2014	2/11/2014	2/12/2014	2/13/2014	2/14/2014	2/8/2014
8	2014	3	3/9/2014	3/10/2014	3/11/2014	3/12/2014	3/13/2014	3/14/2014	3/8/2014
9	2014	4	4/13/2014	4/14/2014	4/8/2014	4/9/2014	4/10/2014	4/11/2014	4/12/2014
10	2014	5	5/11/2014	5/12/2014	5/13/2014	5/14/2014	5/8/2014	5/9/2014	5/10/2014
11	2014	6	6/8/2014	6/9/2014	6/10/2014	6/11/2014	6/12/2014	6/13/2014	6/14/2014
12	2014	7	7/13/2014	7/14/2014	7/8/2014	7/9/2014	7/10/2014	7/11/2014	7/12/2014
13	2014	8	8/10/2014	8/11/2014	8/12/2014	8/13/2014	8/14/2014	8/8/2014	8/9/2014
14	2014	9	9/14/2014	9/8/2014	9/9/2014	9/10/2014	9/11/2014	9/12/2014	9/13/2014
15	2014	10	10/12/2014	10/13/2014	10/14/2014	10/8/2014	10/9/2014	10/10/2014	10/11/2014
16	2014	11	11/9/2014	11/10/2014	11/11/2014	11/12/2014	11/13/2014	11/14/2014	11/8/2014
17	2014	12	12/14/2014	12/8/2014	12/9/2014	12/10/2014	12/11/2014	12/12/2014	12/13/2014

Figure 4-14: A dynamic date table calculating the Nth occurrence of each weekday.

How it works

Cell C6 (see Figure 4-14) contains the following formula:

```
=DATE($A6,$B6,1)+C$4-WEEKDAY(DATE($A6,$B6,1))+($B$2-(C$4>=WEEKDAY(DATE($A6,
    $B6,1))))*7
```

This formula applies some basic math to calculate which date within the month should be returned given a specific week number and occurrence.

To use this table, simply enter the Years and Months you are targeting starting in columns A6 and B6. Then adjust the occurrence number you need in cell B2.

So, if you are looking for the first Monday of each month, enter a 1 in cell B2 and look in the Monday column. If you are looking for the third Thursday of each month, enter a 3 in cell B2 and look in the Thursday column.

Formula 38: Calculate the Date of the Last Weekday of the Month

You can leverage the functions covered in this chapter thus far to build a dynamic date table that automatically provides you with the last instance of a given weekday. For instance, Figure 4-15 illustrates a table that calculates the last Sunday, Monday, Tuesday, and so on for each month listed.

	A	B	C	D	E	F	G	H	I
1									
2			7	6	5	4	3	2	1
3	YEAR	MONTH	Last Sun of the Month	Last Mon of the Month	Last Tues of the Month	Last Wed of the Month	Last Thurs of the Month	Last Fri of the Month	Last Sat of the Month
4	2014	1	1/26/2014	1/27/2014	1/28/2014	1/29/2014	1/30/2014	1/31/2014	1/25/2014
5	2014	2	2/23/2014	2/24/2014	2/25/2014	2/26/2014	2/27/2014	2/28/2014	2/22/2014
6	2014	3	3/30/2014	3/31/2014	3/25/2014	3/26/2014	3/27/2014	3/28/2014	3/29/2014
7	2014	4	4/27/2014	4/28/2014	4/29/2014	4/30/2014	4/24/2014	4/25/2014	4/26/2014
8	2014	5	5/25/2014	5/26/2014	5/27/2014	5/28/2014	5/29/2014	5/30/2014	5/31/2014
9	2014	6	6/29/2014	6/30/2014	6/24/2014	6/25/2014	6/26/2014	6/27/2014	6/28/2014
10	2014	7	7/27/2014	7/28/2014	7/29/2014	7/30/2014	7/31/2014	7/25/2014	7/26/2014
11	2014	8	8/31/2014	8/25/2014	8/26/2014	8/27/2014	8/28/2014	8/29/2014	8/30/2014
12	2014	9	9/28/2014	9/29/2014	9/30/2014	9/24/2014	9/25/2014	9/26/2014	9/27/2014
13	2014	10	10/26/2014	10/27/2014	10/28/2014	10/29/2014	10/30/2014	10/31/2014	10/25/2014
14	2014	11	11/30/2014	11/24/2014	11/25/2014	11/26/2014	11/27/2014	11/28/2014	11/29/2014
15	2014	12	12/28/2014	12/29/2014	12/30/2014	12/31/2014	12/25/2014	12/26/2014	12/27/2014

Figure 4-15: A dynamic date table calculating the last weekday in each month.

How it works

Cell C4 (refer to Figure 4-15) contains the following formula:

```
=DATE($A4,$B4+1,1)- WEEKDAY(DATE($A4,$B4+1,C$2))
```

This formula applies some basic math to calculate which date within the month should be returned given a specific year, month, and week number.

To use this table, simply enter the Years and Months you are targeting starting in columns A4 and B4.

The idea is to use this table in your Excel data models as a place you can link to or simply copy from in order to get the dates you need.

Formula 39: Extracting Parts of a Time

In some situations, you need to be able to pick out a specific part of a time. Excel provides a simple set of functions to parse times out into their component parts. These functions are

> ➤ **HOUR:** Extracts the hour portion of a given time value

> ➤ **MINUTE:** Extracts the minute portion of a given time value

> ➤ **SECOND:** Extracts the second portion of a given time value

Figure 4-16 demonstrates the use of these functions to parse the time in cell C3 into its component time parts.

⬧	A	B	C
1			
2			
3			6:15:27 AM
4			
5		=HOUR(C3)	6
6		=MINUTE(C3)	15
7		=SECOND(C3)	27
8			

Figure 4-16: Extract the parts of a time.

How it works

These functions are fairly straightforward.

The HOUR function returns a number between 0 and 23 corresponding to the hour of a given time. The following formula returns 6:

```
=HOUR("6:15:27 AM")
```

The MINUTE function returns a number between 0 and 59 corresponding to the minutes of a given time. This formula returns 15:

```
=MINUTE("6:15:27 AM")
```

The SECOND function returns a number between 0 and 59 corresponding to the seconds of a given time. This formula returns 27:

```
=SECOND("6:15:27 AM")
```

Formula 40: Calculating Elapsed Time

One of the more common calculations done with time values involves calculating elapsed time — that is, the number of hours and minutes between a start time and an end time.

The table in Figure 4-17 shows a list of start and end times along with calculated elapsed times. Looking at Figure 4-17, you can see that the formula in Cell D4 is

```
=IF(C4< B4, 1 + C4 - B4, C4 - B4)
```

⬛	A	B	C	D
1				
2				
3		Start Time	End Time	Elapsed Minutes:Seconds
4		8:57:50 AM	10:04:39 AM	=IF(C4< B4, 1 + C4 - B4, C4 - B4)
5		4:35:20 PM	4:23:23 PM	23:48
6		8:24:35 AM	4:14:36 PM	7:50
7		3:10:39 PM	9:50:59 PM	18:40
8		2:33:22 PM	2:01:49 PM	23:28
9		8:42:35 AM	11:16:31 AM	2:33
10		11:20:24 AM	9:36:17 AM	22:15
11		3:56:53 PM	2:05:17 PM	22:08
12		3:33:16 PM	10:46:08 AM	19:12
13		12:41:54 PM	1:18:37 PM	0:36
14		11:39:07 AM	11:19:15 AM	23:40

Figure 4-17: Calculating elapsed time.

How it works

To get the elapsed time between a start and end time, all you need to do is subtract the end time from the beginning time. However, there is a catch. If the end time is less than the start time, you have to assume that the clock has been running for a full 24-hour period, effectively looping back the clock.

For such cases, you have to add a 1 to the time to represent a full day. Adding a 1 ensures that you don't have negative elapsed times.

In the elapsed time formula, you use an IF function to check whether the end time is less than the beginning time. If it is, you add a 1 to the simple subtraction. If it's not, you just perform the subtraction:

```
=IF(C4< B4, 1 + C4 - B4, C4 - B4)
```

Cross-Ref

For more detail on the IF function, see Formula 44: Check to See Whether a Simple Condition Is Met, in Chapter 5.

Formula 41: Rounding Time Values

It's often necessary to round time to a particular increment. For instance, if you're a consultant, you may always want to round times up to the next 15-minute increment or down to 30-minute increments.

Figure 4-18 demonstrates how you can round to 15- and 30-minute increments.

The Formula in cell E4 is

```
=ROUNDUP(C4*24/0.25,0)*(0.25/24)
```

The formula in cell F4 is

```
=ROUNDDOWN(C4*24/0.5,0)*(0.5/24)
```

	A	B	C	D	E	F
1						
2						
3		Start Time	End Time	Elapsed Minutes:Seconds	Round Up to Nearest 15 Minutes	Round Down to Nearest 30 minutes
4		8:49:12 AM	10:03:56 AM	1:14	10:15	10:00
5		10:58:31 AM	10:18:55 AM	23:20	10:30	10:00
6		9:23:37 AM	1:48:26 PM	4:24	14:00	13:30
7		8:39:16 AM	4:40:22 PM	8:01	16:45	16:30
8						

Figure 4-18: Rounding a time value to 15- and 30-minute increments.

How it works

You can round a time value to the nearest hour by multiplying the time by 24, passing that value to the ROUNDUP function, and then dividing the result by 24. For instance, the following formula returns 7:00:00:

```
=ROUNDUP("6:15:27 "*24,0)/24
```

To round up to 15-minute increments, you simply divide 24 by .25 (a quarter). The following formula returns 6:30:00:

```
=ROUNDUP("6:15:27 "*24/0.25,0)*(0.25/24)
```

To round down to 30-minute increments, divide 24 by .5 (a half). The following formula returns 6:00:00:

```
=ROUNDDOWN("6:15:27 "*24/0.5,0)*(0.5/24)
```

Cross-Ref

For more detail on the ROUNDDOWN and ROUNDUP functions, see Formula 8: Basic Rounding of Numbers, in Chapter 2.

Formula 42: Converting Decimal Hours, Minutes, or Seconds to a Time

It's not uncommon to import data from an external data source in which the times are recorded in decimal hours. For example, for the representation of one hour and 30 minutes, you see 1.5 instead of the standard 1:30.

You can easily convert to the standard representation by dividing the decimal hour by 24 and then formatting the result as a time.

Figure 4-19 shows some example decimal hours and the converted times.

	A	B	C
1			
2		Decimal Hours	Hours:Minutes
3		11.50	=B3/24
4		13.75	13:45
5		18.25	18:15
6		11.35	11:21
7		12.45	12:27
8		15.60	15:36
9		18.36	18:21
10		18.56	18:33
11		21.83	21:49

Figure 4-19: Converting decimal hours to hours and minutes.

How it works

Dividing the decimal hour by 24 results in a decimal that Excel recognizes as a time value.

To convert decimal minutes into times, divide the number by 1440. The following formula returns 1:04 (one hour and four minutes).

```
=64.51/1440
```

To convert decimal seconds into times, divide the number by 86400. The following formula returns 0:06 (six minutes):

```
=390.45/86400
```

Formula 43: Adding Hours, Minutes, or Seconds to a Time

Because time values are nothing more than a decimal extension of the date serial numbering system, you can add two time values together to get a cumulative time value. In some cases, you may want to add a set number of hours and minutes to an existing time value. In these situations, you can use the TIME function.

Cell D4 in Figure 4-20 contains this formula:

```
=C4+TIME(5,30,0)
```

In this example, you add 5 hours and 30 minutes to all the times in the list.

▲	A	B	C	D
1				
2				
3			Start Time	End time if working 5 hours and 30 minutes
4			3:00:52 PM	=C4+TIME(5,30,0)
5			3:43:03 PM	9:13:03 PM
6			12:30:14 PM	6:00:14 PM
7			8:08:53 AM	1:38:53 PM
8			11:33:56 AM	5:03:56 PM
9			3:55:18 PM	9:25:18 PM

Figure 4-20: Adding a set number of hours and minutes to an existing time value.

How it works

The TIME function allows you to build a time value on the fly using three arguments: hour, minute, and second.

For example, the following formula returns the time value 2:30:30 p.m.:

```
=TIME(14,30,30)
```

To add a certain number of hours to an existing time value, simply use the TIME function to build a new time value and then add them together. The following formula adds 30 minutes to the existing time, resulting in a time value of 3:00 p.m.

```
="2:30:00 PM" + TIME(0, 30, 0)
```

Performing Conditional Analysis

Excel provides several worksheet functions for performing conditional analysis, and in this chapter, we show you how to use some of those functions. Conditional analysis means performing different actions depending on whether a condition is met.

Note

You can download the files for all the formulas at `www.wiley.com/go/101excelformula.`

Formula 44: Check to See Whether a Simple Condition Is Met

A *condition* is a value or expression that returns TRUE or FALSE. Based on the value of the condition, a formula can branch into two separate calculations. That is, when the condition returns TRUE, one value or expression is evaluated while the other is ignored. A FALSE condition reverses the flow of the formula, and the first value or expression is ignored and the other evaluated.

Figure 5-1 displays a list of states and six monthly gas prices. For each price, say that you want to determine whether that state's price in that month is above or below average for all the states for the same month. For higher-than-average prices, you report "High," and for lower than average, "Low". A grid below the data is used to report the results.

```
=IF(C3>AVERAGE(C$3:C$11),"High","Low")
```

| C14 | ▼ | fx | =IF(C3>AVERAGE(C$3:C$11),"High","Low") |

	A	B	C	D	E	F	G	H	I
1									
2		State	Aug-13	Sep-13	Oct-13	Nov-13	Dec-13	Jan-14	
3		California	3.919	3.989	3.829	3.641	3.642	3.666	
4		Colorado	3.569	3.582	3.410	3.231	3.122	3.238	
5		Florida	3.614	3.558	3.388	3.377	3.516	3.486	
6		Massachusetts	3.761	3.703	3.518	3.419	3.520	3.527	
7		Minnesota	3.577	3.540	3.318	3.143	3.113	3.272	
8		New York	3.933	3.879	3.700	3.633	3.736	3.734	
9		Ohio	3.542	3.512	3.317	3.231	3.281	3.336	
10		Texas	3.509	3.383	3.180	3.104	3.171	3.187	
11		Washington	3.855	3.767	3.567	3.373	3.348	3.366	
12									
13									
14		California	High	High	High	High	High	High	
15		Colorado	Low	Low	Low	Low	Low	Low	
16		Florida	Low	Low	Low	High	High	High	
17		Massachusetts	High	High	High	High	High	High	
18		Minnesota	Low	Low	Low	Low	Low	Low	
19		New York	High	High	High	High	High	High	
20		Ohio	Low	Low	Low	Low	Low	Low	
21		Texas	Low	Low	Low	Low	Low	Low	
22		Washington	High	High	High	High	Low	Low	
23									

Figure 5-1: Monthly gas prices by state.

How it works

The IF function is the most basic conditional analysis function in Excel. It has three arguments: the condition; what to do if the condition is true; and what to do if the condition is false.

The condition argument in this example is C3>AVERAGE(C$3:C$11). Condition arguments must be structured to return TRUE or FALSE, and that usually means that there is a comparison operation (like an equal sign or greater-than sign) or another worksheet function that returns TRUE or FALSE (such as ISERR or ISBLANK). In this example, the condition has a greater-than sign and compares the value in C3 to the average of all the values in C3:C11.

Tip

In this formula, the reference to C3 is relative to both columns and rows and will change as the formula is copied to different cells. The C$3:C$11 reference is relative to columns but absolute to rows. This reference will change as it is copied to different columns, but not to different rows.

Cross-Ref

See Chapter 1 for more information on absolute and relative cell references.

If the condition argument returns TRUE, the second argument of the IF function is returned to the cell. The second argument is "High" **and because the value in C3 is indeed larger than the average, cell C14 shows** the word "High".

Cell C15 compares the value in C4 to the average. Because it is lower, the condition argument returns FALSE and the third argument is returned. Cell C15 shows "Low", the third argument of the IF function.

Formula 45: Checking for Multiple Conditions

Simple conditions like the one shown in Formula 44 can be strung together. This is known as *nesting* functions. The value_if_true and value_if_false arguments can contain simple conditions of their own. This allows you test more than one condition where subsequent conditions are dependent on the first one.

Figure 5-2 shows a spreadsheet with two user input fields for the type of automobile and a property of that automobile type. The properties are listed in two ranges below the user input fields. For this example, when the user selects the type and property, you want a formula to report whether the user has identified a coupe, a sedan, a pickup, or an SUV, as follows:

```
=IF(E2="Car",IF(E3="2-door","Coupe","Sedan"),IF(E3="Has
   Bed","Pickup","SUV"))
```

How it works

With some conditional analysis, the result of the first condition causes the second condition to change. In this case, if the first condition is Car, the second condition is 2-door or 4-door. But if the first condition is Truck, the second condition changes to either Has Bed or No Bed. The data validation in cell E3 in Figure 5-2 changes to allow only the appropriate choices based on the first condition. See the "Conditional data validation" sidebar in this chapter for instructions on how to create the data validation in cell E3.

As mentioned previously, Excel provides the IF function to perform conditional analyses. You can also nest IF functions — that is, use another IF function as an argument to the first IF function — when you need to check more than one condition. In this example, the first IF checks the value of E2. Rather than return a value if TRUE, the second argument is another IF formula that checks the value of cell E3. Similarly, the third argument doesn't simply return a value of FALSE, but contains a third IF function that also evaluates cell E3.

	D	E	F	G	H	I	J	K
fx	=IF(E2="Car",IF(E3="2-door","Coupe","Sedan"),IF(E3="Has Bed","Pickup","SUV"))							
	Auto Type:	Truck		Which Auto:	Pickup			
	Auto Property:	Has Bed						
		Car						
		2-door						
		4-door						
		Truck						
		Has Bed						
		No Bed						

Figure 5-2: A model for selecting an automobile.

In Figure 5-2, the user has selected "Truck". The first IF returns FALSE because E2 doesn't equal "Car" and the FALSE argument is evaluated. In that argument, E3 is seen to be equal to "Has Bed" and the TRUE condition ("Pickup") is returned. If the user had selected "No Bed", the FALSE condition ("SUV") would have been the result.

Note

In Excel versions prior to 2007, you can only nest functions up to seven levels deep. Starting in Excel 2007, that limit was increased to 64 levels. As you can imagine, even seven levels can be hard to read and maintain. If you need more than three or four levels, it's good idea to investigate other methods.

 ## Conditional data validation

The user input fields in Figure 5-2 are actually data validation lists. The user can make selections from a drop-down box rather than typing in the values. The Data Validation in cell E3 uses an interesting technique with an INDIRECT function to change its list depending on the value in E2.

The worksheet contains two named ranges. The range named Car points to E6:E7 and the range named Truck points to E10:E11. The names are identical to choices in the E2 Data Validation list. The following figure shows the Data Validation dialog box for cell E3. The Source is an INDIRECT function with E2 as the argument.

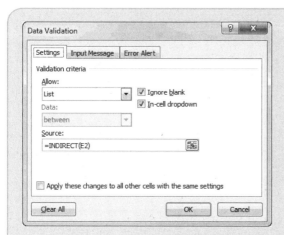

The INDIRECT function takes a text argument that it resolves into a cell reference. In this case, because E2 is "Truck", the formula becomes =INDIRECT("Truck"). Because Truck is a named range, INDIRECT returns a reference to E10:E11 and the values in those cells become the choices. If E2 contained "Car", INDIRECT would return E6:E7 and those values would become the choices.

One problem with this type of conditional data validation is that when the value in E2 is changed, the value in E3 does not change. The choices in E3 change, but the user still has to select from the available choices or your formulas may return inaccurate results.

Alternative 1: Looking up values

When you have too many nested IF functions, your formulas can become long and hard to manage. Figure 5-3 shows a slightly different setup to the auto selecting model. Instead of hardcoding the results in nested IF functions, the results are entered into the cells next to their properties; for example, "Sedan" is entered in the cell next to "4-door".

The new formula is

```
=IF(E2="Car",VLOOKUP(E3,E6:F7,2,FALSE),VLOOKUP(E3,E10:F11,2,FALSE))
```

You can use this formula to return the automobile type. The IF condition is the same, but now a TRUE result looks up the proper value in E6:E7 and a FALSE result looks it up in E10:F11. You can learn more about VLOOKUP in Chapter 6.

f_x	=IF(E2="Car",VLOOKUP(E3,E6:F7,2,FALSE),VLOOKUP(E3,E10:F11,2,FALSE))

D	E	F	G	H	I	J
Auto Type:	Car		Which Auto:	Sedan		
Auto Property:	4-door					
	Car					
	2-door	Coupe				
	4-door	Sedan				
	Truck					
	Has Bed	Pickup				
	No Bed	SUV				

Figure 5-3: A different auto selector model.

Formula 46: Check Whether Condition1 AND Condition2 Are Met

In addition to nesting conditional functions, such functions can be evaluated together inside an AND function. This is useful when two or more conditions need to be evaluated at the same time to determine where the formula should branch.

Figure 5-4 shows a listing of inventory items, their quantities, and the discount that applies when they are sold. The inventory items are structured with three sections divided by hyphens. The first section is the department; the second section determines whether the item is a part, a subassembly, or a final assembly; and the third condition is a unique four-digit number. For this example, you want to assign a discount of 10 percent to only those items that are in department 202 and are final assemblies. All other items have no discount.

```
=IF(AND(LEFT(B3,3)="202",MID(B3,5,3)="FIN"),0.1,0)
```

How it works

The IF function returns 10 percent if TRUE and 0 percent if FALSE. For the condition argument (the first argument), you need an expression that returns TRUE if both the first section of the item number is 202 and the second section is FIN. Excel provides the AND function to accomplish this task. The AND function takes up to 255 logical arguments separated by commas. Logical arguments are expressions that return either TRUE or FALSE. For this example, you use only two logical arguments.

The first logical argument, LEFT(B3,3)="202", returns TRUE if the first three characters of B3 are equal to 202. The second logical argument, MID(B3,5,3)="FIN", returns TRUE if the three digits starting at the fifth position are equal to FIN.

See Chapter 3 for more about text manipulation functions.

Cross-Ref

	f_x	=IF(AND(LEFT(B3,3)="202",MID(B3,5,3)="FIN"),10%,0%)				
	A	B	C	D	E	F
1						
2		Inventory Item	Quantity	Discount		
3		202-PRT-3013	76	0%		
4		201-FIN-1452	69	0%		
5		202-FIN-8206	12	10%		
6		201-FIN-8238	79	0%		
7		203-FIN-8882	16	0%		
8		202-PRT-9587	87	0%		
9		203-FIN-4614	97	0%		
10		201-PRT-2478	25	0%		
11		202-SUB-1955	14	0%		
12		201-SUB-8641	67	0%		
13		202-FIN-9069	40	10%		
14		202-PRT-7937	61	0%		
15		201-SUB-3124	70	0%		
16		203-SUB-4369	16	0%		
17		202-FIN-6273	74	10%		
18		203-SUB-3972	85	0%		
19		203-PRT-3335	84	0%		
20		201-SUB-1022	48	0%		
21		203-FIN-3507	17	0%		
22		203-SUB-8304	31	0%		
23						
24						

Figure 5-4: An inventory listing.

With the AND function, all logical arguments must return TRUE for the entire function to return TRUE. If even one of the logical arguments returns FALSE, the AND function returns FALSE. Table 5-1 shows the results of the AND function with two logical arguments.

Table 5-1: A Truth Table for the AND Function

First Logical Argument	Second Logical Argument	Result of AND function
TRUE	TRUE	TRUE
TRUE	FALSE	FALSE
FALSE	TRUE	FALSE
FALSE	FALSE	FALSE

In cell D3, the first logical condition returns TRUE because the first three characters of the item number are "202". The second logical condition returns FALSE because the middle section of the item number is "PRT", not "FIN". According to Table 5-1, a TRUE and a FALSE condition returns FALSE and 0 percent is the result. Cell D5, on the other hand, returns TRUE because both logical conditions return TRUE.

Alternative 1: Referring to logical conditions in cells

The AND function in Figure 5-4 includes two logical conditions that evaluate to TRUE or FALSE. The arguments to AND can also reference cells as long as those cells evaluate to TRUE or FALSE. When building a formula with the AND function, it can be useful to break out the logical conditions into their own cells. In Figure 5-5, the inventory listing is modified to show two extra columns. These columns can be inspected to determine why a particular item does or does not get the discount.

	A	B	C	D	E	F	G
		fx	=IF(AND(D3,E3),10%,0%)				
1							
2		Inventory Item	Quantity	IsDept202	IsFinalAssembly	Discount	
3		202-PRT-3013	76	TRUE	FALSE	0%	
4		201-FIN-1452	69	FALSE	TRUE	0%	
5		202-FIN-8206	12	TRUE	TRUE	10%	
6		201-FIN-8238	79	FALSE	TRUE	0%	
7		203-FIN-8882	16	FALSE	TRUE	0%	
8		202-PRT-9587	87	TRUE	FALSE	0%	
9		203-FIN-4614	97	FALSE	TRUE	0%	
10		201-PRT-2478	25	FALSE	FALSE	0%	
11		202-SUB-1955	14	TRUE	FALSE	0%	
12		201-SUB-8641	67	FALSE	FALSE	0%	
13		202-FIN-9069	40	TRUE	TRUE	10%	
14		202-PRT-7937	61	TRUE	FALSE	0%	
15		201-SUB-3124	70	FALSE	FALSE	0%	
16		203-SUB-4369	16	FALSE	FALSE	0%	
17		202-FIN-6273	74	TRUE	TRUE	10%	
18		203-SUB-3972	85	FALSE	FALSE	0%	
19		203-PRT-3335	84	FALSE	FALSE	0%	
20		201-SUB-1022	48	FALSE	FALSE	0%	
21		203-FIN-3507	17	FALSE	TRUE	0%	
22		203-SUB-8304	31	FALSE	FALSE	0%	
23							
24							

Figure 5-5: A modified inventory listing.

With these modifications, the result doesn't change, but the formula becomes

```
=IF(AND(D3,E3),10%,0%)
```

Formula 47: Check Whether Condition1 OR Condition2 Is Met

In Formula 46, you apply a discount to certain products based on their item number. In this example, you expand the number of products eligible for the discount. As before, only final assembly products get the discount, but the departments will be expanded to include both departments 202 and 203. Figure 5-6 shows the inventory list and the new discount schedule.

```
=IF(AND(OR(LEFT(B3,3)="202",LEFT(B3,3)="203"),MID(B3,5,3)="FIN"),10%,0%)
```

	fx	=IF(AND(OR(LEFT(B9,3)="202",LEFT(B9,3)="203"),MID(B9,5,3)="FIN"),10%,0%)						
	A	B	C	D	E	F	G	H
1								
2		Inventory Item	Quantity	Discount				
3		202-PRT-3013	76	0%				
4		201-FIN-1452	69	0%				
5		202-FIN-8206	12	10%				
6		201-FIN-8238	79	0%				
7		203-FIN-8882	16	10%				
8		202-PRT-9587	87	0%				
9		203-FIN-4614	97	10%				
10		201-PRT-2478	25	0%				
11		202-SUB-1955	14	0%				
12		201-SUB-8641	67	0%				
13		202-FIN-9069	40	10%				
14		202-PRT-7937	61	0%				
15		201-SUB-3124	70	0%				
16		203-SUB-4369	16	0%				
17		202-FIN-6273	74	10%				
18		203-SUB-3972	85	0%				
19		203-PRT-3335	84	0%				
20		201-SUB-1022	48	0%				
21		203-FIN-3507	17	10%				
22		203-SUB-8304	31	0%				

Figure 5-6: A revised discount scheme.

How it works

You expand the conditional argument to the IF function to account for the changes in the discount scheme. The AND function is restrictive because all the arguments must be TRUE for AND to return TRUE. Conversely, the OR function is inclusive. With OR, if any one of the arguments is TRUE, the entire function returns TRUE. In this example, you nest an OR function inside the AND function, making it one of the arguments. Table 5-2 shows a truth table for how these nested functions work.

Note A truth table is a table used in logic that breaks a large Boolean (True or False) result into its Boolean components. Each row of the table is evaluated independently of the other rows. Truth tables are useful in simplifying complex Boolean results and identifying patterns.

Table 5-2: A Truth Table for an OR Function Nested in an AND Function

OR logical 1	OR logical 2	OR result	AND logical 2	Final result
TRUE	TRUE	TRUE	TRUE	TRUE
TRUE	FALSE	TRUE	TRUE	TRUE
FALSE	TRUE	TRUE	TRUE	TRUE
FALSE	FALSE	FALSE	TRUE	FALSE
TRUE	TRUE	TRUE	FALSE	FALSE
TRUE	FALSE	TRUE	FALSE	FALSE
FALSE	TRUE	TRUE	FALSE	FALSE
FALSE	FALSE	FALSE	FALSE	FALSE

Cell D9 in Figure 5-6 shows a previously undiscounted product that receives a discount under the new scheme. The OR section, OR(LEFT(B9,3)="202",LEFT(B9,3)="203"), returns TRUE because one of its arguments returns TRUE.

Formula 48: Sum All Values That Meet a Certain Condition

Simple conditional functions like IF generally work on only one value or cell at a time. Excel provides some different conditional functions for aggregating data, such as summing.

Figure 5-7 shows a listing of accounts with positive and negative values. You want to sum all the negative balances, which you will later compare to the sum of all the positive balances to ensure that they are equal. Excel provides the SUMIF function to sum values based on a condition.

```
=SUMIF(C3:C12,"<0")
```

How it works

SUMIF takes each value in C3:C12 and compares it to the condition (the second argument in the function). If the value is less than zero, it meets the condition and is included in the sum. If it is zero or greater, the value is ignored. Text values and blank cells are also ignored. For the example in Figure 5-7, cell C3 is evaluated first. Because it is greater than zero, it is ignored. Next, cell C4 is evaluated. It meets the condition of being less than zero, so it is added to the total. This process continues for each cell. When it's complete, cells C4, C7, C8, C9, and C11 are included in the sum and the others are not.

	f_x	=SUMIF(C3:C12,"<0")			
	A	B	C	D	
1					
2		Account	Balance		
3		1510 Equipment	9,863.00		
4		1540 Accumulated Depreciation	(9,502.00)		
5		1690 Land	5,613.00		
6		1915 Other Assets	8,653.00		
7		2320 Wages Payable	(6,937.00)		
8		2420 Current Portion of Long-term Debt	(6,826.00)		
9		2440 Deposits from Customers	(3,717.00)		
10		5800 Cost of Goods Sold, Other	73.00		
11		5900 Purchase Returns and Allowances	(4,443.00)		
12		6300 Charitable Contributions Expense	7,223.00		
13					
14		Negative Balances	(31,425.00)		
15		Positive Balances	31,425.00		
16					

Figure 5-7: Sum values less than zero.

The second argument of SUMIF, the condition to be met, has quotation marks around it. Because this example uses a less-than sign, you have to create a string that represents the expression.

The SUMIF function has an optional third argument called the *sum_range*. So far, you've applied the condition to the very numbers that you're summing. By using the third argument, you can sum a range of numbers but apply your conditions to a different range. Figure 5-8 shows a listing of regions and their associated sales. To sum the sales for the East region, use the formula =SUMIF(B2:B11,"East",C2:C11).

	f_x	=SUMIF(B2:B11,"East",C2:C11)			
	A	B	C	D	
1					
2		South	2,714,745.31		
3		South	1,434,322.83		
4		North	1,983,811.70		
5		East	929,430.78		
6		East	3,154,066.47		
7		South	1,264,430.64		
8		North	4,674,274.42		
9		East	940,684.25		
10		South	2,497,381.24		
11		South	1,728,260.75		
12					
13		Sum on the East	5,024,181.50		
14					

Figure 5-8: List of regions and sales values.

Alternative 1: Summing greater than zero

Figure 5-8, shown previously, also shows the total of all the positive balances. The formula for that calculation is =SUMIF(C3:C12,">0"). Note that the only difference between this formula and the previous example formula is the expression string. Instead of "<0" as the second argument, this formula has ">0". See the "Constructing criteria in SUMIF" sidebar in this chapter for more examples of expression strings.

You don't have to include zero in the calculation because you're summing, and zero never changes a sum. If, however, you were interested in summing numbers greater or less than 1,000, you couldn't simply use "<1000" and ">1000" as your second arguments because you would never include anything that was exactly 1,000. When you use a greater-than or less-than nonzero number in a SUMIF, make the greater-than number a greater than or equal to, such as ">=1000", or make the less-than number a less than or equal to, such as "<=1000". Don't use the equal sign for both, just one. This approach ensures that you include any numbers that are exactly 1,000 in one or the other calculation, but not both.

Constructing criteria in SUMIF

The second argument of SUMIF is named *criteria*. There are also criteria arguments in COUNTIF, SUMIFS, COUNTIFS, AVERAGEIF, and AVERAGEIFS. All these arguments follow the same rules.

In general, the criteria argument is an expression that evaluates to TRUE or FALSE, which means that it includes a comparison operator such as equals (=), not equal (<>), or greater than (>). The exception is that you can omit the equals operator when you're doing an exact match. Non-equal comparisons include less than (<), less than or equal to (<=), greater than (>), greater than or equal to (>=), and not equal to (<>).

Constructing a good criteria argument can be a little tricky, but if you follow a few simple rules, explained in the following table, you'll get it right every time:

To Set a Condition . . .	. . . Follow These Rules	For Example
Equal to a number or cell reference	Don't use an equal sign or any double quotation marks.	=SUMIF(A1:A10,3)
Equal to a string	Don't use an equal sign, but put the string in quotation marks.	=SUMIF(A1:A10,"book")
Non-equal comparison to a number	Put both the operator and the number in double quotation marks.	=SUMIF(A1:A10,">=50")
Non-equal comparison to a string	Put both the operator and the string in double quotation marks.	=SUMIF(A1:A10,"<>Payroll")
Non-equal comparison to a cell reference or formula	Put the operator in double quotation marks and concatenate the cell reference or formula with the ampersand (&).	=SUMIF(A1:A10,"<"&C1)

You can use the TODAY function (to get the current date), or most other functions, in the second argument. The following figure shows a listing of dates and values. To sum a range of numbers that correspond to today, use the formula =SUMIF(B3:B11,TODAY(),C3:C11). To sum only those values that correspond to today or earlier, concatenate the less-than-or-equal-to sign to the function, such as =SUMIF(B3:B11,"<="&TODAY(),C3:C11).

	fx	=SUMIF(B3:B11,TODAY(),C3:C11)		
	A	B	C	D
1				
2		Date	Value	
3		2/1/2014	10	
4		2/2/2014	20	
5		2/3/2014	30	
6		2/9/2014	40	
7		2/5/2014	50	
8		2/1/2014	60	
9		2/9/2014	70	
10		2/5/2014	80	
11		2/10/2014	90	
12				
13		Sum today	110	
14		Sum today and prior	360	
15				
16				

There are two wildcard characters that you can use in the condition argument to SUMIF. The question mark (?) represents any single character, and the asterisk (*) represents zero, one, or any number of characters. The formula =SUMIF(B2:B11,"?o*",C2:C11) sums all the values in C2:C11 that correspond to the values in B2:B11 where the second character is a lowercase "o". If you apply that formula to the data in Figure 5-9, you get the sum for sales in both the North and South regions because both have a lowercase "o" as the second letter and East does not.

Formula 49: Sum All Values That Meet Two or More Conditions

The limitation of SUMIF shown in Formula 48 is that it works with only one condition. In Excel 2010 and later versions, you can use the SUMIFS function when more than one condition is needed.

Figure 5-9 shows a partial listing of countries and their gross domestic product (GDP) from 2000 to 2009. You want to total Brazil's GDP from 2003 to 2006. You use the Excel SUMIFS worksheet function to sum values when two or more conditions must be met, such as Country and Year in this example.

```
=SUMIFS(D3:D212,B3:B212,G3,C3:C212,">="&G4,C3:C212,"<="&G5)
```

How it works

SUMIFS arguments start with the range that contains the value you want to sum. The remaining arguments are in pairs that follow the pattern criteria_range, criteria. Because of the way the arguments are laid out, SUMIFS will always have an odd number of arguments. The first criteria pair is required; without at least one condition, SUMIFS would be no different than SUM. The remaining pairs of conditions, up to 126 of them, are optional.

In this example, each cell in D3:D212 is added to the total only if the corresponding values in B3:B212 and C3:C212 meet their respective conditions. The condition for B3:B212 is that it matches whatever is in cell G3. There are two year conditions because you need to define the first year and last year of your year range. The first year is in cell G4 and the last year is in cell G5. Those two cells are concatenated with greater-than-or-equal-to and less-than-or-equal-to, respectively, to create the year conditions. Only if all three conditions are true is the value included in the total.

fx	=SUMIFS(D3:D212,B3:B212,G3,C3:C212,">="&G4,C3:C212,"<="&G5)						
	A	B	C	D	E	F	G
1							
2		Country	Year	GDP			
3		Australia	2000	399,594		Country	Brazil
4		Australia	2001	377,207		Start Year	2003
5		Australia	2002	423,676		End Year	2006
6		Australia	2003	539,162			
7		Australia	2004	654,968		Total GDP	3,187,415
8		Australia	2005	730,729		Using SUMPRODUCT	3,187,415
9		Australia	2006	777,933			
10		Australia	2007	945,364			
11		Australia	2008	1,051,261			
12		Australia	2009	993,349			
13		Belgium	2000	233,354			
14		Belgium	2001	232,686			
15		Belgium	2002	253,689			
16		Belgium	2003	312,285			
17		Belgium	2004	362,160			
18		Belgium	2005	378,006			
19		Belgium	2006	400,337			
20		Belgium	2007	460,280			
21		Belgium	2008	509,765			
22		Belgium	2009	474,580			
23		Brazil	2000	644,734			
24		Brazil	2001	554,185			
25		Brazil	2002	506,043			
26		Brazil	2003	552,383			
27		Brazil	2004	663,734			
28		Brazil	2005	882,043			
29		Brazil	2006	1,089,255			
30		Brazil	2007	1,366,854			
31		Brazil	2008	1,653,538			
32		Brazil	2009	1,622,311			
33		Canada	2000	739,451			

Figure 5-9: Calculating the gross domestic product of a selected country between two years.

Alternative: SUMPRODUCT

The SUMIFS function was introduced in Excel 2010. Prior to that version of Excel, the best way to sum values with two or more conditions was to use SUMPRODUCT. For this application, the SUMPRODUCT function needs only one argument, but it's a big one. The SUMPRODUCT equivalent of this section's example is =SUMPRODUCT((B3:B212=G3)*(C3:C212>=G4)*(C3:C212<=G5)*(D3:D212)). This formula uses a pairing of ranges and conditions similar to the pairing of arguments in SUMIFS. Each set of parentheses (except the last one) contains a range, a comparison operator, and a comparison value. The last set of parentheses simply contains the range to sum. Excel evaluates each set of parentheses as an *array*. See the "SUMPRODUCT and arrays" sidebar in this chapter to learn how Excel combines arrays using SUMPRODUCT. Unlike SUMIFS, the parentheses aren't required to be in any order. The range to sum could be the first set or somewhere in the middle and the result would be the same.

SUMPRODUCT and arrays

The SUMPRODUCT function operates on `arrays`. Arrays are simply lists of values. In SUMPRODUCT, each value in the array is compared to the right value. For instance, in the example for "Alternative: SUMPRODUCT" for Formula 49, each value in B3:B212 is checked to see whether it equals the value in G3; that is, does the country equal Brazil? When the comparison is made, the result is another array that contains a TRUE or FALSE for every item in the original array. The array B3:B212 has 210 `elements` (individual pieces of data that make up an array are known as elements). When the comparison is complete, the resulting array will also have 210 elements. Most of them will be FALSE, but the 10 of them that were Brazil will be TRUE.

The four sets of parentheses turn into four arrays, and those arrays get multiplied together. The multiplication produces one array with 210 elements. Here's the magic of arrays: When a TRUE is multiplied times something else, it acts like the number 1. When a FALSE is multiplied by something else, it acts like the number zero. That means that if any FALSEs are in a particular element of the four arrays, the resulting array will contain zero for that element because anything times zero is zero. If, however, each of a particular element is TRUE, the element in the resulting array will be equal to whatever that particular element is in D3:D212. The first three 1s will all be multiplied together with the element for column D.

In Figure 5-9, shown previously, row 10 shows the GDP for Australia in 2007 (row 10 is the eighth element of the arrays). When SUMPRODUCT gets to the eighth element, it will evaluate that element against its condition and the resulting calculation will be FALSE * TRUE * FALSE * 945,364 (not Brazil * greater than 2003 * not less than 2006 * the values array), which will further evaluate to 0 * 1 * 0 * 945,364. Because there are FALSE elements, and FALSE elements act like a zero, the resulting calculation, when all the eighth elements of all four arrays are multiplied together, will be zero.

Row 28 tells a different story. All the elements that come from that row will be 1 because Brazil is in the first array, 2005 is greater than 2003, and 2005 is less than 2006. The calculation for that element ends up like 1 * 1 * 1 * 882,043. Row 28 and all the other rows that contain no FALSE elements are summed up and returned by SUMPRODUCT. The SUMPRODUCT function is not as easy to grasp nor does it calculate as quickly as SUMIFS, but when you understand how arrays multiply together, you'll find SUMPRODUCT to be quite handy.

Formula 50: Sum Values That Fall between a Given Date Range

One way that you can use SUMIF with two or more conditions is to add or subtract multiple SUMIF calculations. If the two conditions operate on the same range, this is an effective way to use multiple conditions. When you want to test different ranges, the formulas get tricky because you have to make sure that you don't double count values.

Figure 5-10 shows a list of dates and amounts. You want to find the sum of the values that are between June 23 and June 29, inclusive. The starting and ending dates will be put in cells F4 and F5, respectively.

```
=SUMIF(B3:B20,"<="&F5,C3:C20)-SUMIF(B3:B20,"<"&F4,C3:C20)
```

How it works

This technique subtracts one SUMIF from another to get the desired result. The first SUMIF, SUMIF(B3:B20," <="&F5,C3:C20), returns the sum of the values that are less than or equal to the date in F5, which is June 29 in this example. The conditional argument is the less-than-or-equal-to operator concatenated to the cell reference F5. If that was the whole formula, the result would be 5,962.33. However, you want only values that are also greater than or equal to June 23. You therefore want to exclude values that are less than June 23. The second SUMIF achieves that goal. Sum everything less than or equal to the later date and subtract everything less than the earlier date to get the sum of values between the two dates.

	A	B	C	D	E	F	G
					fx	=SUMIF(B3:B20,"<="&F5,C3:C20)-SUMIF(B3:B20,"<"&F4,C3:C20)	
1							
2		Date	Amount				
3		6/20/2015	843.77				
4		6/21/2015	400.60		Start Date	6/23/2015	
5		6/22/2015	396.54		End Date	6/29/2015	
6		6/23/2015	656.56				
7		6/24/2015	249.77		Sum	4,321.42	
8		6/25/2015	318.04				
9		6/26/2015	935.37		With SUMIFS	4,321.42	
10		6/27/2015	828.11		SUMPRODUCT	4,321.42	
11		6/28/2015	686.07		Reversed	4,321.42	
12		6/29/2015	647.50				
13		6/30/2015	375.00				
14		7/1/2015	991.02				
15		7/2/2015	344.75				
16		7/3/2015	485.97				
17		7/4/2015	580.80				
18		7/5/2015	703.13				
19		7/6/2015	504.85				
20		7/7/2015	596.06				
21							

Figure 5-10: Summing values that are between two dates.

Alternative 1: SUMIFS

If you're using Excel version 2010 or greater, you can use the SUMIFS function to achieve the same result as the preceding formula. You may even find SUMIFS to be more intuitive than the subtraction technique. The formula =SUMIFS(C3:C20,B3:B20,"<="&F5,B3:B20,">="&F4) sums the values in C3:C20 that correspond to the values in B3:B20 that meet the criteria pairs. The first criteria pair is identical to the first SUMIF criteria, "<="&F5. The second criteria pair limits the dates to greater than or equal to the start date.

Alternative 2: SUMPRODUCT

You can use the SUMPRODUCT function in place of SUMIF. The formula =SUMPRODUCT((B3:B20<=F5)*(B3:B20>=F4)*(C3:C20)) returns the same result as SUMIF. See Formula 49 for a detailed explanation of how SUMPRODUCT uses arrays.

Formula 51: Get a Count of Values That Meet a Certain Condition

Summing values isn't the only aggregation you can do in Excel. As with SUMIF and SUMIFS, Excel provides functions for conditionally counting values in a range.

Figure 5-11 shows a partial listing of countries and their gross domestic product (GDP) from 2000 to 2009. For this example, you want to know how many times the GDP was greater than or equal to 1 million. The criteria to be applied will be in cell G3.

```
=COUNTIF(D3:D212,G3)
```

How it works

The COUNTIF function works very similarly to the SUMIF function from Formula 48. The obvious difference, as the name suggests, is that it counts entries that meet the criteria rather than sums them. Another difference is that the formula uses no optional third argument as the SUMIF formula does. With SUMIF, you can sum a range that's different from the range to which the criterion is applied. With COUNTIF, however, doing that wouldn't make sense because counting a different range would get the same result.

The formula in this example uses a slightly different technique to construct the criteria argument. The string concatenation occurs all in cell G3 rather than in the function's second argument. If you had used the same approach as SUMIF in Formula 48, the second argument would look like ">=1000000" or ">="&G3 rather than just pointing to G3. You may also note that the formula in G3, =">="&10^6, uses the exponent operator, or caret (^), to calculate 1 million. Representing large numbers using the caret can help reduce errors caused by miscounting the number of zeros that you typed.

	fx	=COUNTIF(D3:D212,G3)						
	A	B	C	D	E	F	G	H
1								
2		Country	Year	GDP				
3		Australia	2000	399,594		Criterion	>=1000000	
4		Australia	2001	377,207				
5		Australia	2002	423,676		Count	96	
6		Australia	2003	539,162				
7		Australia	2004	654,968		Between	500000	
8		Australia	2005	730,729		And	1000000	
9		Australia	2006	777,933				
10		Australia	2007	945,364		Count	62	
11		Australia	2008	1,051,261				
12		Australia	2009	993,349		SUMPRODUCT	96	
13		Belgium	2000	233,354				
14		Belgium	2001	232,686				
15		Belgium	2002	253,689				
16		Belgium	2003	312,285				
17		Belgium	2004	362,160				
18		Belgium	2005	378,006				
19		Belgium	2006	400,337				
20		Belgium	2007	460,280				
21		Belgium	2008	509,765				
22		Belgium	2009	474,580				
23		Brazil	2000	644,734				
24		Brazil	2001	554,185				
25		Brazil	2002	506,043				
26		Brazil	2003	552,383				
27		Brazil	2004	663,734				
28		Brazil	2005	882,043				
29		Brazil	2006	1,089,255				

Figure 5-11: Count the number of country and year combinations whose gross domestic product meets a specified criterion.

Alternative: SUMPRODUCT

You can also use SUMPRODUCT to count conditionally. Formula 49 discusses how you can use SUMPRODUCT in place of SUMIFS to sum conditionally. It's the same for COUNTIF, with a few minor changes. The formula =SUMPRODUCT(--(D3:D212>10^6)) returns 96 just as COUNTIF did.

You may have noticed that double negative in the function's argument. In Formula 49, we discussed how multiplying TRUE makes it act like a 1 and multiplying FALSE makes it act like zero. This example, however, uses only one condition, D3:D212>10^6, so you have nothing to multiply, and the TRUEs and FALSEs never get converted to 1s and 0s. The double negative performs a mathematical operation on the array, forcing the conversion, but since it's doubled up, it doesn't have any effect on the result. The TRUEs are converted to -1 with the first negation and converted back to 1 with the second. The FALSEs are converted to zero simply because some math is being done, but negation has no effect on zero so it stays the same throughout.

Formula 52: Get a Count of Values That Meet Two or More Conditions

The SUMIF function has its COUNTIF cousin. Of course, Microsoft couldn't introduce SUMIFS for summing multiple conditions without also introducing COUNTIFS to count them. Microsoft did just that in Excel 2010.

Figure 5-12 contains a list of Alpine Skiing medalists from the 1972 Winter Olympics. For this example, you would like to know how many silver medalists have an ö in their name. The letter you're looking for is typed in cell I3, and the type of medal is in cell I4. (See the "Finding the code for a nonstandard character" sidebar for how to obtain the ö character and other nonstandard characters.)

```
=COUNTIFS(C3:C20,"*"&I3&"*",F3:F20,I4)
```

	A	B	C	D	E	F	G	H	I	J
			fx	=COUNTIFS(C3:C20,"*"&I3&"*",F3:F20,I4)						
1										
2		Event	Athlete	Country	Result	Medal				
3		Downhill Men	Bernhard Russi	SUI	01:51.4	GOLD		Name contains	ö	
4		Downhill Men	Roland Collombin	SUI	01:52.1	SILVER		Medal Won	SILVER	
5		Downhill Men	Heini Messner	AUT	01:52.4	BRONZE		Count	3	
6		Slalom Men	Francisco Fernández	ESP	01:49.3	GOLD		SUMPRODUCT	3	
7		Slalom Men	Gustav Thöni	ITA	01:50.3	SILVER				
8		Slalom Men	Roland Thöni	ITA	01:50.3	BRONZE		T	84	
9		Giant Slalom Men	Gustav Thöni	ITA	03:09.6	GOLD		h	104	
10		Giant Slalom Men	Edmund Bruggmann	SUI	03:10.7	SILVER		ö	246	
11		Giant Slalom Men	Werner Mattle	SUI	03:11.0	BRONZE		n	110	
12		Downhill Women	Marie-Thérès Nadig	SUI	01:36.7	GOLD		i	105	
13		Downhill Women	Annemarie Moser-Pröll	AUT	01:37.0	SILVER				
14		Downhill Women	Susan Corrock	USA	01:37.7	BRONZE				
15		Slalom Women	Barbara Cochran	USA	01:31.2	GOLD				
16		Slalom Women	Danièlle Debernard	FRA	01:31.3	SILVER				
17		Slalom Women	Florence Steurer	FRA	01:32.7	BRONZE				
18		Giant Slalom Women	Marie-Thérès Nadig	SUI	01:29.9	GOLD				
19		Giant Slalom Women	Annemarie Moser-Pröll	AUT	01:30.8	SILVER				
20		Giant Slalom Women	Wiltrud Drexel	AUT	01:32.4	BRONZE				
21										

Figure 5-12: The letter ö shows up the names of the1972 alpine skiing Olympic silver medalists three times.

How it works

The criteria_range and criteria arguments come in pairs, just as in SUMIFS. Whereas SUMIFS will always have an odd number of arguments, COUNTIFS will always have an equal number.

The first criteria_range argument is the list of athlete's names in C3:C20. The matching criteria argument, "*" & I3 & "*", surrounds whatever is in I3 with asterisks. Asterisks are wildcard characters in COUNTIFS that stand for zero, one, or more characters of any kind. By including an asterisk both before and after the character, you ask Excel to count all the names that include that character anywhere within the name. That is, you don't care whether there are zero, one, or more characters before ö and you don't care whether there are zero, one, or more characters *after* ö — as long as that character is in there somewhere.

The second criteria_range, criteria argument pair counts those entries in F3:F20 that are SILVER (the value typed into I4). Only those rows in which both the first argument pair and second argument pair match (only rows in which the athlete's name contains ö *and* the medal won was silver) are counted. In this example, Gustav Thöni won the silver in the Men's Slalom and Annemarie Moser-Pröll placed in both the Women's Downhill and the Women's Giant Slalom, for a count of three.

Alternative: SUMPRODUCT

The COUNTIFS worksheet function was introduced in Excel 2010. If you're using an earlier version, you can use SUMPRODUCT to get the same result. The formula =SUMPRODUCT((NOT(ISERR(FIND(I3,C3:C20))))*(F3:F20=I4)) will also return the proper count, although it's a little tougher to read. In Formula 49, you see how SUMPRODUCT multiplies arrays of TRUEs and FALSEs to sum based on conditions. For the example in this section, SUMPRODUCT does the same thing. Everything to the left of the asterisk will turn into an array of 18 TRUEs and FALSEs, and everything to the right will do the same. When a TRUE is used in a mathematical operation, it acts like the number one and FALSE acts like zero. Whenever a FALSE is in either the first or second array, the result will be zero. If both the first and second array contain 1, the formula multiplies 1 * 1 to get a 1 in the final array. The result of multiplying those two arrays together is an 18-element array of 1s and 0s. When SUMPRODUCT adds up the 1s, it effectively counts the rows where both conditions are met.

 ## Finding the code for a nonstandard character

For the example in Formula 52, you can type the ö character into cell I3 by holding down the Alt key and typing 0246 on the numeric keyboard. Don't try to type those numbers on the number keys across the top of your keyboard because it won't work. The number 246 is the ASCII code that represents ö. Every character in this chapter has an ASCII code. When typing the ASCII code to enter a character, be sure to type four digits. If the code is fewer than four digits, type zeros before the number to make it four digits.

In the range H8:I12 in Figure 5-12, you can see a small table of characters and their codes. In cell H8, the formula =MID($C$8,ROW(),1) returns the eighth character from the name in cell C8. (The eighth character was chosen somewhat haphazardly. It was somewhere before the character you're looking for but not too far away.) You copy that formula down a few rows until the character you want to inspect shows up. The character you want is in H10. The dollar signs in $C$8 anchor that cell reference so that it doesn't change as the formula is copied. The ROW() function without an argument returns the row of whatever cells it's in. As the formula is copied down, ROW() returns 8, 9, 10, and so on.

Cell I8 has the formula =CODE(H8). The CODE worksheet function returns the ASCII code for the letter that's passed in. In this example, you can see that a capital *T* is ASCII code 84, a lowercase *i* is ASCII code 105, and *ö* is ASCII code 246. Armed with that knowledge, you can hold down the Alt key and type the code to use that character anywhere you want.

The second array, F3:F20=I4, is pretty straightforward. Each cell in F3:F20 is compared to I4 and a TRUE or a FALSE is included in that array. The first array is a little more complicated than the first. You know that the result needs to be a bunch of TRUEs and FALSEs, so you need to come up with an expression that returns TRUE or FALSE. The FIND function returns the position of a string in another string. For example, FIND("ö","Thöni") returns 3 because "ö" is the third letter in the name "Thöni". If FIND can't find the letter, it returns an error.

The ISERR function returns either TRUE or FALSE depending on whether the expression is any error except #N/A!. Using ISERR gets you close to your goal because it returns TRUE or FALSE. The problem is that it returns the wrong one. It returns TRUE if FIND *can't* find ö in the name, but you want it to return TRUE when it *does* find it. The NOT function comes to the rescue. The NOT function takes a TRUE or a FALSE and turns into the other one. If ö is in the name, FIND returns a number (like the number 10 when it looks at Roland Thöni). Then, ISERR(10) returns FALSE because 10 isn't an error, it's a number. Finally, NOT(FALSE) returns TRUE.

Formula 53: Get the Average of All Numbers That Meet a Certain Condition

After summing and counting, taking an average of a range of numbers is the next most common aggregator. The average, also known as the arithmetic mean, is the sum of the numbers divided by the count of the numbers.

As in the example for Formula 52, Figure 5-13 shows medalists' results from the 1972 Winter Olympics. For this example, you want to determine the average result, but only for skiers from Switzerland. The country code is entered in cell I3 so that it can be easily changed to a different country.

```
=AVERAGEIF(D3:D20,I3,E3:E20)
```

How it works

Excel provides the AVERAGEIF function to accomplish just what you want. Like its cousin the SUMIF function, AVERAGEIF has a criteria_range and a criteria argument. The final argument is the range to average. In this example, each cell in E3:E20 is either included in or excluded from the average, depending on whether the corresponding cell in D3:D20 meets the criteria.

Note   If no rows meet the criteria in AVERAGEIF, the function returns the #DIV/0! error.

Alternative

The AVERAGEIF function simply adds up the average_range for all rows that meet the criteria and then divides by the number of rows. This same result can be had by using the SUMIF function divided by the COUNTIF function. Using the list from Figure 5-13, the formula =SUMIF(D3:D20,I3,E3:E20)/COUNTIF(D3:D20,I3) can also be used to find the conditional average.

	A	B	C	D	E	F	G	H	I
			fx	=AVERAGEIF(D3:D20,I3,E3:E20)					
2		Event	Athlete	Country	Result	Medal			
3		Downhill Men	Bernhard Russi	SUI	01:51.4	GOLD		Country	SUI
4		Downhill Men	Roland Collombin	SUI	01:52.1	SILVER			
5		Downhill Men	Heini Messner	AUT	01:52.4	BRONZE		Average Result	02:12.0
6		Slalom Men	Francisco Fernández	ESP	01:49.3	GOLD		SUMIF and COUNTIF	02:12.0
7		Slalom Men	Gustav Thöni	ITA	01:50.3	SILVER			
8		Slalom Men	Roland Thöni	ITA	01:50.3	BRONZE			
9		Giant Slalom Men	Gustav Thöni	ITA	03:09.6	GOLD			
10		Giant Slalom Men	Edmund Bruggmann	SUI	03:10.7	SILVER			
11		Giant Slalom Men	Werner Mattle	SUI	03:11.0	BRONZE			
12		Downhill Women	Marie-Thérès Nadig	SUI	01:36.7	GOLD			
13		Downhill Women	Annemarie Moser-Pröll	AUT	01:37.0	SILVER			
14		Downhill Women	Susan Corrock	USA	01:37.7	BRONZE			
15		Slalom Women	Barbara Cochran	USA	01:31.2	GOLD			
16		Slalom Women	Danièlle Debernard	FRA	01:31.3	SILVER			
17		Slalom Women	Florence Steurer	FRA	01:32.7	BRONZE			
18		Giant Slalom Women	Marie-Thérès Nadig	SUI	01:29.9	GOLD			
19		Giant Slalom Women	Annemarie Moser-Pröll	AUT	01:30.8	SILVER			
20		Giant Slalom Women	Wiltrud Drexel	AUT	01:32.4	BRONZE			
21									
22									
23									

Figure 5-13: Averaging results based on a country.

Formula 54: Get the Average of All Numbers That Meet Two or More Conditions

In Excel 2010, Microsoft introduced AVERAGEIFS along with SUMIFS and COUNTIFS to allow you to average a range of numbers based on more than one condition.

Continuing the analysis of skiing times as an example (see Formulas 52 and 53), Figure 5-14 shows some results of the 1972 Winter Olympics. In this case, you want to determine the average time based on more than one condition. The country, gender, and medal are entered into cell I3:I5. You want to average only those results that meet all three criteria:

```
=AVERAGEIFS(E3:E20,D3:D20,I3,B3:B20,"*"&I4,F3:F20,I5)
```

How it works

The AVERAGEIFS function is structured very similarly to the SUMIFS function. The first argument is the range to average and is followed by up to 127 pairs of criteria_range/criteria arguments. The three criteria pairs are

➤ D3:D20,I3, which includes only those rows where the country code is SUI

➤ B3:B20,"*"&I4, which includes only those rows where the event name ends with the word "Women"

➤ F3:F20,I5, which includes only those rows where the medal is GOLD

When all three conditions are met, the time in the Result column is averaged.

`=AVERAGEIFS(E3:E20,D3:D20,I3,B3:B20,"*"&I4,F3:F20,I5)`

	Event	Athlete	Country	Result	Medal			
3	Downhill Men	Bernhard Russi	SUI	01:51.4	GOLD		Country	SUI
4	Downhill Men	Roland Collombin	SUI	01:52.1	SILVER		Gender	Women
5	Downhill Men	Heini Messner	AUT	01:52.4	BRONZE		Medal	GOLD
6	Slalom Men	Francisco Fernández	ESP	01:49.3	GOLD		Average Result	01:33.3
7	Slalom Men	Gustav Thöni	ITA	01:50.3	SILVER		SUMIF and COUNTIF	01:33.3
8	Slalom Men	Roland Thöni	ITA	01:50.3	BRONZE			
9	Giant Slalom Men	Gustav Thöni	ITA	03:09.6	GOLD			
10	Giant Slalom Men	Edmund Bruggmann	SUI	03:10.7	SILVER			
11	Giant Slalom Men	Werner Mattle	SUI	03:11.0	BRONZE			
12	Downhill Women	Marie-Thérès Nadig	SUI	01:36.7	GOLD			
13	Downhill Women	Annemarie Moser-Pröll	AUT	01:37.0	SILVER			
14	Downhill Women	Susan Corrock	USA	01:37.7	BRONZE			
15	Slalom Women	Barbara Cochran	USA	01:31.2	GOLD			
16	Slalom Women	Danièlle Debernard	FRA	01:31.3	SILVER			
17	Slalom Women	Florence Steurer	FRA	01:32.7	BRONZE			
18	Giant Slalom Women	Marie-Thérès Nadig	SUI	01:29.9	GOLD			
19	Giant Slalom Women	Annemarie Moser-Pröll	AUT	01:30.8	SILVER			
20	Giant Slalom Women	Wiltrud Drexel	AUT	01:32.4	BRONZE			

Figure 5-14: Averaging on three conditions.

Alternative

You can replace the AVERAGEIFS function with SUMIFS and COUNTIFS. Doing so is useful if you're using a version of Excel prior to 2010, when AVERAGEIFS was introduced. The formula =SUMIFS(E3:E20,D3:D20,I3,B3:B20,"*"&I4,F3:F20,I5)/COUNTIFS(D3:D20,I3,B3:B20,"*"&I4,F3:F20,I5) returns the same result as AVERAGEIFS. Notice how similar the arguments in SUMIFS and COUNTIFS are to those in AVERAGIFS. If it's available, AVERAGEIFS is the preferred method because any changes to the criteria have to be made in only one place.

Using Lookup Formulas

Finding data in a list or table is central to many Excel formulas. Excel provides several functions to assist in looking up data vertically, horizontally, from left to right, and from right to left. By nesting some of these functions, you can write a formula that looks up the correct data even after the layout of your table changes.

Note

You can download the files for all the formulas at `www.wiley.com/go/101excelformula`.

Formula 55: Looking Up an Exact Value Based on a Left Lookup Column

Many tables are arranged so that the key piece of data, the data that makes a certain row unique, is in the far-left column. Although Excel has many lookup functions, VLOOKUP was designed for just that situation. Figure 6-1 shows a table of employees. You want to fill out a simplified paystub form by pulling the information from this table when an employee's ID is selected.

	A	B	C	D	E	F	G	H	I	J
1										
2		ID	Employee Name	Address	Frequency	Salary	Tax Rate	Insurance	401k	
3		154	Paige Jones	427 John A. Creighton Boulevarc	26	42,900.00	15%	100.00	8%	
4		240	Elijah Ward	888 192nd Street Anytown, USA	26	64,600.00	16%	200.00	7%	
5		319	Elizabeth Marshall	530 Dodge Street Anytown, USA	52	72,300.00	24%	300.00	3%	
6		331	Cooper Smith	271 Dodge Street Anytown, USA	12	99,700.00	20%	300.00	5%	
7		428	Isabella Harris	715 136th Street Anytown, USA :	26	57,600.00	25%	100.00	5%	
8		451	Kaylee Perez	772 North 30th Street Anytown,	12	82,800.00	23%	200.00	7%	
9		527	Kimberly Hall	652 Regency Parkway Drive Anyt	12	41,700.00	17%	300.00	4%	
10		540	Jesus Clark	803 Fontenelle Boulevard Anytc	52	83,100.00	18%	200.00	5%	
11		665	Kylie Woods	245 Fontenelle Boulevard Anytc	26	70,400.00	21%	100.00	1%	
12		981	Jackson Stephens	827 Harrison Street Anytown, US	52	50,200.00	18%	100.00	8%	
13										
14										

Figure 6-1: A table of employee information.

The user will select an employee ID from a data validation list in cell L3. From that piece of data, the employee's name, address, and other information will be pulled into the form. The formulas for the paystub form in Figure 6-2 are shown here:

```
Employee Name: =VLOOKUP($L$3,$B$3:$I$12,2,FALSE)
Pay: =VLOOKUP($L$3,$B$3:$I$12,5,FALSE)/VLOOKUP($L$3,$B$3:$I$12,4,FALSE)
Taxes: =(M7-O8-O9)*VLOOKUP($L$3,$B$3:$I$12,6,FALSE)
Insurance: =VLOOKUP($L$3,$B$3:$I$12,7,FALSE)
Retirement: =M7*VLOOKUP($L$3,$B$3:$I$12,8,FALSE)
Total: =SUM(O7:O10)
Net Pay: =M7-O11
```

M3		fx	=VLOOKUP($L$3,$B$3:$I$12,2,FALSE)			
K	L	M	N	O		
1						
2	Employee ID	Employee Name	Check #	Net Pay		
3	319	Elizabeth Marshall	164	$	796.99	
4	Employee Address					
5	530 Dodge Street Anytown, USA 12345					
6		Pay	Deductions			
7		1,390.38	Taxes	251.68		
8			Insurance	300.00		
9			Retirement	41.71		
10						
11			Total	$	593.39	
12						
13						

Figure 6-2: A simplified paystub form.

How it works

The formula to retrieve the employee's name uses the VLOOKUP function. VLOOKUP takes four arguments: lookup value, lookup range, column, and match. VLOOKUP searches down the first column of the lookup range until it finds the lookup value. When the lookup value is found, VLOOKUP returns the value in the column identified by the column argument. In this case, the column argument is 2, and VLOOKUP returns the employee's name from the second column.

Note

All of the VLOOKUP functions in this example have FALSE as the final argument. A FALSE in the match argument tells VLOOKUP to return a value only if it finds an exact match. If it doesn't find an exact match, VLOOKUP returns N/A#. Formula 60, later in this chapter, shows an example of using TRUE to get an approximate match.

The other formulas also use VLOOKUP with a few twists. The address and insurance formulas work just like the employee name formula, but they pull from a different column. The pay formula uses two VLOOKUPs; one divided by the other. The employee's annual pay is pulled from the fifth column and is divided by the frequency from the fourth column, resulting in the pay for one paystub.

The retirement formula pulls the percentage from the eighth column and multiplies that by the gross pay to calculate the deduction. Finally, the taxes formula deducts both insurance and retirement from gross pay and multiplies that by the tax rate, found with VLOOKUP pulling from the sixth column.

Of course, payroll calculations are a little more complex than this, but when you understand how VLOOKUP works, you can build ever more complex models.

Formula 56: Looking Up an Exact Value Based on Any Lookup Column

Unlike the table used in Formula 55, not all tables have the value you want to look up in the leftmost column. Fortunately, Excel provides some functions for returning values that are to the left of the value you're looking up.

Figure 6-3 shows a list of cities and states where the stores are. You want to return the city and store number when the user selects the state from a drop-down box.

```
City:  =INDEX(B3:D25,MATCH(G4,C3:C25,FALSE),1)
Store: =INDEX(B3:D25,MATCH(G4,C3:C25,FALSE),3)
```

G5		f_x	=INDEX(B3:D25,MATCH(G4,C3:C25,FALSE),1)			
	A	B	C	D	E	F	G
1							
2		City	State	Store #			
3		Chandler	AZ	6493			
4		Glendale	CA	4369		State:	NH
5		Fort Collins	CO	4505		City:	Manchester
6		Gainesville	FL	8745		Store:	2608
7		Peoria	IL	6273			
8		Indianapolis	IN	9384		LOOKUP City:	Manchester
9		Lafayette	LA	5654		LOOKUP Store:	2608
10		Grand Rapids	MI	3972			
11		St. Louis	MO	8816			
12		Billings	MT	3331			
13		Raleigh	NC	3335			
14		Manchester	NH	2608			
15		Elizabeth	NJ	4122			
16		Albuquerque	NM	1022			
17		Toledo	OH	7681			
18		Tulsa	OK	8567			
19		Portland	OR	3507			
20		Erie	PA	7326			
21		Providence	RI	4643			
22		Clarksville	TN	8304			
23		Carrollton	TX	7676			
24		Tacoma	WA	4938			
25		Green Bay	WI	1701			
26							

Figure 6-3: A list of stores with their city and state.

How it works

The INDEX function returns the value from a particular row and column of a range. In this case, you pass it your table of stores, a row argument in the form of a MATCH function, and a column number. For the City formula, you want the first column, so the column argument is 1. For the Store formula, you want the third column, so the column argument is 3.

Unless the range you use starts in A1, the row and column won't match the row and column in the spreadsheet. They relate to the top, left cell in the range, not the spreadsheet as a whole. A formula like =INDEX(G2:P10,2,2) would return H3. The cell H3 is in the second row and the second column of the range G2:P10.

Tip   **The second argument of the MATCH function can be only a range that is one row tall or one column wide. If you send it a range that's a rectangle, MATCH returns the #N/A error.**

To get the correct row, you use a MATCH function. The MATCH function returns the position in the list where the lookup value is found. It has three arguments:

➤ **Lookup value:** The value you want to find.

➤ **Lookup array:** The single column or single row to look in.

➤ **Match type:** For exact matches only, set this argument to FALSE or 0.

The value you want to match is the state in cell G4, and you're looking for it in the range C3:C25, the list of states. MATCH looks down the range until it finds "NH". It finds it in the 12th position, so 12 is used by INDEX as the row argument.

With MATCH computed, INDEX now has all it needs to return the right value. It goes to the 12th row of the range and either gets the value from the first column (for City) or the third column (for Store #).

Note   **If you pass INDEX a row number that is more rows than is in the range or a column number that is more columns, INDEX returns the #REF! error.**

Alternative: The LOOKUP function

Although VLOOKUP is the most popular lookup function, the combination of INDEX and MATCH is a close second. A lesser-used alternative is the LOOKUP function. LOOKUP takes these three arguments:

➤ **Lookup value:** The value you want to find

➤ **Lookup vector:** The single column or single row to look in

➤ **Results vector:** The single column or single row to return from

The following formulas are for finding the City and Store # from Figure 6-3:

```
City:  =LOOKUP(G4,C3:C25,B3:B25)
Store: =LOOKUP(G4,C3:C25,D3:D25)
```

The first two arguments of LOOKUP are identical to the first two arguments of MATCH. In fact, LOOKUP works similarly to MATCH in that it finds the position of the lookup value in the lookup vector. Rather than returning that position, however, it returns the value in the same position within the results vector.

To find the city, LOOKUP calculates that "NH" is in the 12th position of the lookup vector (C3:C25) and returns the value in the 12th position of the results vector (B3:B25).

Formula 57: Looking Up Values Horizontally

If the data is structured in such a way that your lookup value is in the top row rather than the first column and you want to look down the rows for data rather than across the columns, Excel has a function just for you.

Figure 6-4 shows a table of cities and their temperatures. The user will select a city from a drop-down box, and you want to return the temperate to the cell just below it.

```
=HLOOKUP(C5,C2:L3,2,FALSE)
```

Figure 6-4: A table of cities and temperatures.

How it works

The HLOOKUP function has the same arguments as VLOOKUP. The *H* in HLOOKUP stands for *horizontal*, and the *V* in VLOOKUP stands for *vertical*. Instead of looking down the first column for the lookup_ value argument, HLOOKUP looks across the first row. When it finds a match, it returns the value from the second row of the matching column.

Alternative

HLOOKUP and VLOOKUP are very similar functions. Just as you can substitute a combination of INDEX and MATCH for VLOOKUP, so can you for HLOOKUP.

```
=INDEX(C2:L3,2,MATCH(C5,C2:L2,FALSE))
```

In this case, the row argument of INDEX is hardcoded to "2", and the MATCH function feeds the column argument. MATCH can look at single rows of values as well as single columns. As before, it returns the position of the matched item.

Formula 58: Hiding Errors Returned by Lookup Functions

So far, you've used FALSE for the last argument of your lookup functions so that you return only exact matches. When you force a lookup function to return an exact match but it can't find one, it returns the #N/A error.

The #N/A error is useful in Excel models because it alerts you when a match couldn't be found. But you may be using all or a portion of your model for reporting, and #N/A errors are ugly. Excel has functions to see those errors and return something different.

	A	B	C	D	E	F	G
	D3	▼	fx	=VLOOKUP(C3,$F$3:$G$11,2,FALSE)			
1							
2		Company	CEO	Salary		Name	2012 Salary
3		Activision Blizzard Inc	Robert A. Kotick	#N/A		David M. Cote	33,247,178
4		CBS Corp	Leslie Moonves	62,157,026		Gregory B. Maffei	45,302,040
5		Cheniere Energy Inc	Charif Souki	#N/A		John H. Hammergren	51,744,999
6		Credit Acceptance Corp	Brett A. Roberts	#N/A		Leslie Moonves	62,157,026
7		Discovery Communications Inc	David M. Zaslav	#N/A		Mario J. Gabelli	68,970,486
8		Disney (Walt) Co	Robert A. Iger	#N/A		Marissa A. Mayer	36,615,404
9		Exxon Mobil Corp	R. W. Tillerson	40,266,501		Mark G. Parker	35,212,678
10		Gamco Investors Inc	Mario J. Gabelli	68,970,486		R. W. Tillerson	40,266,501
11		HCA Holdings Inc	Richard M. Bracken	#N/A		Ralph Lauren	36,325,782
12		Honeywell International Inc	David M. Cote	33,247,178			
13		Jefferies Group Llc	Richard B. Handler	#N/A			
14		Level 3 Communications Inc	James Q. Crowe	#N/A			
15		Liberty Interactive Corp	Gregory B. Maffei	45,302,040			
16		Mckesson Corp	John H. Hammergren	51,744,999			
17		Nike Inc	Mark G. Parker	35,212,678			
18		Nuance Communications Inc	Paul A. Ricci	#N/A			
19		Oracle Corp	Lawrence J. Ellison	#N/A			
20		Pall Corp	Lawrence Kingsley	#N/A			
21		Ralph Lauren Corp	Ralph Lauren	36,325,782			
22		Tesla Motors Inc	Elon Musk	#N/A			
23		Viacom Inc	Philippe P. Dauman	#N/A			
24		Yahoo Inc	Marissa A. Mayer	36,615,404			
25							

Figure 6-5: A report of CEO salaries.

Figure 6-5 shows a list of companies and CEOs. The other list shows CEOs and salaries. A VLOOKUP function is used to combine the two tables. But you obviously don't have salary information for all of the CEOs, and you have a lot of #N/A errors.

```
=VLOOKUP(C3,$F$3:$G$11,2,FALSE)
```

In Figure 6-6, the formula has been changed to use the IFERROR function to return a blank if no information is available. The IFERROR function is known as an *error trapping* function because it recognizes, or traps, errors and provides a way for you to handle them other than simply allowing them to propagate through your formula.

	A	B	C	D	E	F	G
	D3 ▾	fx	=IF(ISNA(VLOOKUP(C3,$F$3:$G$11,2,FALSE)),"",VLOOKUP(C3,$F$3:$G$11,2,FALSE))				
1							
2		Company	CEO	Salary		Name	2012 Salary
3		Activision Blizzard Inc	Robert A. Kotick			David M. Cote	33,247,178
4		CBS Corp	Leslie Moonves	62,157,026		Gregory B. Maffei	45,302,040
5		Cheniere Energy Inc	Charif Souki			John H. Hammergren	51,744,999
6		Credit Acceptance Corp	Brett A. Roberts			Leslie Moonves	62,157,026
7		Discovery Communications Inc	David M. Zaslav			Mario J. Gabelli	68,970,486
8		Disney (Walt) Co	Robert A. Iger			Marissa A. Mayer	36,615,404
9		Exxon Mobil Corp	R. W. Tillerson	40,266,501		Mark G. Parker	35,212,678
10		Gamco Investors Inc	Mario J. Gabelli	68,970,486		R. W. Tillerson	40,266,501
11		HCA Holdings Inc	Richard M. Bracken			Ralph Lauren	36,325,782
12		Honeywell International Inc	David M. Cote	33,247,178			
13		Jefferies Group Llc	Richard B. Handler				
14		Level 3 Communications Inc	James Q. Crowe				
15		Liberty Interactive Corp	Gregory B. Maffei	45,302,040			
16		Mckesson Corp	John H. Hammergren	51,744,999			
17		Nike Inc	Mark G. Parker	35,212,678			
18		Nuance Communications Inc	Paul A. Ricci				
19		Oracle Corp	Lawrence J. Ellison				
20		Pall Corp	Lawrence Kingsley				
21		Ralph Lauren Corp	Ralph Lauren	36,325,782			
22		Tesla Motors Inc	Elon Musk				
23		Viacom Inc	Philippe P. Dauman				
24		Yahoo Inc	Marissa A. Mayer	36,615,404			
25							

Figure 6-6: A cleaner report.

```
=IFERROR(VLOOKUP(C3,$F$3:$G$11,2,FALSE),"")
```

How it works

The IFERROR function accepts a value or formula for its first argument and an alternative return value for its second argument. When the first argument returns an error, the second argument is returned. When the first argument is not an error, the results of the first argument are returned.

In this example, you've made your alternative return value an empty string (two double quotation marks with nothing between them). That keeps the report nice and clean. But you could return anything you want, such as "No info" or 0.

Tip

The IFERROR checks for every error that Excel can return, including #N/A, #DIV/0!, and #VALUE. You can't restrict which errors IFERROR catches or ignores and that can hide errors that you otherwise would not want to hide.

Excel provides three other error-trapping functions: ISERROR returns TRUE if its argument returns any error; ISERR returns TRUE if its argument returns any error except #N/A; ISNA returns TRUE if its argument returns #N/A and returns FALSE for anything else include other errors.

All these error-trapping functions return either TRUE or FALSE and are most commonly used with an IF function.

Alternative: The ISNA Function

IFERROR was introduced in Excel 2010. In older versions, you can use the ISNA function to check for errors.

```
=IF(ISNA(VLOOKUP(C3,$F$3:$G$11,2,FALSE)),"",VLOOKUP(C3,$F$3:$G$11,2,FALSE))
```

The ISNA function returns TRUE if its argument returns the #N/A error and returns FALSE if it doesn't. The IF function checks for the error, returns an empty string if it's there, or returns the value of the VLOOKUP if it's not.

The downside to using ISNA is that you have to include the formula twice: once inside ISNA and once for the third argument of the IF function. This means that Excel has to calculate the same formula twice, and if you have a calculation-intensive workbook, it will be even slower.

Formula 59: Finding the Closest Match from a List of Banded Values

The VLOOKUP, HLOOKUP, and MATCH functions allow the data to be sorted in any order when you want an exact match. You set each of their final arguments to FALSE to force an exact match or to return an error.

These functions also work on sorted data for the times you want only an approximate match. Figure 6-7 shows a method for calculating income tax withholding. The withholding table doesn't have every possible value, but it has bands of values. You first determine which band the employee's pay falls in, and then you use the information on that row to compute the withholding:

```
=VLOOKUP(D15,B3:E10,3,TRUE)+(D15-VLOOKUP(D15,B3:E10,1,TRUE))*VLOOKUP(D15,
    B3:E10,4,TRUE)
```

	A	B	C	D	E	F
1						
2		Wages over	But not over	Base amount	Percentage	
3		-	325	-	0.0%	
4		325	1,023	-	10.0%	
5		1,023	3,163	69.80	15.0%	
6		3,163	6,050	390.80	25.0%	
7		6,050	9,050	1,112.56	28.0%	
8		9,050	15,906	195.56	33.0%	
9		15,906	17,925	4,215.03	35.0%	
10		17,925		4,921.68	39.6%	
11						
12		Bi-weekly wage:		2,307.69		
13		Withholding allowances:		2		
14		Allowance:		303.80		
15		Wage less allowance:		2,003.89		
16		Withholding amount:		216.93		
17						
18						

Figure 6-7: Computing income tax withholding.

How it works

The formula uses three VLOOKUP functions to get three pieces of data from the table. The final argument for each VLOOKUP formula is TRUE, indicating you want only an approximate match.

To get a correct result when using a final argument of TRUE, the data in the lookup column (column B in Figure 6-7) must be sorted lowest to highest. VLOOKUP looks down the first column and stops when the *next* value is higher than the lookup value. In that way, it finds the largest value that is not larger than the lookup value.

Caution

Finding an approximate match with a lookup function does not find the *closest* match. Rather, it finds the largest match that's not larger than the lookup value even if the next highest value is closer to the lookup value.

If the data in the lookup column isn't sorted highest to lowest, you may not get an error, but you will likely get an incorrect result. The lookup functions use a *binary search* to find an approximate match. A binary search basically starts in the middle of the lookup column and determines whether the match will be in the first half or the second half of the values. Then it splits that half in the middle and looks either forward or backward depending on the middle value. That process is repeated until the result is found.

You can see with a binary search that unsorted values could cause the lookup function to choose the wrong half to look in and return bad data.

In the example in Figure 6-7, VLOOKUP stops at row 5 because 1,023 is the largest value in the list that's not larger than the lookup value of 2,003.89. The three sections of the formula work as follows:

➤ The first VLOOKUP returns the base amount in the third column, or 69.80.

➤ The second VLOOKUP subtracts the "Wages over" amount (from the first column) from the total wages.

➤ The last VLOOKUP returns the percentage in the fourth column. This percentage is multiplied by the excess wages, and the result is added to the base amount.

When all three VLOOKUP functions are evaluated, the formula computes, as shown here:

```
=69.80 + (2,003.89 - 1,023.00) * 15.0%
```

Tip

The method the lookup functions use to find an approximate match is much faster than an exact match. For an exact match, the function has to look at every single value in the lookup column. If you know your data will always be sorted lowest to highest and will always contain an exact match, you can decrease calculation time by setting the last argument to TRUE. An approximate match lookup will always find an exact match if it exists and if the data is sorted.

Alternative: INDEX and MATCH

As with all of your lookup formulas, the INDEX and MATCH combination can be substituted. As do VLOOKUP and HLOOKUP, MATCH has a final argument to find approximate matches. MATCH has the added advantage of being able to work with data that is sorted highest to lowest.

Figure 6-8 shows the same withholding table as Figure 6-7 except that the data is sorted in descending order. The VLOOKUP based formula from Figure 6-7 returns #N/A, as shown in cell D16 on Figure 6-8. This is because VLOOKUP looks at the middle of the lookup column, determines that it is higher than the lookup value, and then looks only at values before the middle value. Because your data is sorted descending, no values before the middle value are lower than the lookup value.

The INDEX and MATCH formula in cell D18 of Figure 6-8 returns the correct result and is shown here:

```
=INDEX(B3:E10,MATCH(D15,B3:B10,-1)+1,3)+(D15-
   INDEX(B3:E10,MATCH(D15,B3:B10,-1)+1,1))*INDEX(B3:E10,MATCH(D15,B
   3:B10,-1)+1,4)
```

	A	B	C	D	E	F
1						
2		Wages over	But not over	Base amount	Percentage	
3		17,925		4,921.68	39.6%	
4		15,906	17,925	4,215.03	35.0%	
5		9,050	15,906	195.56	33.0%	
6		6,050	9,050	1,112.56	28.0%	
7		3,163	6,050	390.80	25.0%	
8		1,023	3,163	69.80	15.0%	
9		325	1,023	-	10.0%	
10		-	325	-	0.0%	
11						
12		Bi-weekly wage:		2,307.69		
13		Withholding allowances:		2		
14		Allowance:		303.80		
15		Wage less allowance:		2,003.89		
16		Withholding amount:		#N/A		
17						
18		INDEX and MATCH:		216.93		
19						
20						

Figure 6-8: Calculating withholding using INDEX and MATCH.

The final argument of MATCH can be −1, 0, or 1.

> **−1** is used for data that is sorted highest to lowest. It finds the smallest value in the lookup column that is larger than the lookup value. There is not an equivalent method using VLOOKUP or HLOOKUP.

> **0** is used for unsorted data to find the exact match. It is equivalent to setting the final argument of VLOOKUP or HLOOKUP to FALSE.

> **1** is used for data that is sorted lowest to highest. It finds the largest value in the lookup column that is smaller than the lookup value. It is equivalent to setting the final argument of VLOOKUP or HLOOKUP to TRUE.

Because MATCH with a final argument of −1 finds a value that is larger than the lookup value, the formula adds 1 to the result to get the proper row.

Formula 60: Looking Up Values from Multiple Tables

Sometimes the data you want to look up can come from more than one table, depending on a choice that the user makes. In Figure 6-9, a withholding calculation similar to Formula 59 is shown. The difference is that the user can select whether the employee is single or married. If the user chooses Single, the data is looked up in the Single Person table; if the user chooses Married, the data is looked up in the Married Person table.

	A	B	C	D	E	F
	L36		fx			
1						
2		*Married person*				
3		**Wages over**	**But not over**	**Base amount**	**Percentage**	
4		-	325	-	0.0%	
5		325	1,023	-	10.0%	
6		1,023	3,163	69.80	15.0%	
7		3,163	6,050	390.80	25.0%	
8		6,050	9,050	1,112.56	28.0%	
9		9,050	15,906	1,952.56	33.0%	
10		15,906	17,925	4,215.03	35.0%	
11		17,925		4,921.68	39.6%	
12						
13		*Single person*				
14		**Wages over**	**But not over**	**Base amount**	**Percentage**	
15		-	87	-	0.0%	
16		87	436	-	10.0%	
17		436	1,506	34.90	15.0%	
18		1,506	3,523	195.40	25.0%	
19		3,523	7,254	699.65	28.0%	
20		7,254	15,667	1,744.33	33.0%	
21		15,667	15,731	4,520.62	35.0%	
22		15,731		4,543.02	39.6%	
23						
24						
25			Married or Single:	Single		
26			Bi-weekly wage:	4,038.46		
27		Withholding allowances:		3		
28			Allowance:	455.70		
29			Wage less allowance:	3,582.76		
30			Withholding amount:	716.38		
31						
32						

Figure 6-9: Computing income tax withholding from two tables.

In Excel, you can use *named ranges* and the INDIRECT function to direct your lookup to the appropriate table. Before you can write the formula, you need to name two ranges: *Married* for the Married Person table and *Single* for the Single Person table. Follow these steps to create the named ranges:

1. Select the range B4:E11.

2. Click the Define Name button found on the Formulas tab on the Ribbon. The New Name dialog box shown in Figure 6-10 is displayed.

3. Change the Name text box to Married.

4. Click OK.

5. Select the range B15:E22.

6. Click the Define Name button found on the Formulas tab on the Ribbon.

7. Change the Name text box to Single.

8. Click OK.

Figure 6-10: The New Name dialog box.

There is a data validation drop-down box in cell D25 in Figure 6-9. The drop-down box contains the terms Married and Single, which are identical to the names you just created. You use the value in D25 to determine which table to look in, so the values must be identical.

Here's the revised formula for computing the withholding:

```
=VLOOKUP(D29,INDIRECT(D25),3,TRUE)+(D29-VLOOKUP(D29,INDIRECT(D25),1,TRUE))*
   VLOOKUP(D29,INDIRECT(D25),4,TRUE)
```

How it works

The formula in this example is strikingly similar to Formula 59. The only difference is that you use an INDIRECT function in place of the table's location.

INDIRECT takes an argument named ref_text. The ref_text argument is a text representation of a cell reference or a named range. In Figure 6-9, cell D25 contains the text *Single*. INDIRECT attempts to convert that into a cell or range reference. If ref_text is not a valid range reference (as in this case), INDIRECT checks the named ranges to see whether a match exists. Had you not already created a range named Single, INDIRECT would return the #REF! error.

INDIRECT has a second optional argument named a1. The a1 argument is TRUE if ref_text is in the A1 style of cell references and FALSE if ref_text is in the R1C1 style of cell references. For named ranges, a1 can be either TRUE or FALSE, and INDIRECT will return the correct range.

Caution

INDIRECT can also return ranges from other worksheets or even other workbooks. However, if it references another workbook, that workbook must be open. INDIRECT doesn't work on closed workbooks.

Formula 61: Looking Up a Value Based on a Two-Way Matrix

A two-way matrix is a rectangular range of cells. That is, it's a range with more than one row and more than one column. In other formulas, you've used the INDEX and MATCH combination as an alternative to some of the lookup functions. However, INDEX and MATCH were made for two-way matrixes.

Figure 6-11 shows a table of sales figures by region and year. Each row represents a region and each column represents a year. You want the user to select a region and a year and return the sales figure at the intersection of that row and column.

```
=INDEX(C4:F9,MATCH(C13,B4:B9,FALSE),MATCH(C14,C3:F3,FALSE))
```

C15	▾	fx	=INDEX(C4:F9,MATCH(C13,B4:B9,FALSE),MATCH(C14,C3:F3,FALSE))				
	A	B	C	D	E	F	G
1							
2		Regional Sales Report					
3		Region	2010	2011	2012	2013	Total
4		South	1,525,017	1,504,678	1,227,847	1,019,616	5,277,158
5		Northeast	2,704,237	2,135,564	1,411,782	716,535	6,968,118
6		North	3,563,687	4,441,886	4,805,431	3,716,674	16,527,678
7		West	4,489,700	2,651,064	796,330	2,898,601	10,835,695
8		Mid-Atlantic	2,167,319	1,357,850	776,850	3,024,542	7,326,561
9		Canada	1,861,239	3,578,280	4,069,389	1,475,301	10,984,209
10		Total	16,311,199	15,669,322	13,087,629	12,851,269	57,919,419
11							
12							
13		Region:	North				
14		Year:	2011				
15		Sales:	4,441,886				
16							

Figure 6-11: Sales data by region and year.

How it works

By now, you're no doubt familiar with INDEX and MATCH. Unlike other formulas, you're using two MATCH functions within the INDEX function. The second MATCH function returns the column argument of INDEX as opposed to hardcoding a column number.

Recall that MATCH returns the position in a list of the matched value. In Figure 6-11, the North region is matched, so MATCH returns 3 because it's the third item in the list. That becomes the row argument for INDEX. The year 2011 is matched across the header row, and because 2011 is the second item, MATCH returns 2. INDEX then takes the 2 and 3 returned by the MATCH functions to return the proper value.

Alternative: Using default values for MATCH

To add a twist to your sales lookup formula, you change the formula to allow the user to select only a region, only a year, or neither. If one of the selections is omitted, you assume that the user wants the total. If neither is selected, you return the total for the whole table.

```
=INDEX(C4:G10,IFERROR(MATCH(C13,B4:B10,FALSE),COUNTA(B4:B10)),IFERROR(MATCH
   (C14,C3:G3,FALSE),COUNTA(C3:G3)))
```

The overall structure of the formula is the same, but a few details have changed. The range for INDEX now includes row 10 and column G. Each MATCH function's range is also extended. Finally, both MATCH functions are surrounded by an IFERROR function that will return the Total row or column.

The alternative value for IFERROR is a COUNTA function. COUNTA counts both numbers and text and, in effect, returns the position of the last row or column in your range. You could have hardcoded those values, but if you happen to insert a row or column, COUNTA adjusts to always return the last one.

Figure 6-12 shows the same sales table, but the user has left the Year input blank. Because the column headers have no blanks, MATCH returns #N/A. When it encounters that error, IFERROR passes control to the value_if_error argument, and the last column is passed to INDEX.

C15	▾	*fx*	=INDEX(C4:G10,IFERROR(MATCH(C13,B4:B10,FALSE),COUNTA(B4:B10)),				
			IFERROR(MATCH(C14,C3:G3,FALSE),COUNTA(C3:G3)))				

	A	B	C	D	E	F	G
1							
2		**Regional Sales Report**					
3		Region	2010	2011	2012	2013	Total
4		South	1,525,017	1,504,678	1,227,847	1,019,616	5,277,158
5		Northeast	2,704,237	2,135,564	1,411,782	716,535	6,968,118
6		North	3,563,687	4,441,886	4,805,431	3,716,674	16,527,678
7		West	4,489,700	2,651,064	796,330	2,898,601	10,835,695
8		Mid-Atlantic	2,167,319	1,357,850	776,850	3,024,542	7,326,561
9		Canada	1,861,239	3,578,280	4,069,389	1,475,301	10,984,209
10		Total	16,311,199	15,669,322	13,087,629	12,851,269	57,919,419
11							
12							
13		Region:	Mid-Atlantic				
14		Year:					
15		Sales:	7,326,561				
16							
17							

Figure 6-12: Returning totals from the sales data.

Formula 62: Finding a Value Based on Multiple Criteria

Figure 6-13 shows a table of departmental budgets. When the user selects a region and department, you want a formula to return the budget. You can't use VLOOKUP for this formula, because it accepts only one lookup value. You need two lookup values because the regions and departments appear multiple times.

Cross-Ref See Chapter 5 for a discussion of how SUMPRODUCT uses arrays.

You can use the SUMPRODUCT function to get the row that contains both lookup values.

```
=SUMPRODUCT(($B$3:$B$45=H5)*($C$3:$C$45=H6)*($E$3:$E$45))
```

	H7	▾	ƒx	=SUMPRODUCT(($B$3:$B$45=H5)*($C$3:$C$45=H6)*($E$3:$E$45))				
	A	B	C	D	E	F	G	H	I
1								
2		Region	Department	Manager	Budget			
3		Mid-Atlantic	Legal	Jose Palmer	4,406,018			
4		Canada	Legal	Audrey Washington	2,564,165			
5		North	Logistics	Samantha Allen	1,443,535		Region:	South
6		Mid-Atlantic	Customer Service	Katherine Nichols	2,834,014		Department:	Accounting
7		Pacific Northwest	Quality Assurance	David Gordon	1,119,596		Budget:	697,697
8		Mid-Atlantic	Operational	Lillian Hart	2,949,401		Manager:	Brooke Bailey
9		Mid-Atlantic	Sales	Claire Peterson	2,371,246			
10		East	Inventory	Hannah Porter	3,043,499			
11		Mid-Atlantic	Services	Victoria Gomez	1,621,716			
12		South	Accounting	Brooke Bailey	697,697			
13		Mid-Atlantic	Insurance	Layla Green	1,458,914			
14		North	Sales	Alex Cox	2,922,128			
15		North	Business Development	Genesis Mills	3,699,755			
16		South	Business Development	Isaac Chavez	930,133			
17		Pacific Northwest	Services	Adam Howard	2,609,312			
18		South	Quality Assurance	Evelyn Burns	1,660,933			
19		Mid-Atlantic	Business Development	Jack Black	644,173			
20		Pacific Northwest	Customer Service	Wyatt Harris	4,487,298			

Figure 6-13: A table of departmental budgets.

How it works

SUMPRODUCT compares every cell in a range with a value and returns an array of TRUEs and FALSEs depending on the result. When multiplied with another array, TRUE becomes 1, and FALSE becomes 0. The third parenthetical section in your SUMPRODUCT function does not contain a comparison, because that range contains the value you want to return.

If either the Region comparison or the Department comparison is FALSE, the total for that line will be 0. A FALSE result is converted to 0, and anything times 0 is 0. If both Region and Department match, both comparisons return 1. The two 1s (ones) are multiplied with the corresponding row in column E, and that's the value returned.

In the example shown in Figure 6-13, when SUMPRODUCT gets to row 12, it multiplies 1 * 1 * 697,697. That number is summed with the other rows, all of which are 0 because they contain at least one FALSE. The resulting SUM is the value 697,697.

Alternative: Returning text with SUMPRODUCT

SUMPRODUCT works this way only when you want to return a number. If you want to return text, all the text values would be treated as 0, and SUMPRODUCT would always return 0.

However, you can pair SUMPRODUCT with the INDEX and ROW functions to return text. If you want to return the manager's name, for example, you could use this formula:

```
=INDEX(D:D,SUMPRODUCT(($B$3:$B$45=H5)*($C$3:$C$45=H6)*(ROW($E$3:$E$45))),1)
```

Instead of including the values from column E, the ROW function is used to include the row numbers in the array. SUMPRODUCT now computes 1 * 1 * 12 when it gets to row 12. The 12 is then used for the row argument in INDEX against the entire column D:D. Because the ROW function returns the row in the worksheet and not the row in your table, INDEX uses the whole column as its range.

Formula 63: Finding the Last Value in a Column

Figure 6-14 shows an unsorted list of invoices. You want to find the last invoice in the list. A simple way to find the last item in the column is to use the INDEX function and count the items in the list to determine the last row.

```
=INDEX(B:B,COUNTA(B:B)+1)
```

	F5	▾	*fx*	=INDEX(B:B,COUNTA(B:B)+1)			
◢	A	B	C	D	E	F	G
1							
2		Invoice #	Item Count	Amount			
3		IN6787	53	555.73			
4		IN4374	160	940.56		Last Invoice	Last Amount
5		IN5061	40	3,026.10		IN6513	3,326.98
6		IN4305	146	4,885.94			
7		IN1477	84	969.46			
8		IN5552	97	2,979.33			
9		IN8685	200	2,950.74			
10		IN1491	40	3,970.50			
11		IN2408	155	3,332.94			
12		IN6513	75	3,326.98			
13							
14							

Figure 6-14: A list of invoices.

How it works

The INDEX function when used on a single column needs only a row argument. The third argument indicating the column isn't necessary. COUNTA is used to count the non-blank cells in column B. That count is increased by 1 because you have a blank cell in the first row. The INDEX function returns the 12th row of column B.

Caution

COUNTA counts numbers, text, dates, and anything except blanks. If your data contains blank rows, COUNTA won't return the desired result.

Alternative: Finding the last number using LOOKUP

INDEX and COUNTA are great for finding values when the range doesn't contain any blank cells. If you have blanks and the values you're searching for are numbers, you can use LOOKUP and a really large number. The formula in cell G5 of Figure 6-14 uses this technique.

```
=LOOKUP(9.99E+307,D:D)
```

The lookup value is the largest number Excel can handle (just under 1 with 308 zeroes behind it). Because LOOKUP won't find a value that large, it stops at the last value it does find, and that's the value returned.

Tip

A number like 9.99E+307 is written in *exponential notation.* The number before the E has one number to the left of the decimal and two to the right. The number after the E is how many places to move the decimal point to show the number in regular notation (307 in this case). A positive number means to move the decimal to the right, and a negative number means to move it left. A number like 4.32E-02 is equivalent to 0.0432.

This LOOKUP method has the additional advantage of returning the last number even if the range has text, blanks, or errors.

Formula 64: Look Up the Nth Instance of a Criterion

One of the limitations of VLOOKUP and other lookup functions is that they find only the first occurrence of a matching value in a list. To find the second, third, or subsequent occurrence, you have to use an *array formula.*

Figure 6-15 shows a list of salespeople and sale amounts. Next to this list is a filtered list showing sales for only one salesperson. To create this list with formulas, you can't just use a VLOOKUP, because that will find only the first occurrence. You need to find all the occurrences and list them individually.

The following formula uses a number of functions, including INDEX, SMALL, and ROW. The SMALL function finds the *n*th smallest row that matches the name, and that row is used in INDEX to return the amount on that row.

```
=IF(LEN(E3)>0,INDEX($C$1:$C$26,SMALL(IF(($B$3:$B$26=E3),ROW($B$3:$B$26),"")
    ,ROW()-2),1),"")
```

F3			*fx*	{=IF(LEN(E3)>0,INDEX($C$1:$C$26,			
				SMALL(IF(($B$3:$B$26=E3),ROW($B$3:$B$26),""),ROW()-2),1),"")}			
	A	B	C	D	E	F	G	H
1								
2		Name	Sale Amount		Sales for:	Carlos		
3		Carlos	791.78		Carlos	791.78		
4		Payton	729.87		Carlos	136.41		
5		Rachel	879.54		Carlos	233.59		
6		Payton	876.70		Carlos	661.21		
7		Payton	244.33		Carlos	603.34		
8		Andrew	174.47		Carlos	583.64		
9		Rachel	759.46					
10		Payton	439.01					
11		Andrew	199.15					
12		Rachel	631.77					
13		Carlos	136.41					
14		Carlos	233.59					
15		Andrew	133.56					
16		Andrew	893.97					
17		Carlos	661.21					
18		Rachel	847.75					
19		Andrew	478.51					
20		Payton	524.85					
21		Andrew	174.30					
22		Rachel	414.50					
23		Payton	908.75					
24		Carlos	603.34					
25		Rachel	457.94					
26		Carlos	583.64					

Figure 6-15: A list of sales.

The formula in column E is a bit simpler. It lists the salesperson's name a number of times equal to the times the name appears in the main list. It uses COUNTIF to determine how many times the name appears.

```
=IF(COUNTIF($B$3:$B$26,$F$2)>ROW()-3,$F$2,"")
```

Both the formulas in column E and column D are copied down a sufficient number of times to show all the occurrences.

How it works

The formula in column E repeats the name in F2 if the count of that name is greater than ROW()-3. For cell E3, ROW()-3 returns 0, and "Carlos" is in the main list more than zero times, so the name is shown. In cell E9, however, ROW()-3 returns 6. Carlos's name appears only six times, so the count of his name is not greater than ROW()-3. In that case, an empty string (two double quotes) is returned.

Array formulas

Array formulas are special formulas that work on an array of numbers. For non–array formulas, you enter the formula and press Enter. For array formulas, you enter the formula and press Ctrl+Shift+Enter. (Hold down Ctrl and Shift and press Enter.)

When entered as an array formula, Excel puts curly braces, { }, around the formula. Don't type these braces yourself — it doesn't work that way.

SUMPRODUCT works like an array formula, but you enter it the normal way. SUMPRODUCT only sums the resulting array. If you want to perform an operation on an array other than summing, such as SMALL, MAX, AVERAGE, and so on, use an array formula with the appropriate function.

The formula in column D is an array formula, and you enter it by holding down Ctrl+Shift and then pressing Enter. The formula starts by checking to see whether there is a name in column E. If there isn't, an empty string is returned. If there is a name, an INDEX function is used to return the value of the *n*th instance of the name.

The row argument to INDEX uses the SMALL function. SMALL accepts an array (an array of rows and empty strings in this case) for its first argument and a number indicating the nth smallest value. A 2 in the second argument, for example, would find the second smallest number. For the second argument, you use ROW()-2. Because the data starts in row 3, the formula in row 3 returns the first smallest number, the formula in row 4 returns the second smallest number, and so on.

The SMALL function ignores strings and deals only with numbers. You use an IF statement to return the row number when B3:B26 matches the name. If it doesn't match, an empty string is returned, which SMALL simply ignores. When IF is evaluated for Carlos, the array sent to SMALL looks like this:

```
{3;"";"";"";"";"";"";"";"";"";13;14;"";"";17;"";"";"";"";"";"";24;"";26}
```

That's an array with 24 elements. When Carlos is matched, the row is returned, and SMALL will find the *n*th smallest row. For the formula in cell F5, SMALL returns 14 (the third smallest number in the array) and INDEX returns the value in row 14 (233.59).

Formula 65: Performing a Case-Sensitive Lookup

VLOOKUP and the other lookup functions don't care about capitalization when matching values. Using VLOOKUP to match "Bob" and "bob" will return the same result. When case matters, you use Excel's EXACT function.

Figure 6-16 shows a list of computer ID numbers and the last date someone logged in to that computer. The IDs in row 4 and row 11 are identical except for the case of the two letters in the middle. You want to perform a case-sensitive lookup of the computer ID.

Figure 6-16 also shows the results of two formulas. One uses VLOOKUP, and the other uses EXACT. Although you've selected the computer ID from row 11 in cell F4, VLOOKUP returns the result from row 4. The EXACT formula returns the correct result and is shown here:

```
=INDEX(C1:C12,SUMPRODUCT((EXACT(B3:B12,F4))*(ROW(B3:B12))),1)
```

	A	B	C	D	E	F	G
1							
2		ID#	Last Login				
3		0010857yY880	8/19/2014				
4		0036624Ef119	8/6/2014		ID#:	0036624eF119	
5		0018059Jr916	8/29/2014		VLOOKUP:	8/6/2014	
6		0089112nT313	8/24/2014		EXACT:	8/20/2014	
7		0096605oP997	8/6/2014				
8		0093443rE467	8/12/2014				
9		0021987Kb889	8/14/2014				
10		0001151aU089	8/4/2014				
11		0036624eF119	8/20/2014				
12		0029819Al048	8/25/2014				
13							

F6 fx =INDEX(C1:C12,SUMPRODUCT((EXACT(B3:B12,F4))*(ROW(B3:B12))),1)

Figure 6-16: A list of computer IDs and login dates.

How it works

By now you're familiar with using SUMPRODUCT and ROW to feed INDEX with a row number. This formula uses the EXACT function inside SUMPRODUCT. EXACT takes two arguments and returns TRUE if they are exactly the same (including capitalization).

When EXACT is used in SUMPRODUCT or an array formula, you can compare a range of text values to another value and get back an array of TRUEs and FALSEs. In this case, EXACT returns TRUE only when it compares B11 to F4. That TRUE value is converted to a 1 when multiplied by the array of ROW values, and SUMPRODUCT returns 11. All of the other EXACT results are FALSE and return 0.

The result of SUMPRODUCT, 11, is used as the row argument to INDEX, which returns the value from the 11th row in the range C1:C12.

Formula 66: Letting the User Select How to Aggregate Data

Excel's CHOOSE function is a great way to have different formulas in the same cell and let the user select which formula to use. Figure 6-17 shows a list of sales and three ways to aggregate them. The user can select which aggregator to use by selecting from a drop-down box in cell G7.

```
=CHOOSE(MATCH(G7,G3:G5,FALSE),SUM(D3:D17),COUNT(D3:D17),AVERAGE(D3:D17))
```

	G9	▼		*fx*	=CHOOSE(MATCH(G7,G3:G5,FALSE),SUM(D3:D17),COUNT(D3:D17),AVERAGE(D3:D17))					
⁄	A	B	C	D	E	F	G	H	I	J
1										
2		Date	Ticket #	Sale Amount			Aggregates			
3		8/3/2014	421	179.69			Sum			
4		8/11/2014	352	445.41			Count			
5		8/1/2014	325	653.09			Average			
6		8/11/2014	512	173.59						
7		8/2/2014	666	136.42		Select an aggregate:	Average			
8		8/18/2014	759	285.48						
9		8/12/2014	353	233.02		The Average is:	409.83			
10		8/28/2014	400	599.24						
11		8/13/2014	539	564.32		Subtotal:	409.83			
12		8/13/2014	548	253.34						
13		8/29/2014	414	501.22						
14		8/14/2014	411	396.67						
15		8/9/2014	721	471.73						
16		8/31/2014	784	629.04						
17		8/30/2014	380	625.12						
18										

Figure 6-17: Changing the aggregate from the drop-down box in cell G7.

How it works

The CHOOSE function's first argument is named index_num, and it determines which of the next arguments is returned. It can be a number between 1 and the number of arguments in the function up to 254. The next 254 arguments (only the first one is required) determines what is returned by CHOOSE. If index_num is 1, the second argument is returned; if index_num is 2, the third argument is returned; and so on.

The arguments after index_num are the three ways the user can aggregate the sales data, namely SUM, COUNT, and AVERAGE. The index_num argument is provided by a MATCH function that returns 1, 2, or 3 depending on where the user's choice (G7) falls in the list of aggregates (G3:G5).

If the user selects Sum, MATCH returns 1 and second argument (SUM) is returned. If the user selects Count, MATCH returns 2, and the third argument (COUNT) is returned. In Figure 6-17, the user selected Average, MATCH returned 3, and the fourth argument (AVERAGE) is returned.

Alternative

Another way to use CHOOSE and MATCH is in combination with the SUBTOTAL function. SUBTOTAL has a number of built-in aggregates that can be applied to a range. For example, if the first argument of SUBTOTAL is 9, the range is summed; if the first argument is 2, the range is counted; and if the first argument is 1, the range is averaged.

```
=SUBTOTAL(CHOOSE(MATCH(G7,G3:G5,FALSE),9,2,1),D3:D17)
```

Inside the SUBTOTAL, you can use CHOOSE and MATCH to return the SUBTOTAL aggregate to use. This is more restrictive than simply putting the formula in the CHOOSE function's arguments because you're limited to the aggregates allowed by SUBTOTAL.

Common Business and Financial Formulas

Spreadsheets got their start in the accounting and finance departments back when it was all done with paper and pencil. And even though Excel has grown far beyond a simple electronic ledger sheet, that ledger sheet is still a required tool in business. In this chapter, you look at some formulas commonly used in accounting, finance, and other areas of businesses.

Note

You can download the files for all the formulas at `www.wiley.com/go/101excelformula`.

Formula 67: Calculating Gross Profit Margin and Gross Profit Margin Percent

Gross margin is the money left over after subtracting cost of goods sold from revenue. It's the amount of sales that the business uses to cover overhead and other indirect costs. To compute the gross margin, simply subtract cost of goods sold from revenues. For gross margin percent, divide the gross margin by revenue.

Figure 7-1 shows the financial statements of a manufacturing company. Gross margin appears in cell C5 and gross margin percent appears in cell D5.

```
Gross Margin: =C3-C4
Gross Margin Percent: =C5/$C$3
```

C5		f_x =C3-C4					
	A	B	C	D	E	F	G
1							
2			2013		2012		
3		Revenue	$55,656	100%	$65,875	100%	
4		Cost of Goods Sold	41,454	74%	47,852	73%	
5		Gross Margin	14,202	26%	18,023	27%	
6							
7		Research Development	2,046	4%	2,466	4%	
8		Selling, General, and Administrative Expenses	6,528	12%	6,404	10%	
9							
10		Operating Margin	5,628	10%	9,153	14%	
11							
12		Interest Expense	465	1%	467	1%	
13		Other Income and Expense	1,368	2%	3,197	5%	
14							
15		Net Profit	$3,795	7%	$5,489	8%	
16							
17							

Figure 7-1: A financial statement for a manufacturing company.

How it works

The gross margin formula simply subtracts cell C4 from cell C3. The gross margin percent divides C5 by C3, but note that the C3 reference is absolute because it has dollar signs. Making the reference absolute allows you to copy the formula to other lines on the income statement to see the percentage of revenue, a common analysis performed on income statements.

Alternative: Calculating Markup

Markup is often confused with gross margin percent, but they are different. Markup is the percentage added to costs to arrive at a selling price. Figure 7-2 shows the sale of a single product, the markup applied, and the gross margin realized when sold.

C4		f_x =(C3/C2)-1		
	A	B	C	D	E
1					
2		Cost of product	465.00		465.00
3		Selling price	614.00		683.82
4		Markup	32%		47%
5					
6		Revenue	614.00		683.82
7		Cost of Goods Sold	465.00		465.00
8		Gross Margin	149.00		218.82
9		Gross Margin Percent	24%		32%
10					
11					

Figure 7-2: Markup and gross margin percent from a single product.

The markup is computed by dividing the selling price by the cost and subtracting 1:

```
=(C3/C2)-1
```

By marking up the cost of the product 32 percent, you achieve a 24 percent gross margin. If you want to mark up a product to get a 32 percent margin (as shown in column E of Figure 7-2), use the following formula:

```
=1/(1-E9)-1
```

Using this formula, you would need to mark up this product 47 percent if you wanted your income statement to show a 32 percent gross margin.

Formula 68: Calculating EBIT and EBITDA

Earnings before interest and taxes (EBIT) and earnings before interest, taxes, depreciation, and amortization (EBITDA) are common calculations for evaluating the results of a business. Both are computed by adding back certain expenses to earnings, also known as net profit.

Figure 7-3 shows an income statement and the results of the EBIT and EBITDA calculations below it.

```
EBIT: =C18+VLOOKUP("Interest Expense",$B$2:$C$18,2,FALSE)+VLOOKUP("Income
   Tax Expense",$B$2:$C$18,2,FALSE)
EBITDA: =C20+VLOOKUP("Depreciation Expense",$B$2:$C$18,2,FALSE)+VLOOKUP
   ("Amortization Expense",$B$2:$C$18,2,FALSE)
```

How it works

The EBIT formula starts with net loss in C18 and uses two VLOOKUP functions to find Interest Expense and Income Tax Expense from the income statement. For EBITDA, the formula starts with the result of the EBIT calculation and uses the same VLOOKUP technique to add back Depreciation Expense and Amortization Expense.

You benefit from using VLOOKUP rather than simply using the cell references to those expenses. If the lines on the income statement are moved around, the EBIT and EBITDA formulas don't need to be changed.

Cross-Ref   **See Chapter 6 for more on the VLOOKUP function.**

	C20	▼	f_x	=C18+VLOOKUP("Interest Expense",$B$2:$C$18,2,FALSE)+ VLOOKUP("Income Tax Expense",$B$2:$C$18,2,FALSE)				
⊿	A	B	C	D	E	F	G	
1								
2		Revenue	65,245					
3		Cost of Goods Sold	39,147					
4		Gross Margin	26,098					
5								
6		Selling Expenses						
7		Administrative Expenses	8,213					
8		Depreciation Expense	7,245					
9		Amortization Expense	2,444					
10		Total Operating Expenses	17,902					
11								
12		Operating Income	8,196					
13								
14		Other Expenses	654					
15		Interest Expense	6,215					
16		Income Tax Expense	3,215					
17								
18		Net Income (Loss)	(1,888)					
19								
20		EBIT	7,542					
21		EBITDA	17,231					
22								

Figure 7-3: An income statement with EBIT and EBITDA calculations.

Formula 69: Calculating Cost of Goods Sold

The term *cost of goods sold* refers to the amount you paid for all the goods you sold. It is a critical component to calculating gross margin, as demonstrated in Formula 67. If you use a perpetual inventory system, you calculate cost of goods sold for every sale made. For simpler systems, however, you can calculate it based on a physical inventory at the end of the accounting period.

Figure 7-4 shows how to calculate the cost of goods sold with only the beginning and ending inventory counts and the total of all the inventory purchased in the period.

```
Goods Available for Sale: =SUM(C2:C3)
Cost of Goods Sold: =C4-C5
```

	C6	▼	f_x	=C4-C5	
⊿	A	B	C	D
1				
2		Beginning Inventory	1,235,642.25	
3		Purchases	641,152.77	
4		Goods Available for Sale	1,876,795.02	
5		Ending Inventory	1,111,903.23	
6		Cost of Goods Sold	764,891.79	
7				
8				

Figure 7-4: Calculating cost of goods sold.

How it works

The goods available for sale is beginning inventory plus all the purchases made. It is an intermediate calculation that shows what your ending inventory would be if you didn't sell anything.

The cost of goods sold calculation simply subtracts ending inventory from the goods available for sale. If you had the goods at the start of the period or you bought them during the period but you don't have them at the end of the period, they must have been sold.

Formula 70: Calculating Return on Assets

Return on assets (ROA) is a measure of how efficiently a business is using its assets to generate income. For example, a company with higher ROA can generate the same profit as one with a lower ROA using fewer or cheaper assets.

To compute ROA, divide the profits for a period of time by the average of the beginning and ending total assets. Figure 7-5 shows a simple balance sheet and income statement and the resulting ROA.

```
=G15/AVERAGE(C12:D12)
```

	G18 ▾	*fx* =G15/AVERAGE(C12:D12)						
▲	A	B	C	D	E	F	G	H
1								
2		**Balance Sheet**				**Income Statement**		
3		Cash	$1,186	$124		Revenue	$55,656	
4		Accounts Receivable	3,884	3,026		Cost of Goods Sold	41,454	
5		Inventories	8,355	7,651		Gross Margin	14,202	
6		Total Current Assets	13,425	10,801				
7						Research & Development	2,046	
8		Property and Equipment	4,320	4,516		S,G & A Expenses	6,528	
9		Other Assets	578	322				
10		Total Long-term Assets	4,898	4,838		Operating Margin	5,628	
11								
12		Total Assets	$18,323	$15,639		Interest Expense	465	
13						Other Income and Expense	1,368	
14		Accounts Payable	$1,670	$2,644				
15		Accrued Expenses	1,334	1,431		Net Profit	$3,795	
16		Notes Payable Current	788	761				
17		Total Current Liabilities	3,792	4,836				
18						Return on Assets	22.35%	
19		Notes Payable Long Term	3,177	3,244		Return on Equity	40.13%	
20		Total Liabilities	6,969	8,080				
21								
22		Common Stock	453	453				
23		Additional Paid-in Capital	4,562	4,562				
24		Retained Earnings	6,339	2,544				
25		Total Equity	11,354	7,559				
26								
27		Total Liabilities and Equity	$18,323	$15,639				
28								

Figure 7-5: A return on assets calculation.

How it works

The numerator is simply the net profit from the income statement. The denominator uses the AVERAGE function to find the average total assets for the period.

Alternative: Calculating return on equity

Another common profitability measure is return on equity (ROE). An investor may use ROE to determine whether her investment in the business is being put to good use. As does ROA, ROE divides net profit by the average of a balance sheet item over the same period. ROE, however, uses average Total Equity rather than average Total Assets. The formula to calculate ROE from Figure 7-5 is as follows:

```
=G15/AVERAGE(C25:D25)
```

Formula 71: Calculating Break Even

A business may want to determine how much revenue it will need to achieve a net profit of exactly $0. This revenue result is called break even. To determine it, the business estimates its fixed expenses as well as the percentage of each of its variable expenses. Using those numbers, it can back into a revenue amount that results in break even.

Figure 7-6 shows a break-even calculation. Column C shows either an "F" for a fixed expense or a percentage for an expense that varies as revenue changes. For example, research and development will be spent according to a budget and doesn't change if revenue increases or decreases. On the other hand, if the business pays a commission, the selling expenses will rise and fall with revenues.

The calculations to determine break even (those numbers where column C is blank) are as follows:

```
Operating Margin: =SUM(D15:D18)
Margin Net of Variable Expenses: =SUM(D10:D13)
Gross Margin: =SUM(D7:D8)
Revenue: =ROUND(D8/(1-SUM(C4:C7)),0)
```

The two variable expenses shown in Figure 7-6, Cost of Goods Sold and Selling Expenses, are calculated by multiplying the revenue figure by the percentage. The formulas from Figure 7-6 are as follows:

```
Cost of Goods Sold: =ROUND(D3*C4,0)
Selling Expenses: =ROUND(D3*C7,0)
```

D3	▼	f_x	=ROUND(D8/(1-SUM(C4:C7)),0)		
	A	B	C	D	E
1					
2		**Income Statement**			
3		Revenue		$16,935	
4		Cost of Goods Sold	40%	6,774	
5		Gross Margin		10,161	
6					
7		Selling Expenses	8%	1,355	
8		Margin Net of Variable Expenses		8,806	
9					
10		Research & Development	F	2,046	
11		General & Admin Expenses	F	4,927	
12					
13		Operating Margin		1,833	
14					
15		Interest Expense	F	465	
16		Other Income and Expense	F	1,368	
17					
18		Net Profit	F	$0	
19					
20					

Figure 7-6: A break-even calculation.

How it works

To build the break-even model in Figure 7-6, follow these steps:

1. Enter **0** into cell D18 to indicate zero net profit.

2. Enter the fixed expense amounts in column D next to their labels in column B.

3. Enter the percentage the company pays in commission in cell C7 (**8%** in this example).

4. Enter a percentage equal to 1 minus the expected gross margin in cell C4. In this example, the company expects a 60 percent gross margin percent, so you enter **40%** in C4.

5. In cell D13, enter the formula for Operating Margin shown previously. The Operating Margin must be the sum of Interest Expense and Other Income and Expense. As shown in Figure 7-6, if you estimate Interest Expense to be $465 and Other Income and Expense to be $1,368, Operating Margin must be $1,833 for Net Profit to be zero.

6. In cell D8, enter the formula for Margin Net of Variable Expenses shown previously. This calculation is Operating Margin plus the fixed operating expenses. It will drive the revenue calculation.

7. In cell D7, enter the formula for Selling Expenses shown previously. You haven't entered the revenue formula yet, so this will be zero for now. After revenue is entered, however, the cell will show the correct value.

8. Enter the formula for Cost of Goods Sold in cell D4. As with the Selling Expenses formula, this formula will return zero until revenue is computed.

9. Finally, enter the formula for Revenue in cell D3. The Revenue calculation divides Margin Net of Variable Expenses by 1 minus the sum of the variable percentages. In Figure 7-6, the two variable expenses will be 48 percent (40 percent plus 8 percent) of revenue. Subtracting 48 percent from 100 percent leaves 52 percent, which is divided into the Margin Net of Variable Expenses to get Revenue.

If this company makes a 60 percent gross margin, pays 8 percent in commissions, and has estimated the fixed expenses accurately, it needs to sell $16,935 to break even.

Formula 72: Calculating Customer Churn

Customer churn is the measure of how many customers you lose in a given period. It's an important metric to track for subscription-based businesses, although it's applicable to other revenue models as well. If your growth rate (the rate at which you are adding new customers) is higher than your churn rate, your customer base is growing. If not, you're losing customers faster than you can add them, and something needs to change.

Figure 7-7 shows a churn calculation for a company with recurring monthly revenue. You need to know the number of customers at the beginning and end of the month and the number of new customers in that month.

```
Subscribers lost: =C2+C3-C4
Churn rate: =C6/C2
```

C7 fx =C6/C2

	A	B	C
1			
2		Subscribers at beginning of month:	4,215
3		New subscribers:	614
4		Subscribers at end of month:	4,441
5			
6		Subscribers lost:	388
7		Churn rate:	9.21%
8			

Figure 7-7: Calculating the churn rate.

How it works

To determine the number of customers lost during the month, the number of new customers is added to the number of customers at the beginning of the month. Then the number of customers at the end of the month is subtracted from that total. Finally, the number of customers lost during the month is divided by the number of customers at the beginning of the month to get the churn rate.

In this example, the business has a churn rate of 9.21 percent. It is adding more customers than it is losing, so that churn rate may not be seen as a problem. However, if the churn rate is higher than expectation, the company may want to investigate why it's losing customers and change its pricing, product features, or some other aspect of its business.

Alternative: Annual churn rate

If a business has monthly recurring revenue, it means that customers sign up and pay for one month at a time. For those companies, it makes sense to calculate the churn rate on a monthly basis. Any new customers during the month will not churn in the same month because they've already paid for the month.

A typical magazine, however, signs up subscribers for an annual subscription. A meaningful churn rate calculation for that business would therefore be an annual churn rate. If a business wants to calculate a churn rate for a longer period than its recurring revenue model, such as calculating an annual churn for a business with monthly subscribers, the formula changes slightly. Figure 7-8 shows an annual churn rate calculation.

```
Annual churn rate: =C6/AVERAGE(C2,C4)
```

	A	B	C	D
		C7	f_x =C6/AVERAGE(C2,C4)	
1				
2		Subscribers at beginning of year:	4,215	
3		New subscribers:	7,415	
4		Subscribers at end of year:	10,664	
5				
6		Subscribers lost:	966	
7		Annual churn rate:	12.98%	
8				

Figure 7-8: Annual churn rate of monthly recurring revenue.

The number of lost subscribers is divided by the average of beginning and ending subscribers. Because the period of the churn rate is different from the period of the recurring revenue, some of those 7,415 new subscribers canceled their subscriptions within the year, albeit in a later month than they first subscribed.

Formula 73: Calculating Average Customer Lifetime Value

Customer Lifetime Value (CLV) is a calculation that estimates the gross margin contributed by one customer over that customer's life. The churn rate calculated in Formula 72 is a component of CLV.

Figure 7-9 shows a calculation of CLV using the churn rate previously calculated. The first step is to calculate the average gross margin per customer.

```
Gross margin: =F2-F3
Average customer margin: =F4/AVERAGE(C4,C10)
Customer Lifetime Value: =F6/C7
```

	F7	▼	fx	=F6/C7				
⊿	A	B	C	D	E	F	G
1							
2		Subscribers at beginning of month:	4,215		Monthly revenue	564,810	
3		New subscribers:	614		Cost of goods sold	225,924	
4		Subscribers at end of month:	4,441		Gross Margin	338,886	
5							
6		Subscribers lost:	388		Average customer margin	76.31	
7		Churn rate:	9.21%		Customer Lifetime Value	828.97	
8							
9							

Figure 7-9: Customer Lifetime Value calculation.

How it works

To calculate CLV, follow these steps:

1. Calculate the gross margin as demonstrated in Formula 67: revenue less cost of goods sold.

2. Calculate the average customer margin by dividing the gross margin by the average number of customers for the month. Because the gross margin was earned over the month, you have to divide by the average number of customers instead of either the beginning or ending customer count.

3. Calculate the CLV by dividing the average customer margin by the churn rate.

In this example, each customer will contribute an estimated $828.97 over his or her lifetime.

Formula 74: Calculating Employee Turnover

Employee turnover is a measure of how well an organization is hiring and retaining talent. A high turnover rate indicates that the organization is not hiring the right people or not retaining people, possibly due to inadequate benefits or below-average pay. Separations commonly include both voluntary and involuntary terminations.

Figure 7-10 shows the employment changes of an organization over a 12-month period. New hires are added to and separations are subtracted from the number of employees at the beginning of the month to get the ending employee count.

```
Average monthly employment: =AVERAGE(F3:F14)
Separations: =SUM(E3:E14)
Employee Turnover: =F17/F16
```

	F18			fx	=F17/F16	
	A	B	C	D	E	F
1						
2		Month	Beg. Employees	New Hires	Separations	End. Employees
3		Jan	625	10	7	628
4		Feb	628	2	7	623
5		Mar	623	4	1	626
6		Apr	626	6	3	629
7		May	629	5	1	633
8		Jun	633	5	2	636
9		Jul	636	2	5	633
10		Aug	633	3	5	631
11		Sep	631	2	6	627
12		Oct	627	4	2	629
13		Nov	629	10	5	634
14		Dec	634	8	2	640
15						
16				Average monthly employment		630.75
17					Separations	46.00
18					Employee Turnover	7.29%
19						

Figure 7-10: Monthly employment changes over one year.

How it works

Employee turnover is simply the ratio of separations to average monthly employment. The AVERAGE function is used to calculate the average ending count of employees over the months. Separations are summed using SUM and are divided by the average monthly employments.

The result can be compared to industry averages or companies in the same industry. Different industries experience different turnover rates, so comparing them can lead to poor decisions. You don't have to calculate turnover for a 12-month period, but doing so removes seasonal employment variations that can skew results.

Formula 75: Converting Interest Rates

Two common methods for quoting interest rates are the *nominal* rate and the *effective* rate:

➤ **Nominal rate:** This is the stated rate and is usually paired with a compounding period, for example, 3.75 percent APR compounded monthly. In this example, 3.75 percent is the nominal rate; APR is short for annual percentage rate, meaning the rate is applied on an annual basis; and one month is the compounding period.

➤ **Effective rate:** This is the actual rate paid. If the nominal rate period is the same as the compounding period, the nominal and effective rates are identical. However, as is usually the case, when the interest compounds over a shorter period than the nominal rate period, the effective rate will be higher than the nominal rate.

Figure 7-11 shows 12 compounding periods in the middle of a 30-year loan. The original loan was for $165,000, has a nominal rate of 3.75% APR compounded monthly, and calls for 30 annual payments of $9,169.68 each.

	F21			f_x	=EFFECT(F20,12)	
	A	**B**	**C**	**D**	**E**	**F**	**G**
1							
2		Date	Payment	Principle	Interest	Balance	
3						152,151.73	
4		1/10/2015	-	(475.47)	475.47	152,627.20	
5		2/10/2015	-	(476.96)	476.96	153,104.16	
6		3/10/2015	-	(478.45)	478.45	153,582.61	
7		4/10/2015	-	(479.95)	479.95	154,062.56	
8		5/10/2015	-	(481.45)	481.45	154,544.01	
9		6/10/2015	-	(482.95)	482.95	155,026.96	
10		7/10/2015	-	(484.46)	484.46	155,511.42	
11		8/10/2015	-	(485.97)	485.97	155,997.39	
12		9/10/2015	-	(487.49)	487.49	156,484.88	
13		10/10/2015	-	(489.02)	489.02	156,973.90	
14		11/10/2015	-	(490.54)	490.54	157,464.44	
15		12/10/2015	9,169.68	8,677.60	492.08	148,786.84	
16							
17				Total interest paid		5,804.79	
18				Effective Rate		3.815%	
19							
20				Given Nominal Rate		3.750%	
21				Compute Effective Rate		3.815%	
22							
23				Given Effective Rate		3.815%	
24				Compute Nominal Rate		3.750%	

Figure 7-11: A partial amortization schedule to compute the effective rate.

For each period that the interest compounds but no payment is made, the balance goes up by the amount of interest. When the payment is made, a little of it goes to the last month's interest and the rest of it reduces the principle.

Cell F17 sums all the interest compounded over the year and cell F18 divides it by the beginning balance to get the effective rate. Fortunately, you don't have to create a whole amortization schedule to convert interest rates. Excel provides the EFFECT and NOMINAL worksheet functions to do that job:

```
Effective Rate: =EFFECT(F20,12)
Nominal Rate: =NOMINAL(F23,12)
```

How it works

Both EFFECT and NOMINAL take two arguments: the rate to be converted and the npery argument. The rate to be converted is the effective rate for NOMINAL and the nominal rate for EFFECT. The npery argument is the number of compounding periods in the nominal rate period. In this example, the nominal rate is annual because the term APR was used. A year has 12 months, so your nominal rate has 12 compounding periods. If, for example, you had a loan with an APR that compounded daily, the npery argument would be 365.

Alternative: Computing effective rate with FV

The effective rate can also be computed with the FV function. With such a handy function as EFFECT, you don't need to resort to FV, but it can be instructive to understand the relationship between EFFECT and FV.

```
=FV(3.75%/12,12,0,-1)-1
```

This formula computes the future value of a $1 loan at 3.75 percent compounded monthly for one year and then subtracts the original $1. If you were to take this loan, you would pay back $1.03815 after the year was over. That means you'd owe an additional $0.03815 more than you borrowed, or, effectively, 3.815 percent.

Formula 76: Creating a Loan Payment Calculator

You can use the Excel PMT worksheet function to calculate your monthly payment on a loan. You can hard-code the values, such as the loan amount and interest rate, into the function's arguments, but by entering those values in cells and using the cells as the arguments, you can easily change the values to see how the payment changes.

Figure 7-12 shows a simple payment calculator. The user enters values in C2:C4 and the payment is calculated in C6 with the following:

```
=PMT(C3/12,C4*12,C2,0,0)
```

C6	▾	*fx*	=PMT(C3/12,C4*12,C2,0,0)	
◢	A	B	C	
1				
2		Amount Borrowed:	215,000	
3		Interest Rate:	4.125%	
4		Years	30	
5				
6		Your monthly payment:	($1,042.00)	
7				

Figure 7-12: A simple loan payment calculator.

How it works

The PMT function takes three required arguments and one optional argument:

➤ **rate (required):** The rate argument is the annual nominal interest rate divided by the number of compounding periods in a year. In this example, the interest compounds monthly, so the interest rate in C3 is divided by 12.

➤ **nper (required):** The nper argument is the number of payments that will be made over the life of the loan. Because your user input asks for years and the payments are monthly, the number of years in C4 is multiplied by 12.

➤ **pv (required):** The pv argument, or present value, is the amount being borrowed. Excel's loan functions, of which PMT is one, work on a *cash flow basis*. When you think about present value and payments as cash inflows and outflows, it's easier to understand when the value should be positive or negative. In this example, the bank is loaning you $215,000, which is a cash inflow and thus positive. The result of the PMT function is a negative because the payments will be cash outflows.

Tip

If you want the PMT function to return a positive value, you can change the pv argument to a negative number. That's like calculating the payment from the bank's perspective: The loan is a cash outflow and the payments are cash inflows.

Caution

The most common mistake in financial formulas is a mismatch between compounding periods and payment frequency. In this example, the rate is divided by 12 to make it a monthly rate and the nper is multiplied by 12 to make it a monthly payment. Both arguments are converted to monthly, so they match and you get the correct result.

If you forgot to divide the rate by 12, Excel would think you were entering a monthly rate, and the payment would be way too high. Similarly, if you entered years for the nper and a monthly rate, Excel would think you were paying only once a year.

Excel doesn't really know whether you enter months, years, or days. It cares only that the rate and nper match.

Alternative: Creating an amortization schedule

With the payment amount calculated, you can create an amortization schedule that shows how much of each payment is principle and interest and what the loan balance is after each payment. Figure 7-13 shows a portion of the amortization schedule.

	G11 ▾		*fx* =ROUND(H10*$C$3/12,2)					
	A	B	C	D	E	F	G	H
1								
2		Amount Borrowed:	215,000					
3		Interest Rate:	4.125%					
4		Years	15					
5								
6		Your monthly payment:	($1,603.83)					
7								
8								
9				Pmt No	Pmt Amt	Principle	Interest	Balance
10								215,000.00
11				1	1,603.83	864.77	739.06	214,135.23
12				2	1,603.83	867.74	736.09	213,267.49
13				3	1,603.83	870.72	733.11	212,396.77
14				4	1,603.83	873.72	730.11	211,523.05
15				5	1,603.83	876.72	727.11	210,646.33
16				6	1,603.83	879.73	724.10	209,766.60
17				7	1,603.83	882.76	721.07	208,883.84
18				8	1,603.83	885.79	718.04	207,998.05
19				9	1,603.83	888.84	714.99	207,109.21
20				10	1,603.83	891.89	711.94	206,217.32
21				11	1,603.83	894.96	708.87	205,322.36
22				12	1,603.83	898.03	705.80	204,424.33

Figure 7-13: A partial amortization schedule.

The columns of the amortization schedule are as follows:

➤ **Pmt No:** The number of the payment being made. You enter **1** into D11. Then you enter the formula **=D11+1** into D12 and copy it down to D370. (Your amortization schedule can handle 360 payments.)

➤ **Pmt Amt:** The amount of the PMT calculation rounded to the nearest penny. Although Excel can calculate a lot of decimal places, you can write a check only for dollars and cents. This means that there will be a small balance at the end of the loan. You enter the formula **=-ROUND($C$6,2)** into E11 and fill it down through E370.

➤ **Principle:** The amount of each payment applied to the loan balance. You enter the formula **=E11-G11** into F11 and fill it down through F370.

➤ **Interest:** The amount of each payment that is interest. The balance after the prior payment is multiplied by the interest rate divided by 12. The total is rounded to two decimal places. Enter the formula **=ROUND(H10*$C$3/12,2)** into G11 and fill it down through G370.

➤ **Balance:** The balance of the loan after the payment. Enter the formula **=C2** in H10 to represent the original amount of the loan. Starting in H11 and continuing down to H370, the formula =H10-F11 reduces the balance by the principle portion of the payment.

In the example shown previously in Figure 7-13, the number of years was entered as 15, compared to 30 in Figure 7-12. Reducing the length of the loan increases the amount of the payment.

The final step is to hide rows beyond the loan term. You accomplish this task with conditional formatting that changes the font color to white. A white font color against a white background effectively hides the data. The formula for the conditional formatting follows and is shown in Figure 7-14.

```
=$D12>$C$4*12
```

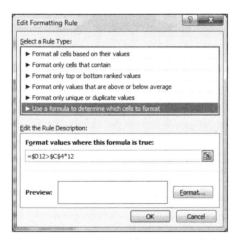

Figure 7-14: Conditional formatting to hide rows.

This formula compares the payment number in column D to the number of years in C4 times 12. When the payment number is larger, the formula returns TRUE and the white font color formatting is applied. When the payment number is less than or equal to the total number of payments, no conditional formatting is applied.

See Chapter 9 for more information on conditional formatting.

Cross-Ref

Formula 77: Creating a Variable-Rate Mortgage Amortization Schedule

In Formula 76, you create an amortization schedule for a loan with a fixed interest rate. There are also loans for which the rate changes at times during the life of the loan. Often these loans have an interest rate that's tied to a published index, such as the London Interbank Offered Rate (LIBOR), plus a fixed percentage. Those interest rates are usually stated as "LIBOR plus 3%," for example.

Figure 7-15 shows an amortization schedule for a loan with a variable interest rate. We added a Rate column to the amortization schedule so that interest rate changes will be obvious. A separate table is used to record when the rate changes.

The Rate column has the following formula to select the proper rate from the rate table:

```
=VLOOKUP(D11,$K$11:$L$23,2,TRUE)
```

The Interest column formula changes to use the rate in column G rather than the rate in C3:

```
=ROUND(I10*G11/12,2)
```

All other formulas are unchanged from the schedule created in Formula 76.

	G11		*fx*	=VLOOKUP(D11,$K$11:$L$23,2,TRUE)									
	A	B	C	D	E	F	G	H	I	J	K	L	N
1													
2		Amount Borrowed:	215,000										
3		Interest Rate:	4.125%										
4		Years	15										
5													
6		Your monthly payment:	($1,603.83)										
7													
8													
9				Pmt No	Pmt Amt	Principle	Rate	Interest	Balance		Interest Changes		
10									215,000.00		Pmt No.	New Rate	
11				1	1,603.83	864.77	4.125%	739.06	214,135.23		1	4.125%	
12				2	1,603.83	867.74	4.125%	736.09	213,267.49		10	3.875%	
13				3	1,603.83	870.72	4.125%	733.11	212,396.77		98	4.000%	
14				4	1,603.83	873.72	4.125%	730.11	211,523.05				
15				5	1,603.83	876.72	4.125%	727.11	210,646.33				
16				6	1,603.83	879.73	4.125%	724.10	209,766.60				
17				7	1,603.83	882.76	4.125%	721.07	208,883.84				
18				8	1,603.83	885.79	4.125%	718.04	207,998.05				
19				9	1,603.83	888.84	4.125%	714.99	207,109.21				
20				10	1,603.83	935.04	3.875%	668.79	206,174.17				
21				11	1,603.83	938.06	3.875%	665.77	205,236.11				
22				12	1,603.83	941.09	3.875%	662.74	204,295.02				
23				13	1,603.83	944.13	3.875%	659.70	203,350.89				
24				14	1,603.83	947.18	3.875%	656.65	202,403.71				
25				15	1,603.83	950.23	3.875%	653.60	201,453.48				

Figure 7-15: A variable-rate amortization schedule.

How it works

The Rate column uses a VLOOKUP with a fourth argument of TRUE. The fourth argument of TRUE requires that the rate table be sorted in ascending order. Then VLOOKUP looks up the payment number in the rate table. It doesn't require an exact match but returns the row where the next payment number is larger than the lookup value. For instance, when the lookup value is 16, VLOOKUP returns the second row of the rate table because the payment number in the next row, 98, is larger than the lookup value.

Cross-Ref   See Chapter 6 for more examples of using VLOOKUP.

The interest rate column formula is very similar to the one used in Formula 76 except that the absolute reference to $C$3 is replaced by a reference to column G (G11 for the formula in row 11).

Alternative: Using dates instead of payment numbers

The two amortization schedules for this section and the previous one use the payment number to identify each payment. In reality, those payments are due on the same day of the month. Using a payment number instead of a date, however, allows the amortization schedule to be used for loans that start on any date. Figure 7-16 shows an amortization schedule using dates.

	D12	▼	f_x	=DATE(YEAR(D11),MONTH(D11)+1,DAY(D11))								
	A	B	C	D	E	F	G	H	I	J	K	L
1												
2		Amount Borrowed:	215,000									
3		Interest Rate:	4.125%									
4		Years	15									
5												
6		Your monthly payment:	($1,603.83)									
7												
8												
9				Pmt No	Pmt Amt	Principle	Rate	Interest	Balance		Interest Changes	
10									215,000.00		Pmt No.	New Rate
11				1/10/2015	1,603.83	864.77	4.125%	739.06	214,135.23		1/10/2015	4.125%
12				2/10/2015	1,603.83	867.74	4.125%	736.09	213,267.49		10/1/2015	3.875%
13				3/10/2015	1,603.83	870.72	4.125%	733.11	212,396.77		2/1/2023	4.000%
14				4/10/2015	1,603.83	873.72	4.125%	730.11	211,523.05			
15				5/10/2015	1,603.83	876.72	4.125%	727.11	210,646.33			
16				6/10/2015	1,603.83	879.73	4.125%	724.10	209,766.60			
17				7/10/2015	1,603.83	882.76	4.125%	721.07	208,883.84			
18				8/10/2015	1,603.83	885.79	4.125%	718.04	207,998.05			
19				9/10/2015	1,603.83	888.84	4.125%	714.99	207,109.21			
20				10/10/2015	1,603.83	935.04	3.875%	668.79	206,174.17			
21				11/10/2015	1,603.83	938.06	3.875%	665.77	205,236.11			
22				12/10/2015	1,603.83	941.09	3.875%	662.74	204,295.02			
23				1/10/2016	1,603.83	944.13	3.875%	659.70	203,350.89			
24				2/10/2016	1,603.83	947.18	3.875%	656.65	202,403.71			
25				3/10/2016	1,603.83	950.23	3.875%	653.60	201,453.48			

Figure 7-16: A date-based amortization schedule.

To modify the schedule to show the dates, follow these steps:

1. Enter the first payment date in cell D11.

2. Enter the below formula in D12 and fill down.

    ```
    =DATE(YEAR(D11),MONTH(D11)+1,DAY(D11))
    ```

3. Change the Pmt No column in the rate table (cells K9:L23) to the date the rate changed.

4. Change the formula in the conditional formatting to the following formula:

    ```
    =$D12>=DATE(YEAR($D$11),MONTH($D$11)+($C$4*12),DAY($D$11))
    ```

Formula 78: Calculating Depreciation

Excel provides a number of depreciation-related worksheet functions including DB, DDB, SLN, and SYD. In this section, you look at calculating straight-line (SLN) and variable-declining balance (VDB) depreciation.

Note

The depreciation for the first and last year of an asset's life is usually different than for the middle year. A *convention* is employed so that a full year's depreciation is not taken for the first year. Common conventions are half-year, mid-month, and mid-quarter. For the half-year convention, the asset is assumed to have been purchased at the halfway point of the year; consequently, one half of a normal year's depreciation is recorded for that year.

Figure 7-17 shows a depreciation schedule for five assets using the straight-line method and a half-year convention. Columns B:E contain the following user-entered data:

➤ **Asset No.:** A unique identifier for each asset. It's not necessary for the schedule, but is handy for keeping track of assets.

➤ **Cost:** The amount paid to put the asset in service. This amount includes the price paid for the asset, any taxes associated with purchase, the cost to ship the asset to its place of service, and any costs to install the asset so that it's ready for use. This amount is also known as basis or cost basis.

➤ **Year Acquired:** The year the asset was put into service. This year may be different from the year the payment was made to purchase the asset. It determines when depreciation starts.

➤ **Useful Life:** The number of years you estimate that the asset will provide service.

The formula in F3:N7 is as follows:

```
=IF(OR(YEAR(F$2)<$D3,YEAR(F$2)>$D3+$E3),0,SLN($C3,0,$E3))*IF(OR(YEAR(F$2)=$
    D3+$E3,YEAR(F$2)=$D3),0.5,1)
```

	A	B	C	D	E	F	G	H	I	J	K	L	M	N	
				fx	=IF(OR(YEAR(F$2)<$D3,YEAR(F$2)>$D3+$E3),0,SLN($C3,0,$E3))*IF(OR(YEAR(F$2)=$D3+$E3,YEAR(F$2)=$D3),0.5,1)									

	B	C	D	E	F	G	H	I	J	K	L	M	N
1													
2	Asset No.	Cost	Year Acquired	Useful Life	12/31/2015	12/31/2016	12/31/2017	12/31/2018	12/31/2019	12/31/2020	12/31/2021	12/31/2022	12/31/2023
3	1	10,400	2010	5	1,040.00	-	-	-	-	-	-	-	-
4	2	14,600	2010	7	2,085.71	2,085.71	1,042.86	-	-	-	-	-	-
5	3	39,400	2012	7	5,628.57	5,628.57	5,628.57	5,628.57	2,814.29	-	-	-	-
6	4	4,900	2015	5	490.00	980.00	980.00	980.00	980.00	490.00	-	-	-
7	5	20,200	2017	5	-	-	2,020.00	4,040.00	4,040.00	4,040.00	4,040.00	2,020.00	-
8	Total				9,244.29	8,694.29	9,671.43	10,648.57	7,834.29	4,530.00	4,040.00	2,020.00	-
9													

Figure 7-17: A straight-line depreciation schedule.

How it works

The main part of this formula is SLN($C3,0,$E3). The SLN worksheet function computes the straight-line depreciation for one period. It takes three arguments: cost, salvage, and life. For simplicity, the salvage value for this example is set to zero, meaning that the asset's cost will be fully depreciated at the end of its useful life.

The SLN function is pretty simple. But this is a depreciation schedule, so you have more work to do. The first IF function determines whether the date for that column (in row 2) is within the asset's useful life. If the year of the date in F2 is less than the year acquired, the asset isn't in service yet and the depreciation is zero. If F2 is greater than the year acquired plus the useful life, the asset is already fully depreciated, and the depreciation is zero. Both of these conditionals are wrapped in an OR function so that if either is TRUE, the whole expression returns TRUE. If both are FALSE, however, the SLN function is returned.

See Chapter 5 for more examples of using IF with OR.

Cross-Ref

The second part of the formula is also an IF and OR combination. These conditional statements determine whether the year in F2 is either the first year of depreciation or the last year. If either is TRUE, the straight-line result is multiplied by 0.5, representing the half-year convention employed here.

All the cell references in this formula are anchored so that the formula can be copied down and to the right and so that the cell references change appropriately. References to row 2 are anchored on the row so that you're always evaluating the date in row 2. References to the columns C:E are anchored on the columns so that Cost, Year Acquired, and Useful Life stay the same as the formula is copied.

See Chapter 1 for more information on relative and absolute cell references.

Cross-Ref

Alternative: Accelerated depreciation

The straight-line method depreciates an asset equally over all the years of its useful life. Some organizations use an accelerated method, which is a method that depreciates at a higher rate at the beginning of an asset's life and a lower rate at the end. The theory is that an asset loses more value when it is first put in service than in its last year of operation.

Excel provides the DDB function (double-declining balance) for accelerated depreciation. DDB computes what the straight-line method would be for the remaining asset value and doubles it. The problem with DDB is that it doesn't depreciate the whole asset within the useful life. The depreciation amount gets smaller and smaller but runs out of useful life before it gets to zero.

The most common application of accelerated depreciation is to start with a declining balance method, and after the depreciation falls below the straight-line amount, the method is switched to straight line for the remaining life of the asset. Fortunately, Excel provides the VDB function, which has that logic built in. Figure 7-18 shows a depreciation schedule using the VDB-based formula as follows:

```
=IF(OR(YEAR(F$2)<$D3,YEAR(F$2)>$D3+$E3),0,VDB($C3,0,$E3*2,IF(YEAR(F$2)=$D3,
   0,IF(YEAR(F$2)=$D3+$E3,$E3*2-1,(YEAR(F$2)-$D3)*2-1)),IF(YEAR(F$2)=$D3,1,I
   F(YEAR(F$2)=$D3+$E3,$E3*2,(YEAR(F$2)-$D3)*2+1)))))
```

F3			fx		=IF(OR(YEAR(F$2)<$D3,YEAR(F$2)>$D3+$E3),0,VDB($C3,0,$E3*2,IF(YEAR(F$2)=$D3,0, IF(YEAR(F$2)=$D3+$E3,$E3*2-1,(YEAR(F$2)-$D3)*2-1)), IF(YEAR(F$2)=$D3,1,IF(YEAR(F$2)=$D3+$E3,$E3*2,(YEAR(F$2)-$D3)*2+1)))))								
A	B	C	D	E	F	G	H	I	J	K	L	M	N
1													
2	Asset No.	Cost	Year Acquired	Useful Life	12/31/2015	12/31/2016	12/31/2017	12/31/2018	12/31/2019	12/31/2020	12/31/2021	12/31/2022	12/31/2023
3	1	10,400	2010	5	681.57	-	-	-	-	-	-	-	-
4	2	14,600	2010	7	1,417.94	1,417.94	708.97	-	-	-	-	-	-
5	3	39,400	2012	7	4,836.26	3,826.49	3,826.49	3,826.49	1,913.25	-	-	-	-
6	4	4,900	2015	5	980.00	1,411.20	903.17	642.25	642.25	321.13	-	-	-
7	5	20,200	2017	5	-	-	4,040.00	5,817.60	3,723.26	2,647.65	2,647.65	1,323.83	-
8	Total				7,915.77	6,655.63	9,478.63	10,286.34	6,278.76	2,968.78	2,647.65	1,323.83	-
9													

Figure 7-18: An accelerated depreciation schedule.

You might have noticed that this formula is a little more complicated than the SLN formula from the previous example. Don't worry, we step through it piece by piece for you. Here's the first part:

```
=IF(OR(YEAR(F$2)<$D3,YEAR(F$2)>$D3+$E3),0,VDB(...))))
```

This first part of the formula is identical to the SLN formula described previously in this section. If the date in row 2 is not within the useful life, the depreciation is zero. If it is, the VDB function is evaluated. Following is the VDB function from the IF function's third argument. There are placeholders for the starting period and ending period arguments of VDB, which we explain later.

```
VDB($C3,0,$E3*2,starting_period,ending_period)
```

The first three arguments to VDB are the same as the SLN arguments: cost, salvage value, and life. SLN returns the same value for every period so that you don't have to tell SLN which period to calculate. But VDB returns a different amount depending on the period. The last two arguments of VDB tell it which period to compute. The life in E3 is doubled, which we explain in the next section.

```
Starting_period: IF(YEAR(F$2)=$D3,0,IF(YEAR(F$2)=$D3+$E3,$E3*2-
   1,(YEAR(F$2)-$D3)*2-1))
```

None of Excel's depreciation functions takes into account the convention. That is, Excel calculates depreciation as if you bought all your assets on the first day of the year. That's not very practical. In this section, you assume a half-year convention so that only half of the depreciation is taken in the first and last years. To calculate depreciation on a half-year convention using VDB, you have to trick Excel into thinking that the asset has twice its useful life.

For an asset with a five-year useful life, the period for the first year goes from 0 to 1. For the second year, the periods span 1–3. The third year spans periods 3–5. That pattern continues until the last year, which spans 9–10 (10 is double the five-year life). The starting period portion of the formula evaluates like this:

> ➤ If the year to compute is the acquisition year, make the starting period zero.

> ➤ If the year to compute is the last year, make the starting period the useful life times two and subtract one.

> ➤ For all other years, subtract the acquisition year from the year to compute, multiply by two, and subtract 1.

The ending period portion of the formula is similar to the starting period portion. For the first year, the ending period argument is set to 1. For the last year, it ends at the useful life times 2 minus 1. For the middle years, it does the same calculation except that it adds 1 instead of subtracting.

By doubling the useful life, say from 7 periods to 14 periods for a seven-year asset, you can introduce the half-year convention into a declining balance function like VDB.

Formula 79: Calculating Present Value

The time value of money (TVM) is an important concept in accounting and finance. The idea is that a dollar today is worth less than the same dollar tomorrow. The difference in the two values is the income you can create with that dollar. The income may be interest from a savings account or the return on an investment.

Excel provides several functions for dealing with TVM, such as the PV function for calculating the present value. In its simplest form, PV *discounts* a future value amount by a discount rate to arrive at the present value. If I promise to pay you $10,000 one year from now, how much would you take today instead of waiting? The following formula and Figure 7-19 show how you would calculate that amount:

```
=PV(C4,C3,0,-C2)
```

	C5	▾		f_x	=PV(C4,C3,0,-C2)	
◢	A	B	C	D	E	
1						
2		Future Value	10,000			
3		Years	1			
4		Discount Rate	6.00%			
5		Present Value	$9,433.96			
6						

Figure 7-19: A present value calculation.

How it works

The present value calculator in Figure 7-19 suggests that you would take $9,434 now instead of $10,000 a year from now. If you took the $9,434 and were able to earn 6 percent over the next year, you would have $10,000 at the end of the year.

The PV function accepts five arguments:

➤ **rate:** Also known as the discount rate, the rate argument is the return you think you could make on your money over the discount period. It is the biggest factor in determining the present value and can also be the hardest to determine. If you're conservative, you might pick a lower rate — something you're sure you can achieve. If you were to use the money to pay off a loan with a fixed rate, the discount rate would be easy to determine.

➤ **nper:** The nper is the period of time to discount the future value. In this example, the nper is 1 year and is entered in cell C3. The rate and the period must be in the same units. That is, if you enter an annual rate, nper must be expressed as years. If you use a monthly rate, nper must be expressed as months.

➤ **pmt:** The pmt argument is the regular payments received over the discount period. When there is only one payment, as in this example, that amount is the future value and the payment amount is zero. The pmt must also the match the nper argument. If your nper is 10 and you enter any nonzero pmt, PV assumes that you'll get that payment amount 10 times over the discount period. The next example shows a present value calculation with payments.

➤ **fv:** The future value amount is the amount you will receive at the end of the discount period. Excel's financial function works on a cash flow basis. That means the future value and present value have opposite signs. For this example, the future value was made negative so the formula result would return a positive number.

➤ **type:** The type argument can be 0 if the payments are received at the end of the period or 1 if the payments are received at the beginning of the period. The type argument has no effect on this example because the payment amount is zero. The type argument can be omitted, in which case it is assumed to be 0.

Alternative: Calculating the present value of future payments

Another use of PV is to calculate the present value of a series of equal future payments. If, for example, you owe $5,000 of rent for an office over the next 10 years, you can use PV to calculate how much you would be willing to pay to get out of the lease. Figure 7-20 shows the present-value calculation for that scenario.

C5			f_x =PV(C4,C3,-C2,0,1)		
	A	B	C	D	E
1					
2		Rent	5,000		
3		Years	10		
4		Discount Rate	3.00%		
5		Present Value	43,931		
6					
7		Year	Rent	PV	
8		1	5,000	5,000	
9		2	5,000	4,854	
10		3	5,000	4,713	
11		4	5,000	4,576	
12		5	5,000	4,442	
13		6	5,000	4,313	
14		7	5,000	4,187	
15		8	5,000	4,065	
16		9	5,000	3,947	
17		10	5,000	3,832	
18				43,931	
19					
20					

Figure 7-20: The present value of a series of future payments.

Here's the PV formula used in Figure 7-20:

```
=PV(C4,C3,-C2,0,1)
```

If your landlord thought he could make 3 percent on the money, he may be willing to accept $43,930 instead of ten $5,000 payments over the next 10 years. The type argument is set to 1 in this example because rents are usually paid at the beginning of the period.

When used on payments, the PV function actually takes the present value of each payment individually and adds up all the results. Figure 7-20 shows the calculation broken out by payment. The first payment's present value is the same as the payment amount because it's due now. The Year 2 payment is due one year from now and is discounted to $4,854. The last payment, due nine years from now, is discounted to $3,832. All the present value calculations are added up. Fortunately, PV does all the heavy lifting for you.

Formula 80: Calculating Net Present Value

The PV function from Formula 79 can calculate the present value of future cash flows if all the cash flows are the same. But sometimes that's not the case. The NPV (net present value) function is the Excel solution to calculating the present value of uneven future cash flows.

Suppose that someone wanted you to invest $30,000 in a new business. In exchange for your investment, you would be entitled to an annual dividend over the next seven years. The estimated amounts of those dividends are shown in the schedule in Figure 7-21. Further suppose that you would like to earn an 8 percent return on your money.

To determine whether this investment is worth your while, you can use the following NPV function to calculate the net present value of that investment:

```
=NPV(C2,C5:C11)
```

	C13	▼	f_x	=NPV(C2,C5:C11)	
	A	B		C	D
1					
2		Desired Return:		8.00%	
3					
4		Date		Expected Future Cash Flow	
5		12/31/2015		4,000	
6		12/31/2016		4,760	
7		12/31/2017		5,664	
8		12/31/2018		6,797	
9		12/31/2019		7,477	
10		12/31/2020		8,225	
11		12/31/2021		9,458	
12					
13		Net Present Value:		33,068	
14					
15					

Figure 7-21: The net present value of expected future cash flows.

How it works

NPV discounts each cash flow separately based on the rate, just as PV value does. Unlike PV, however, NPV accepts a range of future cash flows rather than just a single payment amount. NPV doesn't have an nper argument because the number of values in the range determines the number of future cash flows.

Although the payments can be for different amounts, they are still assumed to be at regular intervals (one year, in this example). Also, as with the other TVM functions in this chapter, the rate period must be consistent with the payment period. In this example, the 8 percent return you'd like is an annual return and the payments are annual, so they match. If you were getting a quarterly dividend, you would have to adjust the rate to a quarterly return.

The NPV for these cash flows calculates to $33,068. Because the required investment to get those cash flows, $30,000, is less than the NPV (and assuming that the estimates are correct), these would be good investments. In fact, this data shows that you would make something more than the 8 percent return you wanted.

Alternative: Positive and negative cash flows

In the previous example, you were asked to make a large, up-front investment to get future cash flows. Another scenario in which you can use NPV is when you make smaller payments at the beginning of the investment period with the expectation of future cash inflows at the end.

Instead of one $30,000 payment, assume that you would only have to invest $15,000 the first year, $10,000 the second year, and $5,000 the third year. The amount you're required to invest goes down as the business grows and is able to use its own profits to grow. By year four, no more investment is required and the business is expected to be profitable enough to start paying a dividend.

Figure 7-22 shows a schedule that you pay in to for the first three years and get money back the last four. The NPV function is the same as before; just the inputs have changed.

```
=NPV(C2,C5:C11)
```

In the first NPV example, the amount invested was not part of the calculation. You simply took the result of the NPV function and compared it to the investment amount. In this example, a portion of the investment is also in the future, so the invested amounts are shown as negatives (cash outflows) and the eventual dividends are shown as positive amounts (cash inflows).

Instead of comparing the result to an initial investment amount, this NPV calculation is compared to zero. If the NPV is greater than zero, the series of cash flows returns something greater than 8 percent. If it's less than zero, the return is less than 8 percent. Based on the data in Figure 7-22, it's a good investment.

	A	B	C	D
			C13 ▾ (f l\l v(L2,L5:L11)	
1				
2		Desired Return:	8.00%	
3				
4		Date	**Expected Future Cash Flow**	
5		12/31/2015	(15,000)	
6		12/31/2016	(10,000)	
7		12/31/2017	(5,000)	
8		12/31/2018	7,000	
9		12/31/2019	9,100	
10		12/31/2020	11,830	
11		12/31/2021	15,142	
12				
13		Net Present Value:	1,197	
14				
15				

Figure 7-22: The net present value of both positive and negative cash flows.

Formula 81: Calculating an Internal Rate of Return

In Formula 80, you calculate the net present value of future expected cash flows and compare it to the initial investment amount. Because the net present value was greater than the initial investment, you knew the rate of return would be greater than the desired rate. But what is the actual rate of return?

You can use the Excel IRR function to calculate the internal rate of return of future cash flows. IRR is very closely related to NPV. IRR computes the rate of return that causes the NP of those same cash flows to be exactly zero.

For IRR, you have to structure the data a little differently. You have to have at least one positive and one negative cash flow in the values range. If you have all positive values, that means you invest nothing and only receive money. That would be a great investment, but it's not very realistic. Typically, the cash outflows are at the beginning of the investment period and the cash inflows are at the end. But it's not always that way, as long as there is at least one inflow and one outflow.

Figure 7-23 shows the same dividend schedule as Formula 80, but you have to include the initial investment for IRR to work. You add the first row to show the initial $30,000 investment. The following IRR formula shows that the investment return is 10.53 percent.

```
=IRR(C3:C10,0.08)
```

C12		f_x	=IRR(C3:C10,0.08)	
	A	B	C	D
1				
2		Date	**Expected Future Cash Flow**	
3		12/31/2014	(30,000)	
4		12/31/2015	4,000	
5		12/31/2016	4,760	
6		12/31/2017	5,664	
7		12/31/2018	6,797	
8		12/31/2019	7,477	
9		12/31/2020	8,225	
10		12/31/2021	9,458	
11				
12		Internal Rate of Return:	10.53%	
13				

Figure 7-23: The internal rate of return of a series of future cash flows.

How it works

The first argument for IRR is the range of cash flows. The second argument is a guess of what the internal rate of return will be. If you don't supply a guess, Excel uses 10 percent as the guess argument. IRR works by calculating the present value of each cash flow based on the guessed rate. If the sum of those present value calculations is greater than zero, it reduces the rate and tries again. Excel keeps iterating through rates and summing present values until the sum is zero. When the present values sum to zero, it returns that rate.

Alternative: Nonperiodic future cash flows

For both the NPV function in Formula 80 and the IRR function shown previously, the future cash flows are assumed to be at regular intervals. That may not always be the case, though. For cash flows at irregular intervals, Excel provides the XIRR function.

XIRR requires one more argument than IRR does: dates. IRR doesn't need to know the dates because it assumes that the cash flows are the same distance apart. Whether they are one day or one year apart, IRR doesn't care. The rate it returns will be consistent with the cash flows. That is, if the cash flows are annual, the rate will be an annual rate. If the cash flows are quarterly, the rate will be quarterly.

Tip

XIRR has a related function for calculating the net present value of nonperiodic cash flows called XNPV. As does XIRR, XNPV requires a matching range of dates.

Figure 7-24 shows a schedule of nonperiodic cash flows. On some days, the investment loses money and requires a cash injection. On other days, the investment makes money and returns it to the investor. Over all the cash flows, the investor makes an annual return of 10.14 percent. The following formula uses XIRR to calculate the return:

```
=XIRR(C3:C17,B3:B17,0.08)
```

	C19	▼	f_x =XIRR(C3:C17,B3:B17,0.08)	
	A	B	C	D
1				
2		Date	Cash Flows	
3		6/1/2015	(6,723)	
4		8/17/2015	(14,856)	
5		11/6/2015	5,856	
6		12/12/2015	(4,171)	
7		1/21/2016	8,039	
8		3/10/2016	(12,384)	
9		5/18/2016	13,860	
10		7/23/2016	(12,894)	
11		8/26/2016	7,196	
12		11/18/2016	14,907	
13		1/9/2017	(6,636)	
14		2/28/2017	3,964	
15		4/25/2017	(13,690)	
16		7/3/2017	6,185	
17		9/22/2017	14,785	
18				
19		Internal Rate of Return:	10.14%	
20				
21				

Figure 7-24: The internal rate of return of nonperiodic cash flows.

Internally, XIRR works much the same as IRR. It calculates the present value of each cash flow individually, iterating through rates until the sum of the present values is zero. It bases the present-value calculations on the number of days between the current cash flow and the one just previous in date order. Then it annualizes the rate of return.

Common Statistical Analyses

Excel is an excellent tool for performing statistical analysis, in part because of the many statistical functions it provides. In this chapter, you look at formulas for analyzing data, such as averages, buckets, and frequency distribution.

Formula 82: Calculating a Weighted Average

You use a weighted average to average values where each value plays a larger or smaller role in the whole set.

Figure 8-1 shows an investment portfolio. For each fund in the portfolio, the total value of the investment and the return on that investment appear. You want to determine the total return on the portfolio. A simple average won't do because each investment contributes a different amount to the whole portfolio. To determine the total return, you can use the following formula:

```
=SUMPRODUCT((C3:C7/$C$8),D3:D7)
```

How it works

To compute the weighted average, the percentage that each investment contributes to the total value of the portfolio is multiplied by that investment's rate of return. The SUMPRODUCT function is ideal for multiplying two sets of values and summing each result. SUMPRODUCT takes up to 255 arguments separated by commas, but you need only two arguments for this formula.

D8		fx	=SUMPRODUCT((C3:C7/$C$8),D3:D7)		
	A	B	C	D	E
1					
2		Investment	Value	Rate of Return	
3		Roboto Bond Fund	72,021.35	2.500%	
4		Duff Small Cap Fund	25,419.31	7.410%	
5		Ziff Value Investor Fund A	97,440.65	4.400%	
6		Cogswell International Fund	88,967.56	5.100%	
7		Sparkle Growth and Income Fund	139,806.15	10.120%	
8		**Weighted Average Return**	423,655.02	6.292%	
9					
10					
11					

Figure 8-1: An investment portfolio with rates of return.

The first argument takes each investment's value and divides it by the total value. This results in five percentages that represent the weight of each investment. For Roboto Bond Fund, the weight is 17 percent and is computed by dividing 72,021.35 by 423,655,02. The second argument is the rates of return.

Cross-Ref

The dollar signs in the $C$8 reference cause that reference to be absolute rather than relative. See Chapter 1 for a discussion of relative and absolute cell references.

SUMPRODUCT multiplies each element of the first argument by the corresponding element in the second argument. The element C3/C8 is multiplied by D3, the element C4/C8 is multiplied by D4, and so on. When all five elements are multiplied, SUMPRODUCT sums the five results.

If you used AVERAGE to find the simple average of the returns, you would get 5.906 percent. That's lower than the weighted average because investments such as Sparkle Growth and Income Fund had both a higher return than average and represent a larger proportion of the portfolio.

Alternative

All the work that SUMPRODUCT does to compute the weighted average could be done with simpler functions in adjacent cells. Figure 8-2 shows the same calculation, but rather than using SUMPRODUCT in one cell, the calculation uses a different process: Each investment's weight is calculated in its own cell, the effect of the rate on the whole is calculated, and those values are summed.

F8		fx	=SUM(F3:F7)				
	A	B	C	D	E	F	G
1							
2		Investment	Value	Rate of Return	Weight	Contribution	
3		Roboto Bond Fund	72,021.35	2.500%	17%	0.425%	
4		Duff Small Cap Fund	25,419.31	7.410%	6%	0.445%	
5		Ziff Value Investor Fund A	97,440.65	4.400%	23%	1.012%	
6		Cogswell International Fund	88,967.56	5.100%	21%	1.071%	
7		Sparkle Growth and Income Fund	139,806.15	10.120%	33%	3.340%	
8		**Weighted Average Return**	423,655.02			6.292%	
9							
10							
11							

Figure 8-2: Expanding a weighted average calculation into adjacent cells.

Formula 83: Smoothing Data with Moving Averages

You smooth data by eliminating or reducing the effects of data points that are statistical anomalies. You can use a moving average to reduce the impact of unusually high or low data points and therefore provide a clearer picture of the overall trend of the data. A moving average works particularly well when the individual data points are erratic.

Figure 8-3 shows a partial listing of golf scores. Anyone who plays the game knows just how erratic scores can be from one round to the next. Figure 8-4 shows a graph of the scores over time. Getting a sense of how this golfer's game is changing is difficult because of the steep peaks and valleys on the chart.

	A	B	C	D	E	F
	E3		fx	=IF(ROW()<12,NA(),AVERAGE(OFFSET(D3,-9,0,10,1)))		
1						
2		Date	Course	Score	Moving Avg	
3		5/13/2013	Tiburon Golf Club	98	#N/A	
4		5/20/2013	Colbert Hills	88	#N/A	
5		5/27/2013	Colbert Hills	84	#N/A	
6		6/3/2013	Colbert Hills	94	#N/A	
7		6/10/2013	Tiburon Golf Club	85	#N/A	
8		6/17/2013	Tiburon Golf Club	88	#N/A	
9		6/24/2013	Tiburon Golf Club	89	#N/A	
10		7/1/2013	Iron Horse Golf Club	84	#N/A	
11		7/8/2013	Tiburon Golf Club	84	#N/A	
12		7/15/2013	Tiburon Golf Club	97	89.1	
13		7/22/2013	Tiburon Golf Club	97	89.0	
14		7/29/2013	Tiburon Golf Club	84	88.6	
15		8/5/2013	Iron Horse Golf Club	86	88.8	
16		8/12/2013	Tiburon Golf Club	89	88.3	
17		8/19/2013	Tiburon Golf Club	89	88.7	
18		8/26/2013	Tiburon Golf Club	93	89.2	
19		9/2/2013	Tiburon Golf Club	90	89.3	
20		9/9/2013	Tiburon Golf Club	90	89.9	
21		9/16/2013	Tiburon Golf Club	85	90.0	
22		9/23/2013	Indian Creek Golf Course	90	89.3	
23		9/30/2013	Iron Horse Golf Club	94	89.0	
24		10/7/2013	Indian Creek Golf Course	93	89.9	
25		10/14/2013	Bent Tree	90	90.3	
26		10/21/2013	Indian Creek Golf Course	100	91.4	

Figure 8-3: A partial listing of golf scores.

You want to create a chart that shows how the scores are progressing by smoothing out the highs and lows. To do this smoothing, you can calculate the moving average of the scores and plot those values on the chart.

The following formula is used to create another data set containing the moving average of the raw golf scores:

```
=IF(ROW()<12,NA(),AVERAGE(OFFSET(D3,-9,0,10,1)))
```

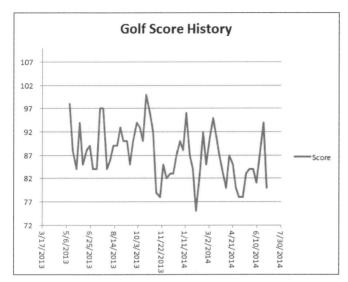

Figure 8-4: A graph of raw golf scores over time.

How it works

This formula uses a number of Excel functions to accomplish the task. First, it uses an IF function to return the #N/A error for the first few scores. The ROW function with no argument returns the row of the current cells. You don't want to start your moving average calculation until you have enough data, so the formula returns #N/A for the first nine rows.

Tip

Excel charts don't show #N/A errors. When Excel encounters an #N/A error, it simply does not plot the data on the chart, potentially leading to breaks in lines or gaps in columns or bars. You use the NA function to return the #N/A error when you want to include such blank areas on your charts.

For the later scores, the AVERAGE function is used to return the arithmetic mean of the prior ten scores. AVERAGE takes up to 255 arguments, but because your values are a contiguous range in this example, you need to supply only one.

You use the OFFSET function to return a particular range that's offset from the starting point. The arguments to OFFSET are

➤ **reference:** the cell where the OFFSET function starts.

➤ **rows:** The number of rows away from the starting cell where the returned range starts. Negative numbers count up the spreadsheet while positive numbers count down.

➤ **cols:** The number of columns from the starting cell. Negative numbers count to the left and positive numbers count to the right.

➤ **height;** How many rows the returned range should have.

➤ **width:** How many columns the returned range should have.

Tip
The height and width arguments of OFFSET must be positive numbers.

If you make cell D12 the reference argument, that's where OFFSET starts counting. The -9 in the rows argument directs OFFSET to count up nine rows to D3. The zero in the cols argument means that OFFSET stays in the same column. After the first two arguments, OFFSET has computed that the start of the returned range will be D3.

The height argument is set to 10, meaning that your range is ten rows in height, or D3:D12. The width argument of 1 keeps the range at one column wide. The result of OFFSET, and what is passed into AVERAGE, is the range D3:D12. As the formula is copied down, the prior ten scores are averaged.

Note
The number of values to include in a moving average varies depending on the data. You may want to show the previous 12 months, 5 years, or another number that makes sense for your data.

In Figure 8-5, the moving average is added to the chart and the line for the raw scores is made lighter so that the average line stands out. Showing the average of the last 10 scores provides a clearer picture of where this golfer's game is headed.

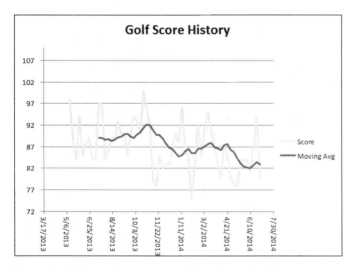

Figure 8-5: The moving average is charted over the raw scores.

Formula 84: Applying Exponential Smoothing to Volatile Data

A moving average, demonstrated in Formula 83, is a great way to smooth data. One problem with moving averages, however, is that they give equal weight to each data point in the set. In a six-week moving average, for example, each week's value is given 1/6 weight. With some data sets, more current data points deserve more weight.

Figure 8-6 shows the demand of a product over 26 weeks. The Demand column shows the actual product sold. The Moving Average column attempts to predict the demand based on a simple six-week moving average. The final column, whose formula follows, uses exponential smoothing to give more weight to recent weeks than past weeks:

```
=(C8*$H$2)+(E8*(1-$H$2))
```

	A	B	C	D	E	F	G	H
					E9 fx =(C8*$H$2)+(E8*(1-$H$2))			
1								
2		Week	Demand	Moving Average	Exponential Forecast		Alpha:	0.30
3		1	412		412			
4		2	634		412			
5		3	990		479			
6		4	1,326		632			
7		5	1,485		840			
8		6	1,589		1,034			
9		7	1,780	1,073	1,201			
10		8	2,510	1,301	1,374			
11		9	3,464	1,614	1,715			
12		10	5,057	2,026	2,240			
13		11	4,956	2,648	3,085			
14		12	7,087	3,226	3,646			
15		13	10,985	4,142	4,679			
16		14	14,830	5,677	6,571			
17		15	14,830	7,730	9,049			
18		16	17,945	9,624	10,783			
19		17	17,406	11,772	12,931			
20		18	27,676	13,847	14,274			
21		19	21,310	17,279	18,294			
22		20	19,606	19,000	19,199			
23		21	18,821	19,795	19,321			

Figure 8-6: The demand of a product over 26 weeks.

How it works

The *alpha* value, shown in cell H2 on Figure 8-6, is the weight given to the most recent data point, or 30 percent in this example. The remaining 70 percent weight is applied to the rest of the data points. The second most recent is weighted 30 percent of the remaining 70 percent (21 percent), the third most recent is weighted 30 percent of 70 percent of 70 percent (14.7 percent), and so on.

The prior week's value is multiplied by the alpha value, and that result is added to the remaining percentage multiplied by the prior forecast. The prior forecast already has all the previous calculations built into it.

The further away a demand value gets, the less it impacts the exponential smoothing forecast. In other words, last week's number is more important than the week before last. Figure 8-7 shows a chart of the demand, the moving average, and the exponential forecast. Note how the exponential forecast responds to changes in demand more quickly than the moving average.

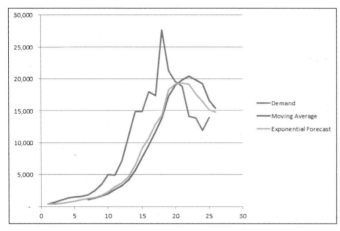

Figure 8-7: A chart comparing raw data, a simple moving average, and an exponential forecast.

Formula 85: Getting the Largest or Smallest Value

Two of the simplest properties of a data set are the largest and the smallest values, also known as the maximum and minimum, respectively. You can use the maximum and minimum to help you grasp the range of the data set.

Figure 8-8 shows the average low temperature by month for the city of Marietta, Georgia. For this example, you want to determine which months have the highest and lowest average temperature. The first formula will find the maximum average low temperature.

```
=MAX(C3:C14)
```

The next formula will return the month that corresponds to the temperature found in the previous formula.

```
=INDEX(B3:B14,MATCH(E5,C3:C14,FALSE),1)
```

	A	B	C	D	E	F	G
1							
2		Month	Avg Low Temp				
3		JAN	33				
4		FEB	36		**Max**	**Min**	
5		MAR	42		70	33	
6		APR	50		**Max Month**	**Min Month**	
7		MAY	59		JUL	JAN	
8		JUN	66				
9		JUL	70				
10		AUG	69				
11		SEP	63				
12		OCT	51				
13		NOV	42				
14		DEC	35				
15							

E5 · (f_x =MAX(C3:C14)

Figure 8-8: Average low temperatures by month.

How it Works

Excel provides two functions for finding the largest and smallest values from a range: MAX and MIN. Both formulas accept up to 255 arguments. Your data is in C3:C14 and that is the range passed into MAX and MIN. MAX returns 70, the largest value in the range, and MIN returns 33, the smallest.

 See Chapter 6 for more information on the MATCH and INDEX functions.
Cross-Ref

To determine to which months those temperatures relate, you start with the INDEX function. The range passed into INDEX is the list of months in B3:B14. The second argument to INDEX is a MATCH function, which returns the position of the lookup value in a list. When you match 70 to the list of temperatures, MATCH returns 7 because 70 is the seventh item in the list. INDEX uses that 7 to return the seventh row of the list of months, or JUL. The same structure is used for MIN to return JAN, the month with the smallest value.

Both MAX and MIN ignore any text in the range, but if there are errors in the range, they return an error. If all of the values in the range are text, MAX and MIN return zero.

Formula 86: Getting the Nth Largest or Smallest Value

The MIN and MAX functions used in Formula 85 are great for finding the largest and smallest values. But sometimes you need to find the second largest or the fifth smallest value.

For this example, Figure 8-9 shows the results of a bowling tournament. The bowlers are sorted alphabetically by name, which makes seeing who the winners are difficult. You want to identify the first through third-place bowlers and their scores. This formula returns the third largest value from the list of scores:

```
=LARGE($C$3:$C$14,ROW(A3))
```

The formula to find the bowler's name uses INDEX and MATCH, similarly to Formula 85:

```
=INDEX($B$3:$B$14,MATCH(F5,$C$3:$C$14,FALSE),1)
```

	F5	▾		*fx*	=LARGE($C$3:$C$14,ROW(A3))			
	A	B	C	D	E	F	G	H
1								
2		Bowler	Score		Position	Score	Bowler	
3		Aidan Knight	352		1st Place	588	Olivia Dunn	
4		Alexa Lee	533		2nd Place	547	Hannah Weaver	
5		Carlos White	389		3rd Place	546	Julian Murray	
6		Dylan Hill	300					
7		Hannah Weaver	547					
8		Jack Price	460					
9		Josiah Stone	511					
10		Julian Murray	546					
11		Justin Mitchell	396					
12		Makayla Simmons	507					
13		Olivia Dunn	588					
14		Vanessa Jackson	384					
15								
16								

Figure 8-9: The results of a bowling tournament.

How it works

The LARGE and SMALL functions are used to find the Nth largest and smallest values in a list. As with the MAX function, you pass a range of values into LARGE. But LARGE has another argument for the "N" in the Nth largest value.

Note

If two values in the list have the same value, LARGE and SMALL return the same value for the Nth value and the Nth + 1 value. So, for example, if two competitors had a score of 588, =LARGE($C$3:$C$14,1) and =LARGE($C$3:$C$14,2) both would return 588.

In cell F3, you use ROW(A1) to determine N. The ROW function returns the row for the cell passed to it — row 1 in this case. You could simply pass the number 1 to the LARGE function, but by using ROW(A1), you can copy this formula down to increase the row. The A1 reference is relative, and when the formula is copied to cell F4, it becomes ROW(A2). That returns 2 and the LARGE function in F4 then returns the second-largest value.

Cross-Ref

See Chapter 1 for more information on absolute and relative cell references.

The LARGE function is appropriate here because higher bowling scores are better. If, instead, you had a list of race times, the SMALL function would be used because lower times are better.

Alternative

Another way to determine the Nth largest or smallest number is the RANK function. The RANK function takes three arguments: the number to be ranked; the list of all the numbers; and the sort order. Figure 8-10 shows another result of a competition, but this time, the lowest time is the winner. It also includes another column to rank each result, and that formula is the following:

```
=RANK(C3,$C$3:$C$14,1)
```

	D3	▼	f_x	=RANK(C3,$C$3:$C$14,1)					
	A	B	C	D	E	F	G	H	I
1									
2		Competitor	Time	Rank		Position	Time	Competitor	
3		Gianna Ruiz	0:20:35	1		1st Place	0:20:35	Gianna Ruiz	
4		Jessica Powell	0:24:22	6		2nd Place	0:21:38	Alexandra Mitchell	
5		Chase Ellis	0:29:26	12		3rd Place	0:21:42	Isaiah Peters	
6		Ayden Taylor	0:27:50	9					
7		Addison West	0:29:13	10					
8		Alexandra Mitchell	0:21:38	2					
9		Natalie Greene	0:29:13	10					
10		Jose Harper	0:24:38	7					
11		Isaiah Peters	0:21:42	3					
12		Carlos Pierce	0:26:56	8					
13		Alexis Coleman	0:23:41	5					
14		Jeremiah Dunn	0:22:50	4					
15									
16									
17									

Figure 8-10: The results of a race.

To determine the rank of Gianna Ruiz, you pass into RANK the time in C3, the total list of times in C3:C14, and the order. The order is 1 in this example because you want the lowest number to have rank 1. If you wanted the highest number to be ranked 1, the final argument would be 0. (See the sidebar "The RANK function and ties" for details on how this function works with tied values.)

In contrast to LARGE and SMALL, which return the actual values, RANK returns the position of the value in the list if the list is sorted according to the last argument. To get the actual values, you need to use INDEX and MATCH just as you did for the names. The formula in cell G3 to return the time of the first-place competitor is as follows:

```
=INDEX($C$3:$C$14,MATCH(ROW(A1),$D$3:$D$14,FALSE),1)
```

The RANK function and ties

When two or more values are a tie, RANK returns the same result for the tied values. For the example in the "Alternative" section for Formula 86, if two racers had a time of 20:35, RANK would return 1 for both. The next lowest time would receive a rank of 3. None of the values would rank 2 because the tied values take up both the 1 and 2 ranking.

Excel 2010 introduced two new functions for handling ties with ranking: RANK.AVG and RANK.EQ. The RANK.EQ function mirrors the results of RANK from prior versions. That is, the same value returns the same ranking. The RANK.AVG function works differently. It returns the average ranking for all values that match.

Assume that the data in Figure 8-10 shows four racers with a time of 21:38, the second lowest time. RANK.AVG returns 1 for the best time and 3.5 for four matching second-place times. Those four times occupy the ranks 2, 3, 4, and 5. The average of those four rankings is 3.5.

Formula 87: Calculating Mean, Median, and Mode

When people refer to the "average," they are usually referring to the arithmetic mean: the sum of the values divided by the count of the values. You can calculate two other averages in Excel: median and mode.

Figure 8-11 shows a list of 20 students and their grades on an assignment. You want to analyze the grades by finding the mean, median, and mode and draw conclusions from the results.

The three formulas that follow calculate the arithmetic mean, median, and mode for the data shown in Figure 8-11:

```
=AVERAGE(C3:C22)
=MEDIAN(C3:C22)
=MODE(C3:C22)
```

How it works

You can see from Figure 8-11 that the mean is 85.1, the median is 90.5, and the mode is 93.0. The mean is computed using the AVERAGE function, which sums all the values in the range and divides by the number of values. How the median and mode compare to the average may provide some insights into the data.

The median is computed using the aptly named MEDIAN function. If all the grades are listed in order, MEDIAN returns the value that's right in the middle. Because you have an even number of grades, no exact middle value exists. In that case, MEDIAN returns the mean of the two values closest to the middle. Figure 8-12 shows that 90 and 91 are the two grades closest to the middle.

G5		fx	=MEDIAN(C3:C22)				
	A	B	C	D	E	F	G
1							
2		Student	Grade	Count of Grades			
3		Addison Gray	96	1			
4		Alex Palmer	90	1		Average	85.1
5		Andrew Stone	98	1		Median	90.5
6		Bryan Wilson	93	4		Mode	93.0
7		Charles Alexander	71	2			
8		Chloe Carpenter	80	2			
9		Christopher Rose	91	2			
10		Connor Hill	93	4			
11		Dylan Edwards	91	2			
12		Ella Bradley	93	4			
13		Grace Mitchell	71	2			
14		Isaac Rice	73	1			
15		Joshua Thomas	93	4			
16		Juan Armstrong	95	1			
17		Kimberly Morales	77	2			
18		Lily Harrison	72	1			
19		Madison Ortiz	80	2			
20		Ryan Long	92	1			
21		Sarah Cunningham	76	1			
22		Sophia Nichols	77	2			
23							

Figure 8-11: A list of students and grades.

K13		fx						
	A	B	C	D	E	F	G	H
1								
2		Student	Grade	Count of Grades				
3		Andrew Stone	98	1				
4		Addison Gray	96	1		Average	85.1	
5		Juan Armstrong	95	1		Median	90.5	
6		Bryan Wilson	93	4		Mode	93.0	
7		Connor Hill	93	4				
8		Ella Bradley	93	4				
9		Joshua Thomas	93	4				
10		Ryan Long	92	1				
11		Christopher Rose	91	2				
12		Dylan Edwards	91	2			90.5	
13		Alex Palmer	90	1				
14		Chloe Carpenter	80	2				
15		Madison Ortiz	80	2				
16		Kimberly Morales	77	2				
17		Sophia Nichols	77	2				
18		Sarah Cunningham	76	1				
19		Isaac Rice	73	1				
20		Lily Harrison	72	1				
21		Charles Alexander	71	2				
22		Grace Mitchell	71	2				
23								
24								
25								

Figure 8-12: The grades listing sorted by grade.

A big difference between the AVERAGE and the MEDIAN indicates that the grades are not evenly distributed through the population. In this case, there appears to be a large gap between the higher-scoring students and the lower-scoring students. In other cases, one unusually large or small number may just be what affects the AVERAGE but not the MEDIAN.

The mode is calculated using the MODE function. MODE returns the grade that appears most frequently. Figure 8-11 shows a count of each grade next to it. From this you can see that 93 occurs four times — the most of any grade. If all the values appear an equal number of times, MODE returns #N/A. If more than one grade appears the same number of times, MODE returns the first one it finds.

Alternative

Excel 2010 introduced two new functions for calculating mode: MODE.SNGL and MODE.MULT. MODE. SNGL works identically to MODE in that it returns the first result if there is more than one. MODE. MULT, on the other hand, returns a vertical array (down the column, not across the row) that includes all the results.

Figure 8-13 shows a list of numbers, and the list has two modes. Both 4 and 2 appear twice in the list. Because MODE.MULT returns an array, you have to select a range that's large enough to hold all the values. In Figure 8-13, three cells were selected even though MODE.MULT had only two values to return. When the range is larger than the values, #N/A is returned in the extra cells.

You enter a formula using MODE.MULT by holding down the Ctrl and Alt keys and pressing Enter. Excel surrounds the formula with curly braces ({}) to indicate that it has been entered as an array formula.

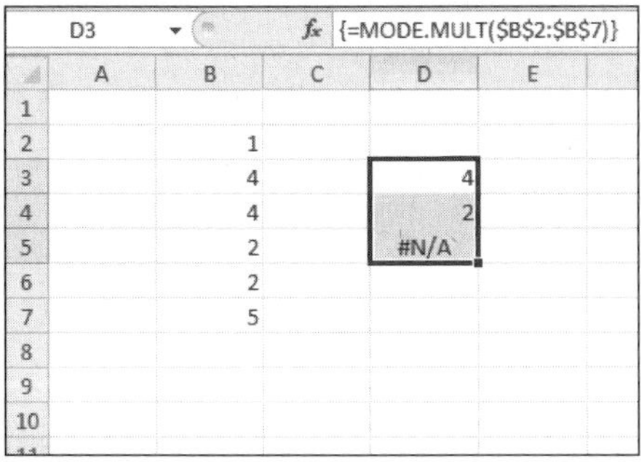

Figure 8-13: The MODE.MULT function returns a list of all the modes of a data set.

Formula 88: Bucketing Data into Percentiles

Separating data into buckets or bins provides insight into how each value compares to the whole.

Figure 8-14 shows a partial list of employees who process a product and the number of defects per 1,000 products that were identified by the Quality Assurance department. For this example, you want to bucket this data into four bins to identify top performers and those employees who may need more training. Excel provides the QUARTILE function to calculate the demarcation line between each quartile. A quartile is a bucket that holds 25 percent of the data.

The following formula is used in cell G3 in Figure 8-14 to find the highest quartile:

```
=QUARTILE($C$3:$C$32,5-ROW(A1))
```

The QUARTILE function provides the demarcation lines. The formula in cell D3 in Figure 8-14 identifies which quartile the value in cell C3 falls into. That formula is then copied down for all of the values. That formula is as follows:

```
=MATCH(C3,$G$3:$G$6,-1)
```

	G3			fx	=QUARTILE($C$3:$C$32,5-ROW(A1))			
	A	B	C	D	E	F	G	H
1								
2		Employee	Defects per 1000	Quartile				
3		Adam Jordan	47	1		Maximum	50.0	
4		Alex Cox	31	3		75th percentile	44.5	
5		Alexa Gonzalez	50	1		50th percentile	31.0	
6		Alyssa Cook	41	2		25th percentile	23.0	
7		Amelia Rivera	30	3				
8		Anna Garcia	30	3				
9		Audrey Cox	23	4				
10		Chloe Marshall	27	3				
11		Eli Green	34	2				
12		Eric Greene	48	1				
13		Evan Stone	17	4				
14		Evelyn Harris	22	4				
15		Gabriel Webb	43	2				
16		Gabriella Davis	45	1				
17		Genesis Bailey	23	4				
18		Isabella Marshall	49	1				
19		Jaden Hart	50	1				
20		Jeremiah Palmer	19	4				
21		Joseph Morgan	17	4				
22		Katelyn Howard	31	3				
23		Kyle Washington	19	4				
24		Lauren Allen	47	1				
25		Layla Gardner	47	1				
26		Lillian Matthews	27	3				
27		Mason Marshall	41	2				
28		Nathaniel Griffin	42	2				
29		Samuel Chavez	21	4				
30		Sean Gomez	39	2				
31		Victoria Freeman	20	4				
32		William Cox	27	3				

Figure 8-14: Identifying quartiles for product defects.

How it works

The QUARTILE function takes a range of values and an integer representing which quartile to return (the quart argument). Acceptable values for the quart argument are 0 for the minimum value, 1 for the 25th percentile, 2 for the 50th percentile, 3 for the 75th percentile, and 4 for the maximum values.

If the quart argument is not in the range 0–4, QUARTILE returns an error. If the quart argument has a decimal, the value is truncated and only the integer portion is used.

The quart argument in this example's QUARTILE function uses the expression 5-ROW(A1). This expression allows the quart argument to decrease by one as the formula is copied down. For cell G3, the expression returns 4 for the maximum value in the range. When the formula is copied down to G3, the A1 reference changes to A2 and the expression returns 5 minus 2, or 3, for the 75th percentile. See the sidebar "The math behind QUARTILE" for more details about the QUARTILE function.

Figure 8-15 shows where QUARTILE divides the sorted data.To find into which quartile each value falls, the MATCH function is used against the range of QUARTILE calculations. Because your quartile data is in descending order, the last argument of MATCH is

```
-1 - Greater than
```

MATCH returns the position in the list in which the value is found, but stops when the next value is less than the lookup value. When attempting to match the value 47, MATCH sees that the second value (44.5) is less than the lookup value and stops at the first position.

	A	B	C	D	E	F
	D3		f_x =MATCH(C3,$K$3:$K$6,-1)			
1						
2		Employee	Defects per 1000	Quartile		
3		Evan Stone	17	4		
4		Joseph Morgan	17	4		
5		Jeremiah Palmer	19	4		
6		Kyle Washington	19	4		
7		Victoria Freeman	20	4		
8		Samuel Chavez	21	4		
9		Evelyn Harris	22	4		
10		Audrey Cox	23	4		7.25: 23+((23-23)*.25)=23
11		Genesis Bailey	23	4		
12		Chloe Marshall	27	3		
13		Lillian Matthews	27	3		
14		William Cox	27	3		
15		Amelia Rivera	30	3		
16		Anna Garcia	30	3		
17		Alex Cox	31	3		14.50: 31+((31-31)*.50)=31
18		Katelyn Howard	31	3		
19		Eli Green	34	2		
20		Sean Gomez	39	2		
21		Alyssa Cook	41	2		
22		Mason Marshall	41	2		
23		Nathaniel Griffin	42	2		
24		Gabriel Webb	43	2		21.75: 43+((45-43)*.75)=44.5
25		Gabriella Davis	45	1		
26		Adam Jordan	47	1		
27		Lauren Allen	47	1		
28		Layla Gardner	47	1		
29		Eric Greene	48	1		
30		Isabella Marshall	49	1		
31		Alexa Gonzalez	50	1		
32		Jaden Hart	50	1		
33						

Figure 8-15: Sorted data and demarcation lines.

Alternative

People debate about the best way to compute quartiles. Prior to Excel 2010, the QUARTILE function, which uses the n%*(count-1) method, was the only function available. Starting with Excel 2010, Excel added the QUARTILE.INC and QUARTILE.EXC functions to provide another method. QUARTILE.INC works exactly as QUARTILE does, but QUARTILE is still available for backward compatibility. The QUARTILE.EXC function uses the n%*(count+1) method.

The QUARTILE.EXC function accepts only a quart argument of 1, 2, or 3. It does not have the 0 or 4 option to return the maximum and minimum values. Figure 8-16 shows the QUARTILE.EXC function applied to the data as well as the revised formula for identifying the quartile of each value. The QUARTILE.EXC formula is as follows:

```
=QUARTILE.EXC($C$3:$C$32,4-ROW(A1))
```

	G4	▼	f_x	=QUARTILE.EXC($C$3:$C$32,4-ROW(A1))				
▲	A	B	C	D	E	F	G	H
1								
2		Employee	Defects per 1000	Quartile				
3		Evan Stone	17	4		QUARTILE.EXC		
4		Joseph Morgan	17	4		75th percentile	45.5	
5		Jeremiah Palmer	19	4		50th percentile	31.0	
6		Kyle Washington	19	4		25th percentile	22.8	
7		Victoria Freeman	20	4				
8		Samuel Chavez	21	4				
9		Evelyn Harris	22	4				
10		Audrey Cox	23	3				
11		Genesis Bailey	23	3				
12		Chloe Marshall	27	3				
13		Lillian Matthews	27	3				
14		William Cox	27	3				
15		Amelia Rivera	30	3				
16		Anna Garcia	30	3				
17		Alex Cox	31	3				
18		Katelyn Howard	31	3				
19		Eli Green	34	2				
20		Sean Gomez	39	2				
21		Alyssa Cook	41	2				
22		Mason Marshall	41	2				
23		Nathaniel Griffin	42	2				
24		Gabriel Webb	43	2				
25		Gabriella Davis	45	2				
26		Adam Jordan	47	1				
27		Lauren Allen	47	1				
28		Layla Gardner	47	1				
29		Eric Greene	48	1				
30		Isabella Marshall	49	1				
31		Alexa Gonzalez	50	1				
32		Jaden Hart	50	1				
33								

Figure 8-16: QUARTILE.EXC applied to the defects data.

The math behind QUARTILE

The QUARTILE function applies a percentage to one less than the count of values to find the two values that surround the demarcation line. Then it interpolates between those two values to find the result.

Using the example for Formula 88, for the 75th percentile, QUARTILE computes .75*(30-1) for the 30 values in Figure 8-14 to get 21.75. Then it sorts the data from lowest to highest and counts down 21 rows from the lowest value. Because the result of the first calculation is not a whole number, it interpolates between the two values. In this case, counting down 21 rows finds the value 43, and the next value is 45. The interpolation uses the decimal portion of 21.75 to find the value that is 75 percent of the way between 42 and 45, or 43+((45-43)*.75).

Similarly for the 50th percentile, QUARTILE computes .5*(30-1) to get 14.5. Counting down from the lowest values, the 50th percentile falls between the Alex Cox's 31 and Katelyn Howard's 31. Because both values are the same, the interpolation is easy and returns 31. Figure 8-15 shows the same employee and defect data sorted with the demarcation lines identified.

Because QUARTILE.EXC does not have a quart argument for returning the maximum, the values in the top quartile are checked to see whether they are greater than the 75th percentile using the following formula:

```
=IF(C3>=$G$4,1,MATCH(C3,$G$4:$G$6,-1)+1)
```

Formula 89: Identifying Statistical Outliers with an Interquartile Range

In Formula 88, you use the QUARTILE function to group data into buckets. Another use of QUARTILE is to identify outliers, that is, values at the extreme ends of the data set.

Figure 8-17 shows another set of employees and the number of defects per 1,000 products. This data set has a wider spread of values than the one for Formula 88. You want to determine which employees are outside a reasonable range (outliers) for further investigation. To identify outliers, this example uses a method called a leveraged interquartile range. An interquartile range is simply the data that lies in the middle 50 percent (between the 75th percentile and the 25th percentile). The "leveraged" part means that you expand that middle range by a factor and establish fences. Any data outside the fence is considered an outlier.

The formulas used in Figure 8-17 are as follows:

```
75th percentile: =QUARTILE.EXC($C$3:$C$22,3)
25th percentile: =QUARTILE.EXC($C$3:$C$22,1)
Interquartile Range: =G4-G5
Fence Factor: 1.5
Upper Fence: =G4+(G6*G8)
Lower Fence: =G5-(G6*G8)
Outliers: =IF(C3<$G$10,"Low",IF(C3>$G$9,"High",""))
```

	D3	▾ (⦁)	*fx*	=IF(C3<$G$10,"Low",IF(C3>$G$9,"High",""))		
◢	A	B	C	D	E	F	G
1							
2		Employee	Defects per 1000	Outliers			
3		Alex Cox	64				
4		Alyssa Cook	104	High		75th percentile	65.5
5		Amelia Rivera	44			25th percentile	42.5
6		Anna Garcia	56			Interquartile Range	23.0
7		Audrey Cox	46				
8		Chloe Marshall	46			Fence Factor	1.5
9		Eli Green	66			Upper Fence	100.00
10		Evan Stone	6	Low		Lower Fence	8.00
11		Evelyn Harris	47				
12		Genesis Bailey	52				
13		Jeremiah Palmer	10				
14		Joseph Morgan	5	Low			
15		Katelyn Howard	46				
16		Kyle Washington	7	Low			
17		Lillian Matthews	46				
18		Mason Marshall	110	High			
19		Samuel Chavez	90				
20		Sean Gomez	101	High			
21		Victoria Freeman	42				
22		William Cox	52				
23							

Figure 8-17: Identifying outliers using a leveraged interquartile range.

How it works

You use the QUARTILE.EXC function to determine the 75th percentile and 25th percentile using *quant* arguments of 3 and 1, respectively. The interquartile range is the difference between these two.

In a non-leveraged interquartile range, you would simply subtract the interquartile range from the 25th percentile to get a lower fence and add it to the 75th percentile to get an upper fence. This method can result in too many outliers, however. By multiplying the interquartile range by a factor (1.5 in this example), you expand the fences to isolate the truly extreme values. Figure 8-18 shows the same data sorted by defects and the demarcation lines of the quartiles, the interquartile range, and the upper and lower fences.

To determine the upper fence, you multiply the fence factor by the interquartile range and add the result to the 75th percentile. The same result is subtracted from the 25th percentile to establish the lower fence.

Tip

You may find that the fence factor of 1.5 excludes values that you consider outliers or includes values that you consider normal. Nothing is magic about 1.5. Simply adjust the factor up or down if it doesn't fit your data.

With your fences established, you use a nested IF formula to determine whether each value is greater than the upper fence or less than the lower fence. The text "High" or "Low" is returned by the nested IF formula for the outliers, and an empty string ("") is returned for those that are inside the fences.

	A	B	C	D	E	F	G	H
			D3 ▼	fx =IF(C3<$K$10,"Low",IF(C3>$K$9,"High",""))				
1								
2		Employee	Defects per 1000	Outliers				
3		Joseph Morgan	5	Low				
4		Evan Stone	6	Low		Leveraged IQR Lower Fence		
5		Kyle Washington	7	Low				
6		Jeremiah Palmer	10					Non-leveraged IQR Lower Fence
7		Victoria Freeman	42					
8		Amelia Rivera	44			25th Percentile		
9		Audrey Cox	46					
10		Chloe Marshall	46					
11		Katelyn Howard	46					
12		Lillian Matthews	46					
13		Evelyn Harris	47					
14		Genesis Bailey	52					
15		William Cox	52					
16		Anna Garcia	56			75th percentile		
17		Alex Cox	64					
18		Eli Green	66					Non-leveraged IQR Upper Fence
19		Samuel Chavez	90					
20		Sean Gomez	101	High		Leveraged IQR Upper Fence		
21		Alyssa Cook	104	High				
22		Mason Marshall	110	High				
23								

Figure 8-18: Leveraged interquartile ranges expand the fences outward.

Formula 90: Creating a Frequency Distribution

Quartiles are a popular way to group data into bins, which is why Excel has a dedicated QUARTILE function. Sometimes, however, you may want to group your data into bins you define.

Figure 8-19 shows a partial list of 50 invoices and the total amount sold on each invoice. For this example, you want to determine how commonly your customers make purchases between $1 and $100, $101 and $200, and so on.

Excel's FREQUENCY function will count all the invoices that fall within the bins you define:

```
=FREQUENCY(C3:C52,F3:F12)
```

How it works

The FREQUENCY function is an array function. Using an array function means that instead of pressing Enter to commit the formula, you must press Ctrl+Shift+Enter. Excel will insert curly braces ({}) around the formula to indicate that it has been array-entered.

FREQUENCY takes two arguments: a range of data to be grouped into bins and a range of numbers that represent the highest amount for that bin. First, enter the bin values in column F. Column E does not affect the formula; it's just there to show the lower bound of the bin.

	G3			*fx* {=FREQUENCY(C3:C52,F3:F12)}				
	A	B	C	D	E	F	G	H
1								
2		Invoice #	Total Sale			Bins	Frequency	
3		IN1288	263.66		-	100	4	
4		IN1388	273.37		100	200	2	
5		IN1395	232.24		200	300	20	
6		IN1518	725.03		300	400	3	
7		IN1793	969.66		400	500	2	
8		IN1860	264.95		500	600	2	
9		IN2239	204.54		600	700	3	
10		IN2379	246.78		700	800	4	
11		IN2782	202.64		800	900	4	
12		IN2887	376.77		900	1,000	6	
13		IN2917	243.42					
14		IN3243	277.74					
15		IN3321	689.93					
16		IN3476	795.39					
17		IN3534	716.55					
18		IN3942	41.68					
19		IN4024	249.15					
20		IN4139	631.67					
21		IN4154	982.17					
22		IN4271	802.17					

Figure 8-19: Calculating the frequency with custom bins.

To enter FREQUENCY into column G, first select the range G3:G12. Although you'll be entering the formula into only G3, committing the formula with Ctrl+Shift+Enter fills in the formula to the entire range selected.

The results of the FREQUENCY formula show that a large number of customers purchase between $200 and $300 per visit.

Alternative

If you attempt to delete one of the cells in the FREQUENCY formula range, Excel will tell you that you "cannot change part of an array." Excel treats FREQUENCY, and all array functions, as one unit. You can change the whole array, just not individual cells within it. If you want to change the bins, you have to delete and reenter the array.

You can also use the COUNTIFS function to create a frequency distribution. Because COUNTIFS is not an array formula, using it makes changing the bins or expanding or contracting the range easier. For the data in Figure 8-19, shown previously, the COUNTIFS function is as follows:

```
=COUNTIFS($C$3:$C$52,">"&E3,$C$3:$C$52,"<="&F3)
```

Cross-Ref   See Chapter 5 for more information on the COUNTIFS function.

In contrast to FREQUENCY, COUNTIFS needs the lower bound of the bin (column E). It counts all the values that are greater than the lower bound and less than or equal to the upper bound. Rather than array-entering this formula, you can simply have it copied down for as many bins as you've defined.

Formula 91: De-Seasonalize your Data before Forecasting

Data that represents sales over one year or more typically contains seasonality. That is, sales in certain parts of a year are predictably higher or lower than average. An important part of forecasting is accounting for the seasonality.

Figure 8-20 shows a chart of five years of monthly sales data. The chart also has a linear trendline showing a steady increase in sales. Probably the most notable information on the chart is the sharp increase in sales every late spring to early summer. If you tried to forecast sales using the linear trend-line, you would surely be understaffed and out of inventory during the busy season.

Figure 8-20: Five years of monthly sales data.

To properly forecast sales for the coming year, you need to de-seasonalize the historical data, determine the trend of the de-seasonalized data, and re-seasonalize the forecast.

Figure 8-21 shows a table of months and a seasonal factor for each month. The seasonal factor shows how much sales in that month historically deviate from average sales. The table shows that sales in January are typically about half (51.37 percent) of average sales, whereas sales in April are more than double (217.24 percent) the average. To calculate the seasonal factor, use the following formula:

```
=SUMPRODUCT((MONTH($B$3:$B$62)=G4)*($C$3:$C$62))/
   SUMPRODUCT(--(MONTH($B$3:$B$62)=G4))/AVERAGE($C$3:$C$62)
```

G	H
Month	Seasonal Factor
1	51.37%
2	66.77%
3	55.48%
4	217.24%
5	199.20%
6	196.28%
7	64.20%
8	70.54%
9	76.31%
10	66.55%
11	72.24%
12	63.83%

Figure 8-21: A table of seasonal factors.

To complete the de-seasonalizing process, you add a new column to the historical data. In this column, each month's sales are divided by the sales factor for that month, returning a de-seasonlized value. Figure 8-22 shows that if all months were equal, January 2008 would have sales of about $13,500. The formula to convert the sales to the seasonal factor is as follows:

```
=C3/VLOOKUP(MONTH(B3),$G$4:$H$15,2,FALSE)
```

f_x | =C3/VLOOKUP(MONTH(B3),$G$4:$H$15,2,FALSE)

	A	B	C	D	E	F
1						
2		Month	Sales	De-seasonal		
3		Jan-08	6,938.24	13,507.71		
4		Feb-08	6,246.32	9,354.65		
5		Mar-08	8,205.83	14,791.73		
6		Apr-08	23,612.64	10,869.20		
7		May-08	28,427.85	14,270.70		
8		Jun-08	22,472.73	11,449.36		
9		Jul-08	7,542.89	11,749.53		
10		Aug-08	9,248.89	13,111.83		
11		Sep-08	10,591.71	13,880.47		
12		Oct-08	8,096.57	12,166.03		
13		Nov-08	8,147.39	11,278.59		
14		Dec-08	9,755.07	15,283.16		
15		Jan-09	7,947.75	15,473.08		
16		Feb-09	9,984.22	14,952.63		

Figure 8-22: Seasonal factors applied back to historical data.

How it works

The seasonal factor formula uses two SUMPRODUCT functions to calculate the average sales for only the month in the cell to the left. The monthly average is then divided by the average of all sales.

 See Chapter 5 for details on how SUMPRODUCT uses arrays.
Cross-Ref

The first SUMPRODUCT sums all the values in C3:C62 whose corresponding cell in B3:B62 has a month equal to the number in G4. For the formula in H4, it sums all the sales for all the Januarys.

The second SUMPRODUCT counts all the Januarys in B3:B62. Recall that SUMPRODUCT returns an array of TRUEs and FALSEs. The double negative converts those TRUEs and FALSEs to 1s and 0s. SUMPRODUCT sums all the 1s (the TRUE values) to return a count of all the Januarys.

Dividing the first SUMPRODUCT by the second is dividing the sum of all January sales by the count of all January sales and results in the average. This average is divided by the average of all sales regardless of month to return the seasonal factor.

Finally, the sales for each month are divided by the seasonal factor. You use a VLOOKUP function to get the seasonal factor from the table. The lookup value uses the MONTH function to return the month's number, and that is matched in the first column of the table.

Formula 92: Create a Trendline Forecast

The main purpose of de-seasonalizing data is to create a forecast. The de-seasonalized data you create in Formula 91 provides the information you need to create a forecast for the next year.

Figure 8-23 shows the bottom of the sales data from Formula 91. Whereas the historical data stopped at Dec-12, you want to forecast sales for 2013. The first step is to use the FORECAST function to extend the de-seasonalized data for 12 more months. The formula to forecast January is the following:

```
=FORECAST(B63,$D$3:$D$62,$B$3:$B$62)
```

How it works

The FORECAST function uses linear regression to predict the future value. It takes three arguments named x, known_y's, and known_x's. The x argument is the month for which you want to predict a value. The known_y's are the de-seasonalized sales data in column D. Finally, the known_x's are the months that relate to the sales data in column B.

	A	B	C	D	E	F
1						
2		Month	Sales	De-seasonal	Re-seasonal	
58		Aug-12	10,617.79	15,052.47		
59		Sep-12	14,963.68	19,609.95		
60		Oct-12	9,801.79	14,728.31		
61		Nov-12	11,733.87	16,243.43		
62		Dec-12	10,739.17	16,824.94		
63		Jan-13		19,081.03	9,800.97	
64		Feb-13		19,184.31	12,809.81	
65		Mar-13		19,298.65	10,706.08	
66		Apr-13		19,409.31	42,165.47	
67		May-13		19,523.65	38,891.95	
68		Jun-13		19,634.30	38,538.09	
69		Jul-13		19,748.65	12,678.11	
70		Aug-13		19,862.99	14,011.06	
71		Sep-13		19,973.65	15,241.20	
72		Oct-13		20,087.99	13,368.69	
73		Nov-13		20,198.65	14,591.03	
74		Dec-13		20,312.99	12,965.55	
75						
76						
77						

Figure 8-23: Forecasts based on de-seasonalized data.

After FORECAST has predicted values for all the months, you need to re-seasonalize the data using the seasonal factors table from Figure 8-21 (refer to Formula 91). The formula to re-seasonalize January is as follows:

```
=D63*VLOOKUP(MONTH(B63),$G$4:$H$15,2,FALSE)
```

When you de-seasonalized the data, you divided by the seasonal factor. Here you do just the opposite: You multiply by the seasonal factor. Because January is historically 53 percent of the average sales, the predicted value is multiplied by 53 percent to become your January forecast. Figure 8-24 shows the newly forecasted data added to the sales chart. By re-seasonalizing the data, you see the predictable second-quarter sales spike.

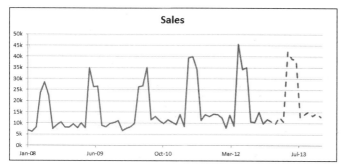

Figure 8-24: Newly forecasted data added to the end of the sales chart.

Using Formulas with Conditional Formatting

9

Conditional Formatting is the term given to the functionality with which Excel dynamically changes the formatting of a value, cell, or range of cells based on a set of conditions you define. Conditional formatting allows you to look at your Excel reports and make split-second determinations on which values are "good" and which are "bad," all based on formatting.

In this chapter, you explore a few examples of how you can use the Conditional Formatting feature in Excel in conjunction with formulas to add an extra layer of visualizations to your analyses.

Note

The Conditional Formatting feature is fairly robust and includes many bells and whistles that we don't cover here. To adhere to the spirit of this book, we focus on the techniques for applying conditional formatting with formulas.

Note

You can download the files for all the formulas at www.wiley.com/ go/101excelformula.

Formula 93: Highlight Cells That Meet Certain Criteria

One of the more basic Conditional Formatting rules that you can create is the highlighting of cells that meet some business criteria. This first example demonstrates the formatting of cells that fall under a hard-coded value of 4000 (see Figure 9-1).

	A	B	C
1			
2			Units Sold
3		January	2661
4		February	3804
5		March	5021
6		April	1001
7		May	4375
8		June	2859
9		July	7659
10		August	3061
11		September	2003
12		October	5147
13		November	4045
14		December	1701
15			

Figure 9-1: The cells in this table are conditionally formatted to show as shaded for values under 4000.

How it works

To build this basic formatting rule, follow these steps:

1. Select the data cells in your target range (cells C3:C14 in this example), click the Home tab of the Excel Ribbon, and then select Conditional Formatting⇨New Rule. The New Formatting Rule dialog box opens, as shown in Figure 9-2.

2. In the list box at the top of the dialog box, click the Use a Formula to Determine which Cells to Format option. This selection evaluates values based on a formula you specify. If a particular value evaluates to TRUE, the conditional formatting is applied to that cell.

3. In the formula input box, enter the formula shown here. Note that you are simply referencing the first cell in the target range. You don't need to reference the entire range.

```
=C3<4000
```

Caution

Note that in the formula, you exclude the absolute reference dollar symbols ($) for the target cell (C3). If you click cell C3 instead of typing the cell reference, Excel will automatically make your cell reference absolute. It's important that you don't include the absolute reference dollar symbols in your target cell because you need Excel to apply this formatting rule based on each cell's own value.

4. Click the Format button. This opens the Format Cells dialog box, where you have a full set of options for formatting the font, border, and fill for your target cell. After you have completed choosing your formatting options, click the OK button to confirm your changes and return to the New Formatting Rule dialog box.

5. Back in the New Formatting Rule dialog box, click the OK button to confirm your formatting rule.

Figure 9-2: Configure the New Formatting Rule dialog box to apply the needed formula rule.

Tip

If you need to edit your conditional formatting rule, simply place your cursor in any of the data cells within your formatted range and then go to the Home tab and select Conditional Formatting⇨Manage Rules, which opens the Conditional Formatting Rules Manager dialog box. Click the rule you want to edit and then click the Edit Rule button.

Formula 94: Highlight Cells Based on the Value of Another Cell

In many cases, you will base the formatting rule for your cells on how they compare to the value of another cell. Take the example illustrated in Figure 9-3. Here, the cells are conditionally highlighted if their respective values fall below the Prior Year Average shown in cell B3.

⊿	A	B	C	D	E
1					
2		Prior Year Average		Month	Units Sold
3		3500		January	2661
4				February	3804
5				March	5021
6				April	1001
7				May	4375
8				June	2859
9				July	7659
10				August	3061
11				September	2003
12				October	5147
13				November	4045
14				December	1701
15					

Figure 9-3: The cells in this table are conditionally formatted to show red for values falling below the Prior Year Average.

How it works

To build this basic formatting rule, follow these steps:

1. Select the data cells in your target range (cells E3:C14 in this example), click the Home tab of the Excel Ribbon, and then select Conditional Formatting⇨New Rule. This opens the New Formatting Rule dialog box shown in Figure 9-4.

2. In the list box at the top of the dialog box, click the Use a Formula to Determine which Cells to Format option. This selection evaluates values based on a formula you specify. If a particular value evaluates to TRUE, the conditional formatting is applied to that cell.

3. In the formula input box, enter the formula shown with this step. Note that you are simply comparing your target cell (E3) with the value in the comparison cell ($B$3). As with standard formulas, you need to ensure that you use absolute references so that each value in your range is compared to the appropriate comparison cell.

```
=E3<$B$3
```

Caution

Note that in the formula, you exclude the absolute reference dollar symbols ($) for the target cell (E3). If you click cell E3 instead of typing the cell reference, Excel automatically makes your cell reference absolute. It's important that you don't include the absolute reference dollar symbols in your target cell because you need Excel to apply this formatting rule based on each cell's own value.

4. Click the Format button. This opens the Format Cells dialog box, where you have a full set of options for formatting the font, border, and fill for your target cell. After you have completed choosing your formatting options, click the OK button to confirm your changes and return to the New Formatting Rule dialog box.

5. Back in the New Formatting Rule dialog box, click the OK button to confirm your formatting rule.

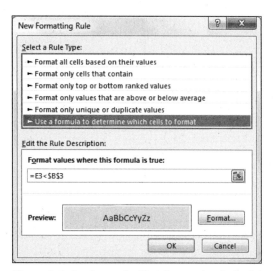

Figure 9-4: Configure the New Formatting Rule dialog box to apply the needed formula rule.

Tip

If you need to edit your conditional formatting rule, simply place your cursor in any of the data cells within your formatted range and then go to the Home tab and select Conditional Formatting⇨Manage Rules. This opens the Conditional Formatting Rules Manager dialog box. Click the rule you want to edit and then click the Edit Rule button.

Formula 95: Highlight Values That Exist in List1 but not List2

You may often be asked to compare two lists and pick out the values that are in one list but not the other. Conditional formatting is an ideal way to present your findings. Figure 9-5 illustrates a conditional formatting exercise that compares customers from 2013 and 2014, highlighting those customers in 2014 who are new customers (they were not customers in 2013).

	A	B	C	D	E	F
1						
2		2013			2014	
3		Customer_Name	Revenue		Customer_Name	Revenue
4		GKNEAS Corp.	$2,333.60		JAMSEA Corp.	$2,324.36
5		JAMSEA Corp.	$2,324.36		JAMWUS Corp.	$2,328.53
6		JAMWUS Corp.	$2,328.53		JAYKA Corp.	$2,328.53
7		JAYKA Corp.	$2,328.53		JUSDAN Corp.	$3,801.86
8		MAKUTE Corp.	$2,334.01		MAKUTE Corp.	$2,334.01
9		MOSUNC Corp.	$2,311.70		MALEBO Corp.	$3,099.45
10		NCUANT Corp.	$2,311.79		MOSUNC Corp.	$2,311.70
11		OSADUL Corp.	$2,311.50		NCUANT Corp.	$2,311.79
12		RRCAR Corp.	$2,315.14		OSADUL Corp.	$2,311.50
13		RULLAN Corp.	$2,332.94		PUNSKE Corp.	$7,220.80
14		SMATHE Corp.	$2,336.59		REBUST Corp.	$14,224.84
15		SOFANU Corp.	$2,333.60		RRCAR Corp.	$2,315.14
16		SUMTUK Corp.	$2,321.61		RULLAN Corp.	$2,332.94
17		TULUSS Corp.	$2,311.96		RUTANS Corp.	$4,175.75
18		UDGUWU Corp.	$2,328.58		SCHOUL Corp.	$5,931.46

Figure 9-5: You can conditionally format the values that exist in one list but not the other.

How it works

To build this basic formatting rule, follow these steps:

1. Select the data cells in your target range (cells E4:E28 in this example), click the Home tab of the Excel Ribbon, and then select Conditional Formatting⇨New Rule. This opens the New Formatting Rule dialog box shown in Figure 9-6.

2. In the list box at the top of the dialog box, click the Use a Formula to Determine which Cells to Format option. This selection evaluates values based on a formula you specify. If a particular value evaluates to TRUE, the conditional formatting is applied to that cell.

3. In the formula input box, enter the formula shown with this step. Note that you use the COUNTIF function to evaluate whether the value in the target cell (E4) is found in your comparison range ($B$4:$B$21). If the value is not found, the COUNTIF function will return a 0, thus triggering the conditional formatting. As with standard formulas, you need to ensure that you use absolute references so that each value in your range is compared to the appropriate comparison cell.

```
=COUNTIF($B$4:$B$21,E4)=0
```

Caution

Note that in the formula, you exclude the absolute reference dollar symbols ($) for the target cell (E4). If you click cell E4 instead of typing the cell reference, Excel automatically makes your cell reference absolute. It's important that you don't include the absolute reference dollar symbols in your target cell because you need Excel to apply this formatting rule based on each cell's own value.

Cross-Ref

For more details on the COUNTIF function, see Formula 51: Get a Count of Values That Meet a Certain Condition, in Chapter 5.

4. Click the Format button. This opens the Format Cells dialog box, where you have a full set of options for formatting the font, border, and fill for your target cell. After you have completed choosing your formatting options, click the OK button to confirm your changes and return to the New Formatting Rule dialog box.

5. In the New Formatting Rule dialog box, click the OK button to confirm your formatting rule.

Figure 9-6: Configure the New Formatting Rule dialog box to apply the needed formula rule.

Tip

If you need to edit your conditional formatting rule, simply place your cursor in any of the data cells within your formatted range and then go to the Home tab and select Conditional Formatting➪Manage Rules. This opens the Conditional Formatting Rules Manager dialog box. Click the rule you want to edit and then click the Edit Rule button.

Formula 96: Highlight Values That Exist in List1 and List2

You may often need to compare two lists and pick out only the values that exist in both lists. Conditional formatting is an ideal way to accomplish this task. Figure 9-7 illustrates a conditional formatting exercise that compares customers from 2013 and 2014, highlighting those customers in 2014 who are in both lists.

▲	A	B	C	D	E	F
1						
2		2013			2014	
3		Customer_Name	Revenue		Customer_Name	Revenue
4		GKNEAS Corp.	$2,333.60		JAMSEA Corp.	$2,324.36
5		JAMSEA Corp.	$2,324.36		JAMWUS Corp.	$2,328.53
6		JAMWUS Corp.	$2,328.53		JAYKA Corp.	$2,328.53
7		JAYKA Corp.	$2,328.53		JUSDAN Corp.	$3,801.86
8		MAKUTE Corp.	$2,334.01		MAKUTE Corp.	$2,334.01
9		MOSUNC Corp.	$2,311.70		MALEBO Corp.	$3,099.45
10		NCUANT Corp.	$2,311.79		MOSUNC Corp.	$2,311.70
11		OSADUL Corp.	$2,311.50		NCUANT Corp.	$2,311.79
12		RRCAR Corp.	$2,315.14		OSADUL Corp.	$2,311.50
13		RULLAN Corp.	$2,332.94		PUNSKE Corp.	$7,220.80
14		SMATHE Corp.	$2,336.59		REBUST Corp.	$14,224.84
15		SOFANU Corp.	$2,333.60		RRCAR Corp.	$2,315.14
16		SUMTUK Corp.	$2,321.61		RULLAN Corp.	$2,332.94
17		THULISS Corp.	$2,311.95		BUTANS Corp.	$4,135.35

Figure 9-7: You can conditionally format the values that exist in both lists.

How it works

To build this basic formatting rule, follow these steps:

1. Select the data cells in your target range (cells E4:E28 in this example), click the Home tab of the Excel Ribbon, and select Conditional Formatting⇨New Rule. This opens the New Formatting Rule dialog box shown in Figure 9-8.

2. In the list box at the top of the dialog box, click the Use a Formula to Determine which Cells to Format option. This selection evaluates values based on a formula you specify. If a particular value evaluates to TRUE, the conditional formatting is applied to that cell.

3. In the formula input box, enter the formula shown with this step. Note that you use the COUNTIF function to evaluate whether the value in the target cell (E4) is found in your comparison range ($B$4:$B$21). If the value is found, the COUNTIF function returns a number greater than 0, thus triggering the conditional formatting. As with standard formulas, you need to ensure that you use absolute references so that each value in your range is compared to the appropriate comparison cell.

```
=COUNTIF($B$4:$B$21,E4)>0
```

Caution

Note that in the formula, you exclude the absolute reference dollar symbols ($) for the target cell (E4). If you click cell E4 instead of typing the cell reference, Excel automatically makes your cell reference absolute. It's important that you don't include the absolute reference dollar symbols in your target cell because you need Excel to apply this formatting rule based on each cell's own value.

Cross-Ref

For more detail on the COUNTIF function, see Formula 51: Get a Count of Values That Meet a Certain Condition, in Chapter 5.

1. Click the Format button. This opens the Format Cells dialog box, where you have a full set of options for formatting the font, border, and fill for your target cell. After you have completed choosing your formatting options, click the OK button to confirm your changes and return to the New Formatting dialog Rule box.

5. Back in the New Formatting Rule dialog box, click the OK button to confirm your formatting rule.

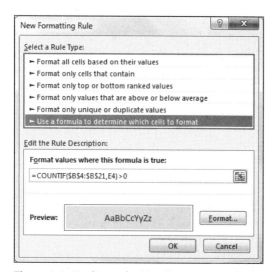

Figure 9-8: Configure the New Formatting Rule dialog box to apply the needed formula rule.

Tip

If you need to edit your conditional formatting rule, simply place your cursor in any of the data cells within your formatted range and then go to the Home tab and select Conditional Formatting⇨Manage Rules. This opens the Conditional Formatting Rules Manager dialog box. Click the rule you want to edit and then click the Edit Rule button.

Formula 97: Highlight Weekend Dates

When working with timecards and scheduling, you often benefit from being able to easily pinpoint any dates that fall on the weekends. The conditional formatting rule illustrated in Figure 9-9 highlights all the weekend dates in the list of values.

◢	A	B
1		
2		**Highlight Weekends**
3		1/23/2012
4		12/28/2009
5		9/26/2010
6		12/8/2014
7		4/25/2010
8		11/7/2012
9		7/31/2014
10		11/24/2014
11		12/28/2010
12		7/28/2011
13		12/17/2014
14		8/3/2014
15		5/1/2011
16		4/2/2011
17		7/17/2009
18		8/12/2009

Figure 9-9: You can conditionally format any weekend dates in a list of dates.

How it works

To build this basic formatting rule, follow these steps:

1. Select the data cells in your target range (cells B3:B18 in this example), click the Home tab of the Excel Ribbon, and then select Conditional Formatting⇨New Rule. This opens the New Formatting Rule dialog box shown in Figure 9-10.

2. In the list box at the top of the dialog box, click the Use a Formula to Determine which Cells to Format option. This selection evaluates values based on a formula you specify. If a particular value evaluates to TRUE, the conditional formatting is applied to that cell.

3. In the formula input box, enter the formula shown with this step. Note that you use the WEEKDAY function to evaluate the weekday number of the target cell (B3). If the target cell returns as weekday 1 or 7, it means the date in B3 is a weekend date. In this case, the conditional formatting will be applied.

    ```
    =OR(WEEKDAY(B3)=1,WEEKDAY(B3)=7)
    ```

Caution

Note that in the formula, you exclude the absolute reference dollar symbols ($) for the target cell (B3). If you click cell B3 instead of typing the cell reference, Excel will automatically make your cell reference absolute. It's important that you don't include the absolute reference dollar symbols in your target cell because you need Excel to apply this formatting rule based on each cell's own value.

Cross-Ref ⌐ui more detail on the WEEKDAY function, see Formula 29: Extracting Parts of a Date, in Chapter 4.

4. Click the Format button. This opens the Format Cells dialog box, where you have a full set of options for formatting the font, border, and fill for your target cell. After you have completed choosing your formatting options, click the OK button to confirm your changes and return to the New Formatting Rule dialog box.

5. Back in the New Formatting Rule dialog box, click the OK button to confirm your formatting rule.

Figure 9-10: Configure the New Formatting Rule dialog box to apply the needed formula rule.

Tip If you need to edit your conditional formatting rule, simply place your cursor in any of the data cells within your formatted range and then go to the Home tab and select Conditional Formatting⇨Manage Rules. This opens the Conditional Formatting Rules Manager dialog box. Click the rule you want to edit and then click the Edit Rule button.

Formula 98: Highlight Days between Two Dates

Some analysis requires the identification of dates that fall within a certain time period. Figure 9-11 demonstrates how you can apply conditional formatting that highlights dates based on a start date and end date. As you adjust the start and end dates, the conditional formatting adjusts with them.

⊿	A	B	C	D	E
1					
2		Start	End		Highlight Days within 2010 and 2012
3		1/1/2010	12/31/2012		1/23/2012
4					12/28/2009
5					9/26/2010
6					12/8/2014
7					4/25/2010
8					11/7/2012
9					7/31/2014
10					11/24/2014
11					12/28/2010
12					7/28/2011
13					12/17/2014
14					8/3/2014
15					5/1/2011
16					4/2/2011
17					7/17/2009
18					8/12/2009

Figure 9-11: You can conditionally format dates that fall between a start and end date.

How it works

To build this basic formatting rule, follow these steps:

1. Select the data cells in your target range (cells E3:E18 in this example), click the Home tab of the Excel Ribbon, and then select Conditional Formatting⟹New Rule. This opens the New Formatting Rule dialog box shown in Figure 9-12.

2. In the list box at the top of the dialog box, click the Use a Formula to Determine which Cells to Format option. This selection evaluates values based on a formula you specify. If a particular value evaluates to TRUE, the conditional formatting is applied to that cell.

3. In the formula input box, enter the formula shown with this step. Note that you use the AND function to compare the date in your target cell (E3) to both the start and end dates found in cells $B$3 and $C$3, respectively. If the target cell falls within the start and end dates, the formula will evaluate to TRUE, thus triggering the conditional formatting.

   `=AND(E3>=$B$3,E3<=$C$3)`

Caution

Note that in the formula, you exclude the absolute reference dollar symbols ($) for the target cell (E3). If you click cell E3 instead of typing the cell reference, Excel automatically makes your cell reference absolute. It's important that you don't include the absolute reference dollar symbols in your target cell because you need Excel to apply this formatting rule based on each cell's own value.

Cross-Ref

For more detail on the AND function, see Formula 46: Check Whether Condition1 AND Condition2 Are Met, in Chapter 5.

4. Click the Format button. This opens the Format Cells dialog box, where you have a full set of options for formatting the font, border, and fill for your target cell. After you have completed choosing your formatting options, click the OK button to confirm your changes and return to the New Formatting Rule dialog box.

5. Back in the New Formatting Rule dialog box, click the OK button to confirm your formatting rule.

Figure 9-12: Configure the New Formatting Rule dialog box to apply the needed formula rule.

Tip

If you need to edit your conditional formatting rule, simply place your cursor in any of the data cells within your formatted range and then go to the Home tab and select Conditional Formatting⇨Manage Rules. This opens the Conditional Formatting Rules Manager dialog box. Click the rule you want to edit and then click the Edit Rule button.

Formula 99: Highlight Dates Based on Due Date

In many organizations, it's important to call attention to dates that fall after a specified time period. With conditional formatting, you can easily create a "past due" report highlighting overdue items. The example shown in Figure 9-13 demonstrates a scenario where the dates that are more than 90 days overdue are formatted in red.

▲	A	B	C
1			
2			
3			Due Date
4			04/25/13
5			05/04/16
6			05/04/14
7			03/28/12
8			04/22/16
9			03/31/13

Figure 9-13: You can conditionally format dates based on due date.

How it works

To build this basic formatting rule, follow these steps:

1. Select the data cells in your target range (cells C4:C9 in this example), click the Home tab of the Excel Ribbon, and then select Conditional Formatting➪New Rule. This opens the New Formatting Rule dialog box shown in Figure 9-14.

2. In the list box at the top of the dialog box, click the Use a Formula to Determine which Cells to Format option. This selection evaluates values based on a formula you specify. If a particular value evaluates to TRUE, the conditional formatting is applied to that cell.

3. In the formula input box, enter the formula shown here. In this formula, you evaluate whether today's date is greater than 90 days past the date in your target cell (C4). If so, the conditional formatting will be applied.

```
=TODAY()-C4>90
```

Caution

Note that in the formula, you exclude the absolute reference dollar symbols ($) for the target cell (C4). If you click cell C4 instead of typing the cell reference, Excel will automatically make your cell reference absolute. It's important that you don't include the absolute reference dollar symbols in your target cell because you need Excel to apply this formatting rule based on each cell's own value.

4. Click the Format button. This opens the Format Cells dialog box, where you have a full set of options for formatting the font, border, and fill for your target cell. After you have completed choosing your formatting options, click the OK button to confirm your changes and return to the New Formatting Rule dialog box.

5. Back in the New Formatting Rule dialog box, click the OK button to confirm your formatting rule.

Tip

If you need to edit your conditional formatting rule, simply place your cursor in any of the data cells within your formatted range and then go to the Home tab and select Conditional Formatting➪Manage Rules. This opens the Conditional Formatting Rules Manager dialog box. Click the rule you want to edit and then click the Edit Rule button.

Figure 9-14: Configure the New Formatting Rule dialog box to apply the needed formula rule.

Formula 100: Highlight Data Based on Percentile Rank

A percentile rank indicates the standing of a particular data value relative to other data values in a sample. Percentiles are most notably used in determining performance on standardized tests. If a child scores in the 90th percentile on a standardized test, this means that his or her score is higher than 90 percent of the other children taking the test. Another way to look at it is to say that the child's score is in the top 10 percent of all the children taking the test.

Percentiles are often used in data analysis as a method of measuring a subject's performance in relation to the group as a whole — for instance, determining the percentile ranking for each employee based on an annual revenue.

In Excel, you can easily get key percentile ranks using the PERCENTILE function. This function requires two arguments: a range of data and the percentile score you want to see.

In the example shown in Figure 9-15, the value in cell D7 is a result of the following formula, which pulls the 75th percentile based on the data in range B3:B20:

```
=PERCENTILE($B$3:$B$20,0.75)
```

This formula tells you that any employee with revenue over $52,651 is in the top 75 percent of performers.

The value in cell D16 is a result of the following formula, which pulls the 25th percentile based on the data in range B3:B20:

```
=PERCENTILE($B$3:$B$20,0.25)
```

This formula tells you that any employee with revenue below $24,656 is in the bottom 25 percent of performers.

Using these percentile markers, this example applies conditional formatting so that any value in the 75th percentile will be colored green and any value in the 25th percentile will be colored red.

	A	B	C	D	
1					
2	Employee_Number	Rev			
3	160014	54,332.63			Green
4	1054	54,147.73			
5	6032	53,621.49			
6	54253	53,433.41		75th percentile	
7	4346	52,990.56		52,651	
8	5530	51,632.42			
9	6655	51,181.69			
10	243	36,376.82			
11	2402	35,620.65			
12	160603	25,733.51			
13	54662	25,381.41			
14	160631	25,373.87			
15	5621	25,148.72		25th percentile	
16	4616	24,492.32		24,656	
17	4442	24,413.54			
18	54646	24,218.90			
19	3544	23,562.85			
20	4112	23,525.89			Red

Figure 9-15: Using Excel's PERCENTILE function to color code performance.

How it works

To build this basic formatting rule, follow these steps:

1. Select the data cells in your target range (cells B3:B20 in this example), click the Home tab of the Excel Ribbon, and then select Conditional Formatting⇨New Rule. This opens the New Formatting Rule dialog box shown in Figure 9-16.

2. In the list box at the top of the dialog box, click the Use a Formula to Determine which Cells to Format option. This selection evaluates values based on a formula you specify. If a particular value evaluates to TRUE, the conditional formatting is applied to that cell.

3. In the formula input box, enter the formula shown with this step. In this formula, you evaluate whether the data in the target cell (B3) is within the 25th percentile. If so, the conditional formatting will be applied.

```
=B3<=PERCENTILE($B$3:$B$20,0.25)
```

Caution　Note that in the formula, you exclude the absolute reference dollar symbols ($) for the target cell (B3). If you click cell B3 instead of typing the cell reference, Excel automatically makes your cell reference absolute. It's important that you don't include the absolute reference dollar symbols in your target cell because you need Excel to apply this formatting rule based on each cell's own value.

4. Click the Format button. This opens the Format Cells dialog box, where you have a full set of options for formatting the font, border, and fill for your target cell. After you have completed choosing your formatting options, click the OK button to confirm your changes and return to the New Formatting Rule dialog box.

5. Back in the New Formatting Rule dialog box, click the OK button to confirm your formatting rule.

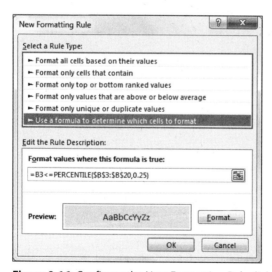

Figure 9-16: Configure the New Formatting Rule dialog box to apply the needed formula rule.

6. At this point, you should be in the Conditional Formatting Rules Manager dialog box. Click the New Rule button.

7. This opens the New Formatting Rule dialog box shown in Figure 9-17. In the list box at the top of the dialog box, click the Use a Formula to Determine which Cells to Format option. This selection evaluates values based on a formula you specify. If a particular value evaluates to TRUE, then the conditional formatting is applied to that cell.

8. In the formula input box, enter the formula shown here. In this formula, you're evaluating if the data in the target cell (B3) within the 75th percentile. If so, the conditional formatting will be applied.

```
=B3>=PERCENTILE($B$3:$B$20,0.75)
```

9. Click the Format button. This opens the Format Cells dialog box, where you have a full set of options for formatting the font, border, and fill for your target cell. After you have completed choosing your formatting options, click the OK button to confirm your changes and return to the New Formatting Rule dialog box.

10. Back on the New Formatting Rule dialog box, click the OK button to confirm your formatting rule.

Figure 9-17: Configure the New Formatting Rule dialog box to apply the needed formula rule.

Tip

If you need to edit your conditional formatting rule, simply place your cursor in any of the data cells within your formatted range and then go to the Home tab and select Conditional Formatting⇨Manage Rules. This opens the Conditional Formatting Rules Manager dialog box. Click the rule you want to edit and then click the Edit Rule button.

Formula 101: Highlight Statistical Outliers

When performing data analysis, you usually assume that your values cluster around some central data point (a median). But sometimes a few of the values fall too far from the central point. These values are called outliers (they lie outside the expected range). Outliers can skew your statistical analyses, leading you to false or misleading conclusions about your data.

You can use a few simple formulas and conditional formatting to highlight the outliers in your data.

The first step in identifying outliers is to pinpoint the statistical center of the range. To do this pinpointing, you start by finding the 1st and 3rd quartiles. A *quartile* is a statistical division of a data set into four equal groups, with each group making up 25 percent of the data. The top 25 percent of a collection is considered to be the 1st quartile, whereas the bottom 25 percent is considered the 4th quartile.

In Excel, you can easily get quartile values by using the QUARTILE function. This function requires two arguments: a range of data and the quartile number you want.

In the example shown in Figure 9-18, the values in cells E3 and E4 are the 1st and 3rd quartiles for the data in range B3:B20.

Taking these two quartiles, you can calculate the statistical 50 percent of the data set by subtracting the 3rd quartile from the 1st quartile. This statistical 50 percent is called the interquartile range (IQR). Figure 9-18 displays the IQR in cell E5.

Now the question is, how far from the middle 50 percent can a value sit and still be considered a "reasonable" value? Statisticians generally agree that IQR*1.5 can be used to establish a reasonable upper and lower fence:

> The lower fence is equal to the 1st quartile – IQR*1.5.

> The upper fence is equal to the 3rd quartile + IQR*1.5.

As you can see in Figure 9-18, cells E7 and E8 calculate the final upper and lower fences. Any value greater than the upper fence or less than the lower fence is considered an outlier.

At this point, the conditional formatting rule is easy to implement.

	A	B	C	D	E	F
1						
2	Employee_Number	Rev				
3	1054	900		Quartile 1	4350	=QUARTILE(B3:B20,1)
4	6032	1000		Quartile 3	6483	=QUARTILE(B3:B20,3)
5	54253	1300		IQR	2133	=E4-E3
6	160014	1500				
7	4346	4300		Upper Fence	9682.5	=E4+(E5*1.5)
8	5530	4500		Lower Fence	1150.5	=E3-(E5*1.5)
9	6655	4600				
10	243	5500				
11	2402	5600				
12	160603	6000				
13	54662	6100				
14	160631	6200				
15	4112	6432				
16	5621	6500				
17	4616	7143				
18	4442	7790				
19	3544	8100				
20	54646	9842				

Figure 9-18: Highlighting outliers with conditional formatting.

Cross-Ref

For more detail on the quartile and interquartile ranges, see Formula 89: Identifying Statistical Outliers with an Interquartile Range, in Chapter 8.

How it works

To build this basic formatting rule, follow these steps:

1. Select the data cells in your target range (cells B3:B20 in this example), click the Home tab of the Excel Ribbon, and then select Conditional Formatting⇨New Rule. This opens the New Formatting Rule dialog box shown in Figure 9-19.

Figure 9-19: Configure the New Formatting Rule dialog box to apply the needed formula rule.

2. In the list box at the top of the dialog box, click the Use a Formula to Determine which Cells to Format option. This selection evaluates values based on a formula that you specify. If a particular value evaluates to TRUE, the conditional formatting is applied to that cell.

3. In the formula input box, enter the formula shown here. Note that you use the OR function to compare the value in your target cell (B3) to both the upper and lower fences found in cells $E$7 and $E$8, respectively. If the target cell is greater than the upper fence or less than the lower fence, it's considered an outlier and thus will evaluate to TRUE, triggering the conditional formatting.

```
=OR(B3<$E$8,B3>$E$7)
```

Caution Note that in the formula, you exclude the absolute reference dollar symbols ($) for the target cell (B3). If you click cell B3 instead of typing the cell reference, Excel automatically makes your cell reference absolute. It's important that you don't include the absolute reference dollar symbols in your target cell because you need Excel to apply this formatting rule based on each cell's own value.

4. Click the Format button. This opens the Format Cells dialog box, where you have a full set of options for formatting the font, border, and fill for your target cell. After you have completed choosing your formatting options, click the OK button to confirm your changes and return to the New Formatting Rule dialog box.

5. Back in the New Formatting Rule dialog box, click the OK button to confirm your formatting rule.

Tip

If you need to edit your conditional formatting rule, simply place your cursor in any of the data cells within your formatted range and then go to the Home tab and select Conditional Formatting⇨Manage Rules. This opens the Conditional Formatting Rules Manager dialog box. Click the rule that you want to edit then click the Edit Rule button.

⊙ Index

About the Authors

Michael Alexander is a Microsoft Certified Application Developer (MCAD) and the author of several books on advanced business analysis with Microsoft Access and Microsoft Excel. He has more than 15 years of experience in consulting and developing Microsoft Office solutions. Mike has been named a Microsoft MVP for his ongoing contributions to the Excel community. In his spare time, he runs a free tutorial site, www.datapigtechnologies.com, where he shares Excel and Access tips.

Dick Kusleika has been awarded as a Microsoft MVP for 12 consecutive years and has been working with Microsoft Office for more than 20. Dick develops Access- and Excel-based solutions for his clients and has conducted training seminars on Office products in the United States and Australia. Dick also writes a popular Excel-related blog at www.dailydoseofexcel.com.

Dedication

Mike Alexander

To my 12 fans at datapigtechnologies.com.

Dick Kusleika

To my Excel protégés, Kim and Jodene.

Authors' Acknowledgments

Our deepest thanks to the professionals at John Wiley & Sons, Inc. for all the hours of work put into bringing this book to life. Thanks also to Mike Talley for suggesting numerous improvements to the examples and text in this book. Finally, a special thank you goes out to our families for putting up with all the time spent locked away on this project.

Publisher's Acknowledgments

Senior Acquisitions Editor: Katie Mohr

Project Editor: Susan Christophersen

Copy Editors: Susan Christophersen and Virginia Sanders

Technical Editor: Mike Talley

Editorial Assistant: Claire Johnson

Sr. Editorial Assistant: Cherie Case

Project Coordinator: Erin Zeltner

More great Excel guides from Mr. Spreadsheet!

Need to know more about Excel? John Walkenbach has it covered.

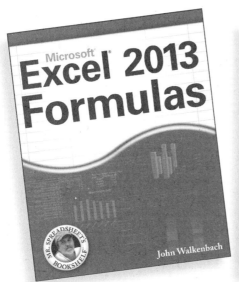

978-1-118-49044-0

978-1-118-49039-6

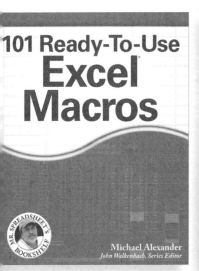

978-1-118-28121-5

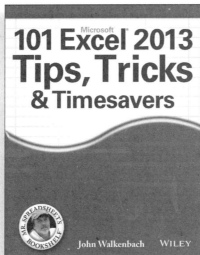

978-1-118-64218-4

978-1-118-49042-6

Available in print and e-book formats.